GOD MONEY

LOST AND FOUND IN THE CRYPTO WILDERNESS

LEGAL DISCLAIMER

The events, stories, and experiences described in this memoir are based on the author's personal recollections of events. While the author has attempted to ensure accuracy, memory is inherently subjective and imperfect. Some events, conversations, and timelines may have been condensed or reconstructed.

To protect the privacy and confidentiality of individuals and entities involved, certain details, including but not limited to financial figures, investment amounts, returns, company names, and identifying characteristics have been altered or anonymized. In some cases, composite characters have been created from multiple real individuals.

All financial data, performance metrics, and monetary amounts presented in this book should not be considered as actual historical records. These figures have been modified and should not be relied upon for any investment decisions or financial analysis. Any specific trading strategies, investment approaches, or market activities described herein may be incomplete, simplified, or modified for narrative purposes.

This memoir is intended for entertainment and informational purposes only and does not constitute financial, investment, legal, or business advice. The author and publisher make no representations or warranties regarding the accuracy, completeness, or reliability of the information contained herein.

This book contains descriptions of drug use, addiction, and other mature themes. Neither the author nor publisher endorses or encourages illegal activities of any kind. Any descriptions of such activities are provided solely for narrative purposes.

Any similarities to actual persons, living or dead, or to actual companies, institutions, or business entities are either coincidental or have been altered to protect privacy. The author and publisher disclaim any liability for any financial or other losses incurred by readers who may rely on the information contained in this book.

Nothing in this book should be construed as investment advice or as a recommendation to invest in cryptocurrency or any other asset class. Past performance, whether actual or modified, is not indicative of future results. Readers are encouraged to conduct their own due diligence and seek professional advice before making any investment decisions.

The views, opinions, and strategies described in this book are those of the author alone and do not necessarily reflect the views of the publisher or any other entity mentioned in the book.

ACKNOWLEDGEMENTS

To my family. And to Lila, Chris, Luke, Johnny, Ben, Davis, my classmates at USF and Stanford who read the book in its rough and painful early drafts and offered invaluable feedback. To all the residents, priests and teachers at the Rochester Zen Center and the Great Vow Zen Monastery who did so much to support me in clearing my mind and energizing me to complete the manuscript after a nearly two year hiatus. Special thanks to my former agent Adam Chromy and current publisher and editor Amelie Lasker at Alexandria Labs.

TABLE OF CONTENTS

CHAPTER ONE –
MAY 25TH, 2017

"You cannot serve both God and money."

– Luke 16:13

[Time sent]: 05/21/17, 10:34 P.M.

[To]: <Twain dorm, Kappa Alpha pledges, Kappa Alpha members, Roble dorm, Lagunitas dorm, economics department, Rugby team>

[From]: <Dpatrick@stanford.edu>

Subject: The Investment Opportunity of a Lifetime.

Body:

Dear friends,

I just filed paperwork with the SEC to establish a private investment trust investing in cryptocurrencies. Already have 500k in commitments (half of which is my own money), capping at $1m. $5,000 minimum, no

annual fees with just 20 % carried interest
and just 12-month lock up (I'm practically
running a charity here).

Contact if interested and I will send you
a 2-page prospectus and if you are still
interested we can meet in person to discuss
more in detail.

Yours truly,

Dean "crypto is the next dot-com" Patrick

I was a junior at Stanford when I sent that email. In addition to violating the 1934 U.S. Securities Act by soliciting investment from nonaccredited investors, a Class C felony, it was filled with lies. There was no paperwork filed, no $500,000 in commitments, not even a two-page prospectus. All I had was a nose full of hubris and an appreciation for the power of artificial scarcity. In four months, the cryptocurrency market had hockey-sticked from $16 billion to $80 billion. A $1 million fund could net me nearly $3 million in fees if growth held steady for another year, making me wealthier than my parents and all but my most affluent peers.

From the moment I sent that email all notions of body and time dissolved into the narrowed universe of my computer screen glowing in my dark room. Hours melted away, a declining high the only metric of passing time–a dullness in the head and the first arrivals of hunger and fatigue–swiftly rectified with a deft toot from my hefty bag.

I refreshed as fast as my thumb could click, wrapped in a sweat-soaked blanket.

A flicker. A new email. My eyes bulged as I read the subject line: "Take my money!"

I slid down in bed—head bent high on a pillow with my laptop resting on arched thighs—a posture I had maintained more or less continuously for the past six weeks, breaking only at my body's most urgent requests. My room had a sink where I peed and window blinds I cinched tight to block out sunlight and imaginary, invasive eyes.

Moments later, another email: "I'm in!" A giddiness simmered.

Then a third: "Where do I send the money??"

I panicked. There was nothing in my background to prepare me for this, no investment banker father or uncle with connections–my Dad spent his entire early career in the commercial fishing industry.

But the mind, I had come to believe, was nothing more than a machine; one that could be coaxed with drugs into astounding feats of creativity and even genius. For the past two months I had been consuming a buffet of pills and powders ordered off the deep web.

The deep web is the dank underbelly of the internet, protected by a fortress of encryption that disguises personal identities and enables websites that coordinate online drug markets and brothels. Accessible through a privacy-focused browser built by the US Navy to protect the identity of its intelligence officers, the dark web relies on the United States Postal Service to ship hundreds of millions of dollars worth of drugs annually to all fifty states and beyond. Beholden to the Fourth Amendment of the US Constitution, the USPS is not allowed to inspect packages without a warrant, making it the perfect drug mule for thousands of online dealers.

Crypto, among other things, is the dark web's currency, with Bitcoin being the preferred option thanks to its broad adoption.

With access to the world's greatest drug dealer, I used my body as a laboratory to concoct the optimal mix of uppers and downers to induce creative flow. I had landed on cocaine, with some Xanax or opiates to take the edge off whenever my heart complained too much.

I threw off the covers and grasped for the bag of powder at my bedside. Almost supine, I dumped a pea-sized rock onto my phone screen, crushing it with a credit card and organizing it into a shapely line before inserting a rolled twenty into my nostril and devouring it. After wiping a drop of sweat off my keyboard, I googled "How to start an investment fund."

My girlfriend, Sarah, who I had only started dating a few months earlier, had grown agitated by my erratic behavior—unresponsive days followed by 2 a.m. texts. She was my year, a straight-A Biology major from Palo Alto. Strawberry blonde hair and green eyes and sundresses and from a rich family and therefore knew the other rich kids, their language, their interests. But she was kind and lacked pretentiousness. When she wasn't studying her focus shifted to having "fun."

"There's a Theta mixer tonight. Are you coming??"

"I can't; I'm working on something big."

"You're ALWAYS working, come out and have some FUN!!"

"I can't. Sorry. I love you."

I threw "love" around freely, not knowing what it meant. I doubted whether Sarah knew either.

"Okay, I'm rooting for you! Love you too," she responded.

I was a little annoyed that she hadn't written "I" before the word "love," but I let it go.

In the month before the email my obsessive absence fed her suspicion of me.

"I never see you on campus anymore, are you even going to class??"
She texted me.

I didn't respond.

Later that day, she entered my room to find me sleeping at 3 pm.

"What are you doing? You should be in class!"

I groaned, my body ached all over and my torso felt soldered to the
bed, unable to muster the energy to turn over and face her. The
window was open and the sunburnt air fragranced with the smell of
asphalt wafted into the room. Every so often the silence was interrupted by shouts or screeching bike tires.

"At least I'm not cheating on you," I grumbled.

"I never thought you were cheating! But you can't just lay there; you
told me you were working!"

"I work at night and sleep during the day."

"That's no way to live."

"It works for me."

"But you'll fail all your classes!"

"I don't care about that."

"You have some serious issues."

I didn't answer and after a few moments, she turned and left,
shutting the door with force.

But now the fund was to absolve me of everything. After two hours
of googling, I learned many ways to start a fund; some required tests
and registration, some didn't. The Financial Industry Regulatory

Authority's website described one test (the series-7) as "measuring the degree to which each candidate possesses the knowledge needed to perform the critical functions of a general securities representative." I dismissed these as yawning credentials suitable for a retirement planner, but the formalities of traditional finance couldn't hold back anyone who wanted to get rich in crypto. After all, both the crypto and traditional finance world march to the same beat: *Buy low, sell high.* However the old respected lawyers, while the new answered only to code.

Besides, there was a much better legal alternative: regulation D, which allowed me to circumvent the most onerous regulation as long as my investors made more than $200k a year. Stanford students wouldn't count, but many of their parents would.

My inspiration for the fund had come a month earlier. I had invested my life savings, $5,000, into an initial coin offering ("ICO"), the IPO of the crypto world, in an Ethereum-based company called Pythia. Pythia had raised $12.5 million in less than fifteen minutes. A news report from Coindesk headlined the event: "ICO Insanity? $300 Million Pythia Valuation Sparks Market Reaction." The header image showed three 20-pound notes going up in flames, with Queen Elizabeth's face slashed through with fire. Crypto had already developed a reputation for attracting lofty valuations seemingly ungrounded in inconvenient and elusive "real-world value." Even Coindesk, an industry rag not averse to publishing aggressive predictions, forecasted that Pythia was destined for a rapid descent back to earth.

Despite Coindesk's pessimism, I learned from Reddit that over-the-counter deals valued Pythia tokens at over $1 billion. In just days, Pythia would be listed on a public exchange, and most online commentators speculated that it would go even higher. I knew I could sell my tokens for an enormous profit—allowing me to reinvest the earnings in the half-a-dozen Pythia-sized ICOs launching monthly, multiplying my profits until I could buy a place on St. Mark[1] and retire by my twenty-second birthday. The fund would supercharge my personal returns and gain me friends for life.

I viewed sleep like a NASCAR driver views pit stops: as a nuisance to be minimized. The coke blew away the natural inclination of my reddened eyes to shut after three sleepless nights, and I immediately got to work on an investment prospectus.

After half an hour I got up and walked to the sink, pissed, and came back to bed. A rare silence had descended on the dorm, which I noted for only a second before picking up my laptop and getting to work. I began at two in the morning, and by three I had finished a draft of a two-pager filled with the financial language I had picked up in my economics classes. After sending it off to my prospective investors, I laid back to relax, settling my hands on my shrunken stomach. I had been an athlete—a wing and center on the Rugby team. Now I would probably snap in half after the first hit, but I didn't care. I was going to be rich. And at Stanford I had learned that money beat muscle every time.

A rustle at my window disturbed me and I sat up. The street lights danced with my window curtains, flapping in the unusually gusty night air, the only sound in the otherwise still night.

I began to gasp but stifled it at the last moment to avoid making a sound. An ogreish shape had formed in the network of shadows playing on the floor. I kept my body still as I tuned every sense to the figure in the window, which was growing more menacing by the breath. The curtains made another violent flap and my crackling nervous system, coiled tightly in anxious anticipation, suddenly snapped at the sound. I sprang out of bed and lunged at the window,

---

1   Caribbean island and playground for the ultra wealthy.

tearing back the curtain and swinging a desperate right hook where I had seen the ogre just a moment before. But I swung at air; the ogre had disappeared. I stuck my head out my window and looked down at the terrace a floor below, but before my eyes could adjust to the night, I leapt back. From the terrace, the ogre launched a midget through the window, over my shoulder and into my room. I swung around to grab him but he moved so fast I couldn't get a clear view of him. For the next hour I tore my already disgusting room apart, trying to catch him. I emptied my closet and drawers, fearing he may have taken refuge in my furniture, sending underwear, T-shirts, books and pencils flying. Then the piles of clothes and books became potential hiding places and I dove on them, flinging them onto my bed, which in turn became another hiding place, and on it went in a desperate cycle of ever-increasing entropy. I moved my bed to the other side of the room and sent my dresser crashing down, kicking it furiously to try to drive the midget out.

There was banging on my door.

"Hey what's going on there? Keep it down!"

"Shut the fuck up I'm looking for something!" I screamed back.

Finally I landed on a more level-headed approach. I used my phone and laptop as surveillance cameras, angling them on my dresser such that every part of the floor was being recorded. Any move the midget made would be caught on camera, and I would have the evidence I needed to call in the authorities. I stood on my bed to try to command the best possible view, dripping sweat, lost in time, waiting to leap. Suddenly there was a flash of movement and I threw myself from the bed. The bastard had escaped me again, but he was on camera. Righteous and terrified, I grabbed my phone and dialed 911 as I burst into the dorm hallway wearing only filthy blue gym shorts, an ounce of cocaine swinging in my pockets.

CHAPTER TWO – 2002

I was in second grade when Mom took us out of school, but the seeds of rebellion against the penitentiary for innocent children were already sown within me. Even as a child, I sensed that any deviation from the norm nurtured something unique within. I was an avid reader of Landmark Books featuring big shots from Joan of Arc to Davy Crockett, each of whom stamped their names in the history books by rejecting the standard path.

I was the youngest son, and not happy about it. Adults, my mom's friends in particular, would cry, "You're the baby!" when they found out I was the youngest. I would turn red and sputter back, "But I'm not a baby!"

To make her announcement, Mom called her three boys into the living room. My oldest brother, Tyler, wore thick glasses and memorized long passages from *Les Misérables*, reading in Costco while shuffling behind Mom's shopping cart. He was also slightly on the spectrum. As a child, he had difficulty understanding emotions and went through a phase of holding me down and kissing me continuously as I kicked and screamed. It was not an outpouring of unreciprocated love that led to this unusual scene, however, but calculated torture. One day, fed up with kiss attacks, I grabbed a log from our wood pile and smashed his glasses while they were still on his face.

But Tyler was also prone to periods of genuine love and affection for us and the animals that grew steadily in number as our childhood went on. While we were still in school, my mom bought two chickens that we named, in an example of groupthink's downward effect on creativity– "Cluck One" and "Cluck Two." Tyler would spend hours after school rubbing Cluck One's stomach as it splayed its head back in pleasure. They became best friends before a Possum attack ended the union.

Evan, on the other hand, was the silent assassin, poking us under the table and crying helplessly when we retaliated overtly. But he was also a peacemaker and a helpful son. My parents gave us each an allowance of ten dollars a week, and I started paying Evan to do my chores. One morning, Mom saw Evan carrying my laundry up the stairs.

"Chores are for building work ethic, not making money!"

"But isn't the point of a work ethic to make money?" I asked.

"Just do your chores."

Mom was careful to dole out unconditional love when appropriate. "I would be happy if you lived under a bridge as long as you were happy!" she told us on many occasions. And she would sing us to sleep many nights: "You are my sunshine, my only sunshine. You make me happy when skies are gray..."

"I had a meeting with the school principal about Tyler," Mom said, opening the meeting. "He's been having some issues at school, and the principal told me that 'smart kids just have to get used to being bored,'" she said, nodding to Tyler, then in fifth grade. "I decided to take your education into my own hands, so you will be homeschooled from now on."

The three of us cheered and clapped, and Mom smiled, relieved at our rapid acquiescence. The principal's words, "Smart kids just have to get used to being bored," were branded on her psyche as a mantra to rouse the furious energy needed to implement her novel education system.

The second purpose of our meeting was to make clear that School Mom was to be obeyed. More than once, I goofed off too much during school hours before being silenced by the forbidding "wait until your father gets home." One day things devolved unusually far, aided by our Holland Lop bunny, Puff, and the trail of pellet-sized droppings he'd deposited around the living room. I'd collected them and spelled Tyler's name, calling him over to reveal my creation, at which point he grabbed the poo and started force-feeding me before my screams sent Mom rushing into the living room.

A few hours later, Dad walked up the steps to the house after a long day and slumped down his bag as if it were his own body, only to face the imminent duty of paddling his boys "with their pants down" (for our particularly naughty behavior). Having been absent for the original offense, it was a task he completed hesitantly and with a light enough hand that I feigned cries to satisfy my mother, who was standing with her arms folded in the next room, and to encourage extra softness on the part of Dad.

Despite his soft paddling, Dad was an effective enforcer. Capable of swinging from jovial chatter to plate-smashing anger at the careless spill of a water glass. He was the primary source of financial stability and emotional instability in my childhood. He worked hard, but was often overwhelmed by the enormous pressure of being a sole provider for a family of five. I became an expert at assessing his emotional state by the sounds of his steps as he approached the house: heavy, and I would run to my room; light, and I would come up to greet him. The way the door was opened was the great reveal:

aggressive, and it was best to not be seen; light, and good money had been made that day.

If hungry, which he often was when he came home, even a poorly worded question could light the fuse. At meal times, he would grow steadily happier as the food hit his stomach, and my shoulders would relax, confident that the evening would pass in peace.

The power that Dad's anger had over the household was awe inspiring, and probably addictive—we would do anything to appease him if a storm blew in. When he raged—at one point smashing up much of the kitchen, including several plates (dinner was late, and he was hungry)—I hid in the living room and whimpered while my mom tried to stop the rampage.

Around the age of seven, I began having a recurring dream, a fantasy, in which his anger finally went too far. Dad would drag me out into the street and stand over me, holding my shirt with his left hand and pounding away with his right. Women would scream and the cops would come, tackling him to the ground, cuffing him and taking him away. Afterward, I would be free.[2]

But when Dad was at work, I relaxed. We lived in Sunnyvale, CA, and had a small house on a quarter-acre lot with a big avocado tree in back whose produce we would use as baseballs to the consternation of our parents. Tyler and I would walk around the block, using sticks as "wappers," mowing down any plant that came in our path.

---

2   I hope the reader doesn't think my father was a bad man. I don't know if he was always a good man, but he certainly is one now. True, he often acted out of rage and reactivity. However, over time he made a conscious effort to change for our family's sake. But he never shirked his responsibilities and in many ways he is a hero. He gave up the freedom I know he yearned for and never stopped working to improve our lives. He came from little, and did his best. The older I get the more I find myself forgiving him and looking up to him. In fact, I find myself striving to live up to the standard he has set, and to work on my own anger which still threatens the relationships in my life.

We got into one neighbor's flower garden and heard shouts from the window.

"What the hell are you kids doing??"

Tyler and I took off running, turning our heads to catch sight of a middle-aged man in a bathrobe chasing us off in his slippers.

In addition to her teaching, Mom had a habit of infusing her every endeavor with a grandiosity that greatly exceeded her capacity. She would declare an intention to write books or start great businesses, and then weeks would pass.

"How's the book, Mom?"

"Not good, honey. I have all these incredible ideas in my head, but when I put them on the page they turn to mush."

The great exception to this was her children, where she rose to the level of her own grand ambitions. Her teaching style was warm but sensible, firm yet open. I loved spending time with her, and with the exception of the occasional poop calligraphy, she was generally delighted by us.

Six months after being taken out of school, a diesel dually pickup arrived in our driveway and was joined the following day by a Lance sit-on-top camper. My brothers and I excitedly piled into the cab as the "for sale" sign in front of our house was taken down. We pulled out of the drive and headed north for Alaska.

"How long will we be gone?"

"Five, maybe six months," Dad replied, "and forty-nine states."

I was in an exalted state. I'd been born with a road bug, and the series of dramatic moves that year, from Mom taking us out of school to my dad leaving his job, had culminated in the ultimate adventure. Any change was good; monotony the enemy.

Soon my senses adjusted to the buzz and rattle of the freeway, and the adrenaline of the new adventure dissolved into a stable new medium of existence. Dad was the driver and map reader, maintaining a usually light-hearted chatter of facts and figures.

"Some of these Redwoods are over 1,000 years old, boys."

"Almost as old as you, Dad."

"That's right."

He was at his most pleasant on the road, at home in moving space with a mission to the day and a team to lead. His temper had virtually evaporated without the stress of work, and so we all relaxed with him. Mom was teacher and keeper of the peace.

"Can you quiet them down back there?" Dad would ask after a thigh poke gone awry.

Mom would twist to the backseat. "Would you boys like to do math right now?"

"No, Mom."

"Then settle down."

"Okay, Mom."

Tyler was a Game Boy player who maintained a monk-like equanimity in the face of natural wonders and three-hour traffic jams. Evan was Dad's buddy, chattering along with him about the national parks and local flora and fauna. I was a restless troublemaker trying to get my share of attention in a family of elders.

"Mom, Tyler is farting back here."

"That's okay. It's natural."

wack

"Mom, Tyler hit me."

"Tyler, don't hit Dean."

wack

"Mom!"

"Okay, that's it! Evan you sit in the middle. Any more trouble and we're replacing the Game Boys with math books."

We drove through California and saw the towering redwoods, whose fallen branches served as wappers for Tyler and me to chase each other with. At our campsite I stole off alone, finding a gun-shaped stick and hiding behind fallen logs as Davy Crockett, picking off Indians. I must have killed thousands of them. I was a legend.

We stopped at Crater Lake, where we all earned our first "junior ranger" badge, a pursuit which quickly became a centerpiece of the homeschool curriculum. The badges were awarded after completing a worksheet based on information in the visitor center, filled out under the watchful eye of Dad.

"What did you put for B?" I would ask Evan.

"I'm not telling you."

"I'll give you my fries the next time we stop at Burger King."

"Deal."

Some badges were prized more than others, the crème being "BIG HOLE" (all caps) National Battlefield in Montana, whose badge I pinned to my shirt for an entire week.

From Crater Lake, we drove northwest into Western Washington to take the ferry from Seattle to Juneau. The first night Mom got seasick and gave us $20 in quarters for the arcade so she could vomit in peace. In Alaska we visited Dad's old Ocean Beauty cannery, where he had served as packer and then plant manager in a twenty-year career that largely preceded my birth. It was part nostalgia, part networking, because after the trip ended he took a job at a remote cannery on Kodiak Island. From Alaska, we descended south through Canada and into Idaho, then due east through Montana toward the eastern shore. Once a week, we would go out to eat.

"Dad, why can't we eat out more?"

"Too expensive. This trip is costing us too much as it is."

"How do I make a lot of money when I get older?"

"You work hard and get a good job."

As we stopped at over one hundred national parks, I failed to find the wonder that clearly filled the soul of my dad. His face, along with Evan's, would slacken in awe at a waterfall or compelling tree.

I preferred to sail around the world in my mind rather than focus on the reality of the rolling ocean on the ferry to Alaska or the vast landscapes of the American West. And in the woods I was the invincible legend of battle. I wanted to be a hero, someone whose accomplishments were impossible to ignore. Waterfalls did nothing for me.

Three months in, we stopped at my grandfather's property in Upstate New York. He held court in his living room, wisely rocking in his chair and attempting to engage his three prepubescent grandchildren in conversation.

"What do you boys want to be when you grow up?" He directed the question to my oldest brother, Tyler, then nine.

"An underwater photographer!" Tyler answered smartly, beaming with the fresh inspiration of a recent visit to Monterey Bay Aquarium.

I pondered my answer. *Not president. That's boring.*

"I want to be..." Evan began.

"A billionaire!" I blurted out, cutting off Evan.

Everyone at the table laughed.

"I'm serious! When I grow up I'm going to be a billionaire."

"Why wait?" My father said, smiling down at me. "You can be the first eight-year-old billionaire!"

"We believe you, honey," said my mom reassuringly. "Then you can buy all of us everything we want."

I smiled.

Years later, I read *Bad Blood*, the story of Elizabeth Holmes, the Theranos founder who dropped out of Stanford at nineteen to revolutionize blood testing before being sentenced to seventeen years in jail for securities fraud and medical malfeasance. When Holmes was eight, her parents asked her what she wanted to be when she grew up.

"A billionaire!" she had replied.

CHAPTER THREE – MAY 25TH, 2017

"There's a midget in there stealing everything!" I bellowed to the small crowd of groggy-eyed onlookers that had formed in the hallway, "An ogre too!" Barefoot, I grabbed one half-conscious student by his pajama shirt and shook him. "Take a look, man! I'm getting invaded!"

To my dormmates I must have seemed zombie-like–reeling forward with fluttering, bloodshot eyes, emaciated from weeks on uppers with a face coated in wild hair wearing only snot-covered gym shorts. My appearance was reflected back to me in a look of alarmed terror that spread across my new friend's face. I let go of his shirt and bounded off toward my open door before checking myself and leaping by the doorway, my cell phone in my right hand, unconscious of the worried dispatcher's questioning. I reached the end of the hallway before turning and running back, jumping again when I reached my door.

"In there!" I shouted to the four or five students who had gathered as I sailed in front of my door, "If I walk by, the ogre will pull me in!" Unbeknownst to me, there was a frenzy of alarmed discussion amongst my dorm mates, which I learned about later. Someone was immediately sent for the resident fellow, the faculty member living in the dorm, and a couple guys contemplated tackling me before thinking better of it.

After a few more laps around the hall, the faculty resident fellow appeared. He was in his early 40s and was scratching his tangled hair as he approached. He had a slight slouch and wore a green pullover fleece, light blue pajama pants and round glasses with hair-thin black frames. I recognized him immediately although I had never met him and stopped running. There was finally someone with authority present who could help me. He studied me seriously for a few moments before his eyes softened with concern. I explained the situation.

As I was talking he leaned across my doorway, peering into my room.

"Don't go in there; the ogre will get you!" I yelled, gripping his shirt and pulling him away.

"When's the last time you got some sleep?" He asked, startled.

"It's been three or four days. Can't remember. I can't sleep now. I just launched a hedge fund. Plus I have to deal with this ogre."

"Tell me more about this hedge fund."

Surprised at his lack of interest in the ogre, I hesitated for a moment, but the thought of the hedge fund snapped me back to my newfound obsession, and within seconds, I forgot about the monster entirely.

"You can issue assets, called tokens, with blockchain technology. And I plan to invest in them as early as possible and then sell them after they go public. Basically, you can get venture capital level returns; we're talking up to 100X in some cases, in a month!"

"That actually sounds like a fascinating opportunity. Do you have any investors?"

His eyes were bright with interest and a furious excitement took hold of me that he might become my first official investor. "Not yet, but dozens of people have expressed interest. I'll raise money in the next few days and begin investing immediately. You're welcome to invest as well."

Before he could answer, our conversation was cut short by the authoritative clump of police boots.

"Is this the kid?" They asked the resident fellow, pointing at me.

"Yes this is him, don't worry he's calm now."

"Why don't you take a seat in the hallway while we look at your room?" I slumped down obediently against the wall in the hallway as the police inspected my room. I sighed deeply as I waited for the sounds of gunshots or a scramble that would indicate the resolution of the midget and ogre problem. Suddenly I remembered the cocaine and grew paranoid that the bags would slip out of my pockets in front of the police. I shoved my hands in to make sure they stayed put.

"Nothing here," one cop said, returning to the hallway, "kid's out of his mind."

"Take your hands out of your pockets," he said, turning to me.

"But the midget, he must have escaped—"

"Take your hands out of your pockets," he took another step towards me.

"They're cold," I responded, looking up at him pleadingly. In my pockets, I worked my hands into fists while using my fingers to separate the coke bags from my sweaty palms. I needed to buy time.

"But you're sweating."

"Cold sweat."

"Uh-huh."

Thank god I was a Stanford student, the cultural image of potential and good intentions that kept the police from searching and arresting me on the spot. But in situations like these you can't apologize for any edge you have; you have to squeeze every drop of "privilege."

"Listen, sir, I was just working on launching a hedge fund and then a midget popped through my window and started stealing everything I own!"

"Don't play games with me, son."

"You really don't believe me? I have a tape! I'm recording it right now!"

He sighed. "Take your hands out of your pockets," the cop said as he lifted his cuffs, "or you're putting these on and coming with me."

"Yes, sir." I slid my hands out, spreading my palms in front of the cop to show him they were empty. The coke bags had stayed put.

"Now. I think it's best if you go to the hospital."

"I'm not sure that's necessary, sir," I answered.

"It's either that or the police station."

"I'll go to the hospital, sir."

CHAPTER FOUR - 2005

Our road trip ended after five months and we moved to a hippie compound (complete with goats, bees, chickens, pet rats, a bunny, and a garden that supplied most of our vegetables in the summer and fall) thirty minutes northeast of Seattle.

The next three years of homeschooling were some of the happiest of my life. I spent hours a day watching clouds pass by as my peers toiled in their classrooms. At least an hour a day of reading was the bedrock of our education, and self-directed learning was the norm.

About a year after the move, Mom decided that farm life would be a core part of our curriculum, including the harsh lesson of "where meat really comes from." One of our chickens, Martha, was in henopause–her egg production had dropped from daily to weekly. Martha had become economically unviable, and since Mom's syllabus demanded at least a loose adherence to market economics, we were forced to look upon poor Martha not as a living being but as a losing asset to liquidate.

"I found a great recipe for chicken stew," Mom said, declaring that the following morning would be Martha's last. "I can't handle the actual act of killing her," Mom said, "it's up to you." When morning came I went out into the chicken coop and scooped up Martha. She was calm and trusting as I carried her out of the coop and into the yard, ensuring I moved far enough to spare the others the trauma. Mom was standing ten feet away, looking on apprehensively.

"I'm just going to snap her neck, I guess," I said, looking to Mom for confirmation. She nodded gravely. I wanted it to be quick and painless for Martha, which meant I had to use all my strength to snap her neck cleanly. With my right hand, I gripped Martha's throat; taking a deep breath I summoned as much power and resolve as my ten-year-old body possessed and jerked her neck down while pinning the rest of her body to my chest. It was as if I had set off a bomb–Martha's neck stretched like an unfurled Slinky, and she erupted from my arms in a clucking frenzy, running with her head dragging on the ground. I turned to Mom for guidance, but she was already fleeing, her face buried in her hands, screaming, "oh my god! Oh my god! Oh my god!"

My only thought was to end Martha's suffering. I chased her down, picked her up by the neck and swung her body like a lasso before slamming it against the ground in a series of violent blows until she shuddered and lay still.

After a few seconds, I set Martha down; all movement had stopped–finally dead.

The next time we decided to kill one of our animals we took it to a butcher. A more palatable middle ground for Mom who had learned she was constitutionally ill-fitted for the more macabre aspects of farm life. This time it was one of our male goats–Dragon–a eunuch lacking economic value. Dragon returned from the butcher as a box of meat wrapped in white paper, marked according to the cut. Mom didn't touch any of the meat, and I had set my fork down after a couple of bites when I became nauseous. That was the last lesson we had in farm economics.

Not long before Martha's death, I met my best friend, Camron, at a homeschool school. The homeschool school was a paradox that had formed when a parent collective set up an unorthodox supplementary school where their children could learn from credentialed teachers and interact with peers. I went twice a week to the portables on the edge of a local junior high school and took improv and art classes taught by teachers who were semi-retired or simply fed up with the public school grind.

On my first day at the homeschool school, I was nine and nervous, standing shiftily after class waiting for my mom to get me.

"Hi. I'm Camron."

 I looked up at a freckled face framed with jet-black hair. He was a little chubby and wore a plaid shirt with loose jeans. His face was so kind and open that my nerves broke, and I smiled broadly.

"Hi. I'm Dean."

I took his outstretched hand and he shook mine vigorously.

"You're homeschooled too?" Camron asked.

"Yeah. My mom took me and my brothers out of school last year."

"That's great. I left school last year too. I love being homeschooled. Do you love it?"

"Yeah. I really like it. How old are you?"

"I'm ten. My birthday's August 20th. How old are you?"

"I'm nine. My birthday's November 15th."

"Oh, so we're only a few months apart! I like Kaitlyn. Do you like any girls?"

"I don't know. I don't like girls too much."

The truth was that I liked girls, but I was afraid of them and it was easier to pretend I simply had no interest. I sensed that humor was the key to unlocking them, but they laughed so unpredictably that I had all but given up hope.

"You will when you turn ten. When I turned ten, I started liking a lot of girls. What music do you like?"

"I don't listen to music much. My mom plays Celtic music in the car sometimes."

He stared at me with an expression of confusion mixed with concern.

"Celtic music? What's that?"

"I don't really know."

Our conversation continued for a long time, and we were so absorbed in each other that we were oblivious to the arrival of Camron's Mom.

"Aw, looks like you found a friend, Camron!" Camron's mom, Monica, had walked up, breaking our trance.

"Yup! This is Dean."

"Mm. Looks to me like you're in love!"

"I'm not in love, Mom, but he's my friend!"

I blushed at the mention of the word love, but in retrospect it was a good word for it. There was something about Camron that slotted perfectly into my being and mine into his. I felt his inner assurance and relative sophistication with girls and music, and he could make me laugh on command. Talking to him felt like talking to a long-lost brother, and our schoolyard meeting was the start of the closest friendship I've ever had. Years later, at Stanford, I wrote Camron a letter that read, "If nothing good ever happens in my life again, our relationship alone will have made my life a happy one."

CHAPTER FIVE – MAY 26TH, 2017

I was escorted out by a team of EMTs into the dorm parking lot. The predawn darkness was diffused with burning white street lights reflecting off the cars and onto my gaunt but active face. I submitted to being strapped down to the gurney, good-naturedly, flushed with the cocaine that still surged through me,

"I don't understand why you're taking me to the hospital." I said, "I feel great."

"Yeah, you seem fine to me."

I kept up a spiel of incessant chatter as the ambulance rode down the hill to the Stanford hospital.

"I'm starting a hedge fund investing in new cryptocurrency launches, I'm going to be rich!"

"Can we invest?"

"Absolutely, I take check or cash."

"Cool. We'll find you once this is all over."

A state of pure happiness had come over me. A strangely spiritual, totally detached perspective that removed every venomous bite of reality. Clinging to nothing; as if all my self-reflective parts were simply offline. When we arrived at the hospital, it was nearly four a.m. and I was met by a blinkered staff attempting to reach their shift's end. A psychiatrist came by and examined me, and I explained to her that a misunderstanding had taken place in my dorm.

"There was a midget and ogre in there stealing everything I owned. People refused to believe me."

She studied me gravely and wrote something down on a notepad before being replaced by a nurse to take blood work.

The nurse inserted the needle and walked away. For several long seconds, I stared at the needle as if in a dream; the exhausted nurse had stuck it in lopsided, and it rode a growing blood swell away from my forearm.

"Why didn't you say something?" The nurse asked, rushing back to my side.

"I was just looking at it."

The nurse pulled the needle and the blood swell erupted, turning my forearm into a purple and pink subway map of bruised capillaries.

What happened next is blanketed in a haze of waking sleep, and the pain of withdrawals gnaws. I recall the bewildering shuffle of hospital staff escorting me through buildings and up elevators, removing my clothing, and strip-searching me.

A male nurse removed the large packet of cocaine from my shorts.

"Give me that bag back." I lunged at him, but he sidestepped me like a matador.

"Can I get some help in here?" He called out.

"Fuck you," I spluttered as two other nurses gently gripped me, I was too weak to resist much. Then I blacked out.

CHAPTER SIX — MAY 27TH, 2017

*"As Gregor Samsa awoke one morning from uneasy
dreams he found himself transformed in his bed into
a gigantic insect."*

— Franz Kafka, The Metamorphosis

Many hours later, I awoke to a screaming headache and a painful stiffness in my legs and back. I sat up and bent my torso forward to stretch my hamstrings before a rush of shame and loathing stunned me, and my arms went limp at my sides. I wasn't so much lost in thought as frozen in a block of self-hatred. After a few moments, I broke the trance and grabbed at my empty pockets, then groped around the room for my coke bag before remembering the robbery the night before.

I got out of bed to find the nurse to demand my coke bag before stopping myself. I sat back down and recalled vague images of doctors and nurses trying to calm me as I punched and kicked furniture, at one point literally banging my head against a wall. The previous night's blackout had not been complete, but my few memories were dream-like, broken and faint, and I couldn't piece together a coherent sequence of events. I remembered someone saying the term "psychiatric hold" to me. Of all the night's terrible memories, the most painful was when some kind of doctor had said to me that my "hedge fund" was a psychotic fantasy. This had led to the head banging.

A plump, smiling nurse in maroon scrubs interrupted my ruminations by pushing a metal cart into the room. For the first time, I took in my environment. The room was brightly lit with white LEDs, and the late May California sun blazed through the steel-barred porthole windows dotting the wall behind me.

The room was beige, with a small wooden desk in the corner. A single bed was lodged against the wall, hedged in by a ruffled wraparound curtain. A checkered beam of light streamed onto my feet.

The nurse pulled back the curtain and smiled warmly. "Hello, Dean. It's time for your check-in. We usually do this at 8, but let you sleep in today."

"Thanks, I feel totally refreshed."

"I need to check your blood pressure."

"Right, go ahead."

As she secured the velcro straps and started squeezing the pump I caught the title of the book on my desk: *Living with Schizophrenia*.

You gotta be kidding me; they're quick with the diagnoses here.

The track marks from my botched bloodwork the night before had grown more vivid overnight. The nurse eyed them cautiously as she took my vitals.

"You have to be more careful if you use a needle."

"This is from bloodwork."

"Okay, honey."

I was wearing turquoise cotton two-piece pajamas with flood pants six inches too short. Laser printed on the breast pocket was the bright red lettering "G2/H2." A baseball-sized indent was in the wall plaster to the right of my head.

"Were you taking any medication before arriving here?"

"I was on a lot of drugs."

"Who prescribed them?"

"I did."

"Mm. Any prescribed by a doctor?"

"No."

A moment later, another nurse with a good body came in with a tray of pills and set it on the table next to my bed.

"What am I taking?"

"An antipsychotic and an antidepressant," she answered with a tinge of sympathy in her voice. Both nurses watched me to make sure I swallowed. But I was a willing patient.

After the nurses left, I went back to sleep for a couple more hours and awoke in a foul mood. I walked out into the hall and nearly ran into a massive man with an unkept beard pounding his fist against a wall.

"Where is Dr. Tracy?" he bellowed. "I need to change one of my prescriptions!"

No shit, I thought.

I carefully avoided eye contact as I slid past him to get to the nurse. Stationed behind a stainless-steel cart carrying vital monitors, she wheeled from room to room doing midday rounds. It was the second nurse, the one with the pills and the good body. It was time to get myself out of the ward.

"Hey there! Do you mind telling me who oversees patient discharge?"

"The physician in charge of the ward makes all discharge decisions. Unfortunately, he's gone for the weekend, and the weekend doctor won't be here till tomorrow morning."

"I'm not really meant to be here, I'm starting a hedge fund and plan on making a lot of money really soon. Is there anyone I can see earlier?"

"Sorry, you'll have to wait until tomorrow."

I felt a rush of anger so strong it took every ounce of restraint not to scream.

"I can't wait till tomorrow; I'm not supposed to be here!" I said with a shaking voice.

She shrugged.

I was about to continue my protests before a bell rang, signaling it was time for lunch. A cart filled with plastic cloche-covered plates appeared, and we lined up in our pajamas, soothed into obedience by the promise of food. I realized I was ravenous, and the savory smell distracted me from my indignation. I accepted the plates and plastic forks and sat at one of the round tables, keeping my head down to avoid eye contact with the other inmates.

I removed the lid and began devouring a steaming plate of meatloaf with mashed potatoes and broccoli. I finished the first portion in ninety seconds before returning for a second plate.

The plump nurse nodded approvingly as I came for seconds. "That's good, honey. You look like you need to eat." I liked her; she cared.

After a second helping, I looked around and watched an older Asian man slip his fork into his pajama pants. He saw me and turned, whispering, "Done with fork?"

"Yeah."

"Give it me?"

"Why not." I handed him the fork, and he slipped it into his pants before nodding thanks to me. I felt like I had just joined in a grand conspiracy.

"Can I have your fork, please?" a nurse asked when she came to collect my plate.

"I gave it to him."

"Hector, are you stealing forks again?" The nurse turned toward him.

"No."

"Hector, stand up." The nurse walked over to Hector and began shaking his pants like a sail in high wind, and half a dozen forks clattered to the ground.

Hector began to shout, "Fuck you! Fuck you! Fuck you!"

A couple people laughed, two or three clapped inscrutably, most ignored it entirely.

As I walked around G2/H2, I saw the depths of my predicament. Doors marked "High Elopement Risk," bars on the windows, meals with plastic silverware, and the chronic wail–moan–whimper of one or more distressed patients reinforced the fact that I had been wronged.

But when Sarah walked into the ward and smiled at me, my heart flipped. I had no idea she was coming and she looked so fresh and warm that the expression on her face alone caused tears to roll down my face. She came up to me and hugged me.

"Aww, don't cry. How are you feeling?"

"Good now that you're here. I can't believe they have me locked up in this place."

"What happened?"

"My room was broken into. And I called the police and they thought I was crazy."

She stared at me for a beat. "Well, you have been doing a lot of drugs."

"I know. I guess they realized I was vulnerable and decided to strike."

A flash of wariness appeared on her face but she quickly recovered her former smile.

"I'm just happy you're alright. And it's good you get a chance to rest and recover a bit. You need it."

"Listen, I'm going to get cleaned up and then I'm going to launch this fund and get so rich."

Her smile grew wider. "That's the spirit. Let's go play a game. By the way, you look cute in those pajama pants."

"Stop it."

"You do!"

After our game Sarah and I went back to my room. My roommate was in, but we closed the curtain. She went down on me, her head bobbing up and down for several minutes. I finished and felt like a new man. Afterward, the nurse came up to me and said Sarah wasn't allowed in my room anymore.

The next morning, I rose at eight and after my check-in with the nurses I was granted permission to see the weekend doctor.

"Since I wasn't around when you were admitted to the ward," began the doctor, "I have no independent ability to assess your level of improvement over the past 36 hours, so I can't release you. Besides, your tox report was frankly disturbing."

"My tox report?" I asked.

"We tested you on intake and found you were positive for cocaine, alprazolam, amphetamine, MDMA, methylphenidate, OxyContin, marijuana—" he hesitated, "and Quaaludes? What is that?"

I stared at the doctor, surprised that someone almost certainly north of fifty didn't know Quaaludes.

"Have you seen *Wolf of Wall Street*?"

"No."

"Leonardo DiCaprio overdoses on Quaaludes—which are a better version of Xanax—while his yacht sinks."

"So you're trying to be that guy?"

I laughed. "It's not the worst outcome for me."

"Listen. I'm worried about your stability," he continued. "Let me put you on a higher dose of an antidepressant to steady your mood."

"So, I guess I'm stuck in here then?"

"At least through the weekend."

It was Memorial Day weekend, which meant three more days.

"I got on the first flight after I heard what happened," my mother gushed after rushing into the ward that afternoon with Evan. "We're just so happy you're okay."

"It's great to see you, Dean," said Evan, hugging me cautiously.

"Your father had to work," Mom added, "but he wanted to be here."

"Listen," I said. "The reason I'm in here, the reason I started using a lot of stimulants and not sleeping and 'went a little crazy'"—I added air quotes to "went a little crazy," which made them both laugh—"was because I was working on launching a hedge fund."

My mom's eyes widened. "Whoa! Crypto has done so well since you started talking about it, it makes sense for you to turn it into a business." She had expressed in the past that she felt my unhappiness, and consequent drug use, stemmed from a lack of ambition and focus on big goals. And I could see her wheels turning now–seizing on the fund as the solution to my problems.

Sarah came by again, and we all sat down to board games.

"So what are you going to call the fund?" Sarah asked.

"Psych Ward Capital?" my brother proposed, laughing.

"How about 'G2/H2'?" I responded with a big grin. Everyone laughed.

"G2H2 Capital," my mom mused, "I like it."

"That's what I'll call it," I said.

"Your Dad's on the phone!" my mother announced, handing me the phone.

"Hey, Dad."

"Dean, I'm sorry to hear about what happened. How are you managing?"

"A lot better with everyone here. But the worst part is being cooped up. I can't go outside."

"I had a similar experience after my vasectomy."

I snorted. "Your what?"

"My vasectomy. I had to lie in bed for three days. It was the worst."

I chuckled. "Thanks, Dad."

In a strange way I started to enjoy it. All the attention from my family was focused on me, it felt good. The food wasn't bad and I liked wearing pajamas all day.

Forty-eight well-behaved hours after my initial intake, I was granted yard privileges. I joined the noontime procession of ten patients into the hospital atrium for an hour of unstructured exercise in the sun. The atrium consisted of a quarter-acre square plot of grass flanked on all sides by the enormous Stanford psychiatric buildings. I contemplated making a break for it as we passed the "High Elopement Risk" doors. The staff member escorting us was a limping middle-aged smoker, and I could outrun him on one leg. But I was afraid and preferred to wait for a legal discharge.

Outside, I grabbed a half-deflated football from a G2/H2 branded bucket and invited my roommate—a schizophrenic (and, as I later learned, the actual owner of the *Living With Schizophrenia* book)—to play. The ball missed me by fifteen feet every time he threw. Nonetheless, I spotted a quivering grin struggling onto his face despite the dulling effects of his antipsychotic meds.

"Hey, I'm Dean," I said, breaking the game to approach him. He didn't respond, but just smiled meekly and stared at the ground. "Look, you have a powerful arm, but you are having some trouble controlling it. Can I show you how to throw?"

He seemed to nod.

"Release the ball once your arm forms a ninety-degree angle, letting it roll off your fingers so it spirals."

I modeled the correct form for him before placing the ball in his hands and guiding him through it.

"Okay, give it a shot," I said, stepping back a few feet. He fired off a clumsy sideways spiral, but it landed in my hands.

"Hey, that's great!" I shouted. "That's your best throw yet!" I tossed the ball back, backpedaled a few more feet, and he threw it back to me. I kept backpedaling until we were on almost opposite sides of the atrium. "You're better than Brady!" I shouted after a particularly tight spiral. His quivering smile transformed into a wide grin and we both started to laugh.

"Time to head inside!" our chaperone shouted.

After returning the ball to the bucket, I patted my new friend on the back. He turned and smiled at me, extending his hand and patting my back too. When I returned to my room I sat down on the bed, flushed with joy. It was the happiest I had felt in months.

Two days later, the doctor from my intake agreed to meet with me.

"I'm impressed with your recovery Dean; after four days rest you look like a completely different person." He was young for a doctor, probably in his early 40s, and had a serious intelligent face with a strong jawline and week-old stubble. His body was in average shape, like most doctors, and he wore glasses with brown frames that magnified his eyes which seemed full of genuine, almost paternal concern as opposed to the evil, unbelieving expression that my vague memories had attached to him.

"Many of the patients who are permanently committed here had drug-induced psychosis, just like you. Not everyone recovers. I don't want to make this a scared straight talk, but you have to stop using drugs. You have shown a propensity for major psychosis, if you continue to use it's only a matter of time before you go so far you never come back."

"I understand; thank you for telling me."

He signed my release papers and handed me over to an attendant nurse who reached behind a counter and handed me my street clothes. My mom had made sure to supply the ward with fresh clothes, a pair of jeans and a polo. I thought about demanding my coke bag back but I knew it was futile. The main thing was that I was free, and it was easy enough to order more drugs on the outside.

The first thing I did after leaving the ward was head to the gym. You die each time you enter a binge, a total neurological collapse that leads, ultimately, like a phoenix out of the ashes, to rebirth.

My favorite way to induce the feeling of psychological rebirth was to sweat. And there is no sweat like a drug sweat. I ran on for close to an hour, and the sweat and steam that came off me cleared the adjacent treadmills.

Coming into the psych ward I felt like a screwdriver had been plunged into my back and cranked my muscles tight as steel wire, and now the slow release of that tension felt like the best massage in the world. The tree leaves sparkled in the wind, and the air itself pulsed with meaning as I walked out of the gym. *Life really is beautiful,* I thought.

Back in my dorm, I checked the Pythia price and found that it had risen 600 percent. I had made $30,000 on my first ICO. I went on the deep web and ordered a half-ounce of cocaine. There was no way I was starting G2H2 sober.

CHAPTER SEVEN – 2006

"Okay, boys. Up and at 'em!"

It was 6:30 in the morning, and Dad was standing in the doorway, rapping drywall with his knuckles.

I rolled over on the top bunk, rubbing my eyes. "Do we have to go to the early service?"

"Yes!" he answered, laughing.

"Dad's a maniac," I whispered to Evan, already dressed after emerging from the bottom bunk, "why does he always make us go to the early service?"

"I kind of like the early service."

Annoyed at not having a partner in misery, I pulled myself down the wooden ladder and into the kitchen.

The next forty-five minutes were a whirl of collared shirts being dug out of closets, the popping of eggs frying in cast iron and neighborhood dogs barking in a discordant Sunday morning symphony.

A fight broke out in the car ride over. I poked Tyler's thigh, calling it a "womper" referencing the imaginary bass tones when I jiggled it. He smacked me in retaliation and I cried out only to be silenced by menacing threats from Dad. I waited a minute or two to start the whole cycle over and by the time we arrived the entire family was shaking with tension. I enjoyed the anxious air, happy to have companions in my native restlessness.

We marched into church, three boys with parents in tow, doing our best to act like any other well-bred, God-fearing family taking their place in the pews. During a-cappella service, I made sure to stand several bodies apart from my tone-deaf dad.

I read the hymn book in a whisper. My legs were tired and I wanted to sit down. To kill time I shifted to poke Evan in the butt. He ignored me. But today I was bored enough to risk guaranteed retaliation by poking the bear himself. I reached over and sunk a pointer into Tyler's butt, just under the button on the back of his slacks. I clenched my jaw as I dug it in as hard as I could. Quick as a snapping mouse-trap his pointer and thumb were on me, bearing down on my forearm in a red-hot pinch.

The pressure mounted, and I fought a scream. Tyler didn't slacken. I bit my lip and snuck a look at Mom, whose eyes were closed, lost in song. Finally the pain overwhelmed me and I cried out. Curious eyes swiveled in our direction, and Mom swore with her face, turning on Tyler, gripping him by the shoulders and placing her body in between us. I flushed with the high of the drama that carried me through the end of the service.

Finally, the pastor took the pulpit. I threw myself into the chair and stuck my palm up on Evan's seat—but he predicted the move and gently shifted it out of the way before sitting down.

The pastor went on stage and thanked everyone for singing so beautifully.

"I always say, if you are going to come for just one part of the service, skip the sermon and come for worship."

He was trying to be humble, but I could tell he didn't mean it. He began with a slide show that presented pictures of a split rock on the bank of the Red Sea and high-tide marks from Noah's flood. Pictographic evidence that the stories in the bible were real, historical events. I liked looking at pictures instead of listening to an old man talk. Our church was very concerned with reassuring us that the Bible was a historical document and that Jesus really did exist. That especially suited Dad, who would snort incredulously whenever the pastor said something he considered stupid. After the slideshow the pastor started on evolution.

"The scientists want you to believe that our ancestors are fish. Now, I don't know about you, but I like to eat fish, not invite them to my family reunion."

Everyone laughed, including Dad.

Just before my 11th birthday, Mom announced we were changing to a new church, Canyon Hills Community Church. A child of the '70s Jesus Revolution, Canyon Hills was a nondenominational church with a rock band-led gospel service that traded hymn books for ten-foot karaoke screens. The pastor was half Christ-muse, half stand-up comedian, and his flock included cortado-sipping, ripped jeans-wearing hipsters. In retrospect, the move to Canyon Hills was our family's first step out of Christ's door. But for many in the packed service, it was their first step in. We had left the austere practitioners of the faith for a community that ostensibly welcomed all. There were tearful confessions from women who'd had abortions, men who had "repented" of their homosexuality, and addicts who had turned their lives around by gripping tight the helping hand of Christ.

The best part of Canyon Hills was the youth service. Instead of a small classroom, we sat in stadium seating and watched high-definition screens where we learned about the world religions and the importance of Christianity. Every Wednesday night we were granted entrance into the hallowed "youth center," complete with an arcade and half-court basketball. We arrived at 6 pm and played for an hour before being shepherded into the pews as payment for our fun. Canyon Hills made Christianity cool. My faith grew with each passing Sunday to the point that I declared to my parents that I was switching my profession from billionaire to missionary.

But as my faith grew so did my sensitivity to the skepticism around me. "It's important to keep a critical mind when you listen to the sermon," Mom said on the car ride home one day, "just because the pastor said it doesn't make it true."

"The truth is," Tyler said, whispering to me, " the only reason we go to church is because Mom and Dad do. If we were born in the Middle East, we'd be Muslims."

I begged Camron to come to Wednesday night service, and he agreed, seduced by the prospect of an hour of communal gaming, and soon became a regular attendee. I immediately got to work on him, trying to persuade him of the veracity of the bible and the saintliness of Jesus.

"Once you take Jesus into your heart," I told him, "you'll feel his loving presence immediately." A doubt rose in my heart as I spoke; it was a doubt that had grown stronger ever since Tyler's remark that we could have been born Muslim.

As Camron and I walked into the youth center my eyes widened and my heart rate quickened as we plunged into the sensory deluge of flashing lights and blaring Christian rock.

"Let's go play table hockey!" I yelled, my energy surging.

"Okay!"

We got to the tables, and two girls our age were already playing. I felt my attention laser in on one of the girls. She was blonde and wore a light green spaghetti strap top. I felt my cheeks flush and my stomach turn. Camron said something to me, but I didn't hear him.

"Do you guys want to play us two-on-two?" Spaghetti strap asked us, smiling.

I tried to speak but my mouth felt full of peanut butter.

"Sure!" Camron said, saving me.

The game began and I grabbed the striker, locking in with a focus that surprised me. The puck came to me and I lashed at it like a striking cobra, slamming it into the girls' goal.

"Woah!" Spaghetti strap said, "You're pretty good."

"Thanks," I murmured, blushing.

As the game progressed, I felt an overwhelming desire to speak to her, but I couldn't think of anything to say. I decided to focus on impressing her with my play, hoping she would just throw herself at me.

Thankfully, Camron also played well and we won ten to three.

"Well played!" Spaghetti Strap's friend said.

"See you guys later!" Spaghetti strap said, smiling.

Suddenly I felt an almost irresistible desire to kiss her, it was an emotion more potent than I had ever felt before, and in a rush of fear and self-loathing I shoved it down. These were the kinds of thoughts that could send me to hell.

"What's the matter?" Camron asked, noticing my pained expression.

"Oh nothing, let's go play Basketball."

Before long a voice came over the speaker announcing it was time for service.

We filed into the pews and sat through the gospel service and sermon. I paid close attention to the youth pastor's words to atone for my dirty thoughts. And when the youth pastor made his regular altar call: "Anyone who would like to give their life to Jesus Christ, please come forward," I nudged Camron, "You should do it!"

To my surprise he nodded and stepped out into the aisle. Approaching the elevated stage where the pastor stood looking down on him, I saw Camron bow his head and repeat the words I knew so well–accepting Jesus Christ into his heart.

"How do you feel?" I asked him when he returned.

"The same," he said, shrugging.

I laughed, then grew solemn.

"You're joking?"

"No, I swear I don't feel different at all."

I didn't acknowledge it inwardly, let alone express it outwardly, but Camron's words drove the first nail into the coffin of my faith. I would continue attending Church for two more years, but every Sunday after that meant less to me than the one before.

CHAPTER EIGHT - JUNE 2017

"Dude, I need in on this," said George, pulling up in front of the Roble dorm. He looked at me through his Ray-Bans as he leaned out of the window of his Lexus. "This idea is genius. The work-to-reward ratio is off the charts. Dumping on these fucking retard retail investors is exactly what I'm about," George cackled, and I faked a smile.

"But I mean, I get it. It's not just about that. I think the idea of decentralized fundraising is brilliant too. Listen, man. I think we should partner on this thing."

"Partner on what thing?"

"The fund, obviously. Look, this is your baby. I'm not talking 50/50 here. This isn't an equal partnership. But I can bring something to the table. Connections. Another set of eyes and ears. Say I take 30 percent. 70/30. What do you say?"

"Let's make it 20."

"Twenty. Man, 20 isn't a lot... let me think it over."

I was hesitant to work with George. We'd met through sports; I was on the rugby team, and he played lacrosse. He was a border-line sociopath with a trust fund–an ugly combination. But I felt I needed him. His father had a controlling interest in a multi-billion dollar commodity empire.

George idolized his father and found intrinsic pleasure in ethically fraught financial schemes. George was friends with an officer of the Stanford Biomedical Club, which received a large funding grant from the university to purchase microscopes and other medical equipment. George convinced his friend to request funding for unnecessary equipment. He then sold the equipment online and split the money with his accomplice friend. He only made a couple thousand dollars, but he relished pulling one over on Stanford, howling with laughter as he exhaustively listed every micro-step of his swindle. Trust funders need a herculean cover story to push off the boulder of stigma they find themselves under. "Real estate investor" is a common choice, but George felt called to more disreputable exploits.

I had heard rumors that George's anti-social bent found physical expression on the field, apparently giddily taking a lacrosse stick to the back of opponents' knees, cackling at the sometimes catastrophic injuries that would result. His teammates said he wasn't any good, a B-squad player, but he didn't care. Breaking the rules on the field when the ref wasn't looking gave him the same thrill as exploiting a bureaucratic loophole to steal a few bucks. Lacrosse is a complex game with nuance and grace. But in the eyes of the raw observer, it is twenty helmeted bodies swirling around the field like so many molecules in a just-opened coke that spent the afternoon rolling in the backseat. Random, spectacular and messy. Like a regulator, a referee can see only a tiny fraction of the action occurring on the field. They can grasp only a few, ball-adjacent actions, leaving a wide surface area for unsupervised knee cracks.

In lacrosse, as in life, George was always looking to get one over on the world. Money had no seriousness in George's life. But he had grown up idolizing a man, his father, Boris, who saw the world through a single financial lens. I later learned through George's ex that she'd ended things with him after he shared a story about a road trip he took with his father in southeast Asia. Apparently, a car had cut them off, igniting Boris's fury. Instead of letting it go, he tailed the driver for miles, swerving aggressively, flashing his high beams, and honking relentlessly, until the terrified man pulled over on the side of a deserted stretch of road.

Boris followed, got out of his car, and walked up to the driver's window, grinning. He didn't touch the man—he didn't have to. He just stood there, staring, letting the silence stretch, watching the driver's hands tremble on the wheel. Then, finally, he leaned in and whispered something through the open window—something George's ex never repeated but said had made the man nod frantically and drive off as fast as he could.

Even worse, said his ex, was how George had bragged about the event. Laughing about how his father had "broken" the man, how he'd taught him a lesson. She said he seemed to relish his dad's behavior as proof of their superiority. The only law, the only ethic, was what one could get away with.

But I only knew what George told me and what I could glean from our interactions–and something about him drew me to him irresistibly. I felt that, against all evidence, he was not a bad person. He had a charm and an innocence that betrayed the fact that his upbringing probably had much more to do with his anti-social behavior than his fundamental nature. And I liked the fact that George trusted me enough to share his unseemly behavior with me. I could trust him to be untrustworthy, which was preferable to more obscure malevolence. He also made me laugh, which provided a welcome relief from the pressure that had been growing since I'd sent the email about the fund. He was also the first person who was not a family member or my girlfriend who was enthusiastic about the fund, and I had always had difficulty saying no to people who showed me even a little kindness. He agreed to my twenty percent offer, and our partnership began.

I spent the first night out of the ward with Sarah. Sex was another escape that allowed me to disappear for a moment. Wrapped in her arms afterward, I could prolong the feeling of transcending myself. I craved this feeling more than ever as I was increasingly disturbed by a vague sense that the dream of the hedge fund did not come from within me but from an all-powerful outside force. But the email had been sent; I had my ticket and it was time to board. After leaving Sarah the next morning, I met up with George for a scheduled phone call with Boris.

George seemed nervous.

"Do you know what you're going to say?" He asked me, breathing rapidly and shifting uncomfortably.

"I'm just going to tell him about the fund."

"Yeah but do you have your pitch down?"

"I got it down."

George dialed the number, set the phone down and rubbed his hands together expectantly. Boris answered.

After a few pleasantries, George started hyping the fund. "You're going to love this, Dad. Dean's got his hands on a money-making machine. Tell him about Pythia, Dean!"

As I described the details of the Pythia investment, I could hear Boris's breath pick up, like a bear eyeing a salmon soaked in honey.

"I only have one question," he asked. "Could you have made the same return on a $500,000 investment as you made on a $5,000 investment?"

"Yes. But $500K is the maximum amount I would invest. The liquidity typically isn't there for seven figures." A strange confidence came over me, my voice was steady, almost bored, and I said "seven figures" like it was a nominal sum I played with regularly.

Liquidity refers to the amount of money flowing through a market; the more liquidity, the easier it is to offload a large investment without changing the price of an asset. A few hundred thousand dollars is to a liquid market, like US treasury bonds, what a glass of water is to the Mississippi River. If the water level is the price of an asset, a glass of water won't alter the Mississippi. But ICO markets were trickles; even ten thousand dollars could change the market— and a hundred thousand could kill your profit entirely. While my $5,000 glass didn't dent the Pythia market, Boris had a water tank the size of a small mountain.

Boris offered to review deals on a case-by-case basis and invest $200-$500k in investments he approved of. More importantly, he introduced us to a Miami lawyer, who quoted us $17,000 to set up the fund. The New York lawyers we spoke to all quoted at least $65,000, so we went with the one in Miami.

After we hung up, I returned to my room. The fund was becoming real, but I still felt like the college student who couldn't pass his econ classes. I reached for the bag, tapping out a mini-avalanche of powder onto the glass of my phone screen and studied what fell. Satisfied, I used my debit card to crush any rocks into snortable powder. My lips grew wet and my hands shook slightly as I carved out three fat worms. I retrieved a dollar bill from my desk, crusted and curled like a dead leaf, and shoved my pinkie into one end, screwing it into a tight roll with my other hand. I felt a pang of satisfaction at my skill executing the ritual. This was something I was good at. I plugged my right nostril to test the suction of the left. The air thudded listlessly against mucus. Automatically, I flipped the plug to test the right nostril and was pleased to find the air whistled clean. In a single motion, I brought the bill to the right nostril, plugged the left, bent over and sucked up the line. I closed my eyes and bent my head back as the powder tore through my nostril, mixing with mucus before dripping down the back of my throat as a thick white ecstatic goo. I kept my eyes closed, savoring, savoring, before opening my eyes to let out a half-laugh, half-scream.

Vague, grandiose thoughts raced before a vivid fantasy crystalized in my mind's eye–I was standing behind a lectern, smiling, delivering a lecture on how great my life was going. Each part of the lecture broke off into a secondary fantasy where I was at once on a tropical island surrounded by beautiful women and in Stockholm receiving the Nobel Prize in Economics.

The fantasy returned to the lecture hall where women were cooing in the audience, my old professors looked at me admiringly, and my parents and friends beamed at me.

Then suddenly, I snapped back to reality, reaching down to massage the coke bag, which gratefully was bursting with powder. All work would stop the moment that bag emptied. And work could not stop.

I directed my brain, roaring like a buzzsaw from the coke, to respond to emails. I set up a half-dozen investor meetings for the week and then spent a couple of hours polishing my investment plan.

After finishing all the productive work I could think of, I opened Poloniex, my crypto exchange of choice. The price of Ethereum had pumped to $200, up from less than $50 a month earlier. With grandiose fantasies whipping through my now undirected mind, I wanted to make some money fast.

Using the profits from Pythia as collateral, I borrowed 1,500 $ETH (Ethereum tokens) on a 10:1 margin. Margin, for the uninitiated, is investing nitrous. It's a way to increase your buying power by taking out a short-term loan using your assets as collateral. Since you're borrowing from the exchange itself, the exchange will automatically close your position to recoup its loan if it detects any danger of defaulting. Since I had borrowed ten times my collateral, my potential gains were magnified tenfold, as were my potential losses. As soon as the margin was on the books I felt like I had swallowed lightning; each flicker of the Ethereum price sent shockwaves through my nervous system. I was alive.

Then the Ethereum market did what it did best: it moved. First up, $205. My lips grew wet and my heart thumped like shoes in a dryer. $202. *Still up.* $200. *Breakeven; it's bound to go up again now.* $197. My heart sank but I did not give up hope, I was still well within my margin. $199. *We're heading back up.* Then a massive sell order of 10,000 $ETH devoured the buy side of the order book: $187. I pounded the sides of my bed like a toddler. The price rebounded almost instantly to nearly $200, but the damage was done. The exchange executed a forced liquidation, seizing what was left of the loan as well as over half my initial collateral.

I got up and used the bathroom, draining a glass of water then looking into the mirror with loathing. But at least I had coke. I returned to my bed and did another line before remembering I had a meeting with Paul Milgrom, my academic advisor, in half an hour. Milgrom was a star in the economics department, on the shortlist for the Nobel Prize (which he would go on to win several years later), and I was hungry to bring him on as a fund advisor.

I walked to the cafeteria coffee machine and downed back-to-back cups. I walked outside and squinted in the sunlight pounding the pavement with an awful vibration. I strode past palm trees and dodged bikes as I headed towards Coupa, a pop-up café with seats vibrating with the gesticulations of people convinced they are interesting. Google founder Sergey Brin was said to frequent it, although I had never seen him. I tried to cool my nerves by visualizing Milgrom naked. I imagined his old, wrinkled body lecturing in front of a class, the girls screaming in horror at the sight of his dick.

When I arrived, Milgrom was already there. He wore a brown leather cowboy hat and smiled the satisfied smile of a tenured professor atop the economics establishment. He rose when he saw me and shook my hand warmly. We sat down and Milgrom took a long sip of coffee before speaking.

"What can I do for you young man?"

I knew I couldn't come right out and ask Milgrom what I wanted. I had to seduce him in his own language of academics.

"Well, I wanted to talk to you about conducting research in the cryptocurrency market."

Milgrom's smile dimmed slightly. "And what about the cryptocurrency market, exactly?"

"New cryptocurrencies are launching daily, and I was wondering if you would work with me to study price discovery and market formation."

"What a ridiculous idea," Milgrom said, almost under his breath, "cryptocurrencies are nothing but a fad."

"You really think so?"

"Yes I do. They are unregulated and totally unconnected with real-world value. There is little to learn from these markets and I predict they will disappear entirely by next year. I'd advise you to focus your energy elsewhere. As for me, I need to be getting back to work." He stood, grabbed his cowboy hat, placed it on his head, and nodded at me.

"Thank you for your time, sir," I said, staring at my feet and blushing like an idiot.

"You know," he started to say, evidently not hearing me, "now and then I take a meeting with an undergraduate in order to... give back to the community, but I'm not sure I will continue to do so."

Milgrom walked away and I sat, burning with shame. An acquaintance of mine came up to me and we exchanged a few words. I realized he was asking me about the fund and I mentioned I had found a good lawyer in Miami before awkwardly asking him where he was headed next. I felt like I was in a dream, forgetting what I said the instant it left my mouth. After several minutes we waved goodbye to each other and I walked back to my dorm.

A week later my luck changed. The wealthy parents of my frat brothers and Rugby acquaintances descended on campus for graduation. I went around campus and met with the fathers of the students who had responded to my email. I secured $200,000 from a private equity magnate, $300,000 from a prominent venture capitalist, and a series of other six-figure checks usually handed out over beers, reminiscences of "when I was your age," and generally lighthearted probing to see if I was "the real deal." Between the cocaine and my newfound proximity to wealth and power, my nervous system was in a frenzied state. I was getting more yesses than nos and at each affirmation my esteem for the powers of cocaine grew, the miracle drug that had granted me the confidence to strut into the halls of power. Without it I was an anxious C-student happy making $15/hour. By the time the confetti was cleaned up from graduation, I had my $1 million in commitments. George graduated and Stanford immediately approved my leave-of-absence request, apparently happy to be rid of me. George and I planned to meet in New York City in a month to officially kick things off.

Sarah had a summer internship at a cancer research lab in San Francisco, and I visited her before I left. Her Dad lent us his BMW 650i for a weekend at her family's Santa Cruz beach house.

"My big hedge fund manager, ready to head off to the Big Apple!" She said laughing when I met her at her house in Palo Alto.

"And you're gonna cure cancer! Talk about a power couple."

"That's right, baby."

We hopped in her Dad's car and roared off to Santa Cruz. I felt like I had already made it driving with the top down on 85. Cars merged out of the way as we raced by, Sarah's hair flapping in the wind.

The house was huge, four bedrooms all to ourselves right on the beach with a hot tub overlooking the ocean. "This sure beats the psych ward," I said, laughing when we walked in.

"Please don't talk about that place anymore; it makes me feel weird."

"Me too."

"My Dad had an eighty-foot sloop out here but he sold it when he got tired of sailing."

"I'll buy us one once the fund takes off," I told her.

"I don't care what you buy as long as you stay off those drugs. They aren't good for you."

"I know, I will."

Sarah went out to the beach and I told her I was just going to jump in the shower before joining her. I went into the bathroom, turned on the shower and did a thick line off the sink.

Three days later, I was on a plane to New York.

CHAPTER NINE - 2007

The decline in my faith combined with a rise in adolescent hormones culminated in a sexual revolution, my personal 60s. Avoiding dirty music was the first pillar of Christian morality to fall. For a few months I had been listening, thanks to Camron's influence, to pop-rock. One song in particular, a breakup ballad, had a lyric that went, "I miss rolling around with you between these sheets," which I knew was cause for damnation. I had memorized the song and would yank out my headphones to avoid hearing the offending lyrics.

But now I let the lyrics roll. Like a pile of dry tinder, even this little spark set me on fire. My insides twisted and rolled as this forbidden desire, hitherto buried deep down, came exploding to the surface. I couldn't take it any longer. I had to know what a woman looked like naked.

My family had one shared computer. A Macbook sat in our living room day and night, a portal to all the dark and beautiful aspects of humanity, my one window into the Sodom and Gomorrah I now yearned for.

That evening, after my parents had gone to bed and my brothers were tucked safely in their rooms, I approached the computer. I had to maintain absolute stealth, I knew what I was doing was shameful and utterly forbidden. Hell on earth was still possible, and my parents could send me there whenever they wished.

Filled with a fearful excitement I was compelled forward by a new, surprising force. This force, which came from below and surged up, could not be reasoned with. It was primal and all-pervasive–growing stronger as I crept forward, wincing at every squeaking floorboard. I held my breath to make sure there was no stirring in my family's rooms. When I was sure that all was still, I cracked open the laptop slowly, until it was at full mast. I went to the search bar and typed: "Nude Women."

My heart was pounding. I had a foreboding that what I was about to see would change my life forever. The room was dark except for the glow of the laptop, which lit upon my face and focused my attention like a magnifying glass the sun.

I clicked on the first result and was slightly disappointed to see a wall of text. I scrolled down and then I saw it. It was a black and white photo of a woman, she was pregnant and her hands cupped the bottom of her belly. But what attracted my attention were two giant breasts draped over her distended stomach. I was overwhelmed with shock. There was something wrong with her. On the end of her breasts were two nipples, which couldn't be right. I scrolled further down, and saw another woman, this one wasn't pregnant, but she also had nipples. I had believed that only men had nipples, and that women's breasts were perfectly rounded like two giant eggs. I felt disgusted, exited the window and shut the laptop, returning to my room to contemplate the implications of my shattered worldview.

The next morning, I awoke to my Mom's cry from the living room. "Boys get in here!" I left my room as if I were walking to my trial. My brothers were already there when I arrived, forming a semicircle around the computer with my Dad standing behind, arms folded.

"Nude women??" She asked with anger and fear in her voice. "Who searched that?"

My face turned white, Tyler and Evan shrugged their shoulders with looks of genuine innocence. Mom looked around at all of us suspiciously, her eyes settling on me for a few moments, studying my face. "I don't want to see any more searches like this on the computer."

I told Camron about what happened. He laughed.

"You just gotta clear the search history!"

"Clear the search history?"

"It guarantees your Mom can't find out what you're looking at; let me show you."

Thank god for Camron.

The following year Tyler entered public school. Mom knew her limits, high school math was too much for an English major, and so Tyler enrolled in tenth grade at the high school. He didn't seem happy about it, but I was excited. I figured he would be getting laid constantly. I had never seen people getting laid, and his room being next to mine, I took my Dad's largest flathead screwdriver and punched a hole through the wall so I could watch. I wanted to study so I would know what to do when my time came. But a year went by and he never did bring a girl home, and the hole went unused until Dad discovered it.

Evan ratted me out.

"Dean made the hole so he could watch Tyler doing stuff with girls."

To my surprise, he didn't get mad. He just patched the hole and told me not to do it again. "Drywall is hard to repair," he said. I guess he understood why I did it.

The next year Evan went to public school, but he didn't bring back any girls either. Finally, a year later, it was my turn. I wasn't a total recluse, I was in the Boy Scouts and had been playing youth football since I was ten. Plus I had Camron and the homeschool school. But public school stood before me like a new world—images of girls and sports and a vague premonition of drugs and other, mysterious adult dark arts appeared in my mind's eye in a kaleidoscope of adolescent delights. I knew I was naive, and I couldn't wait to find out what I was missing.

I arrived for my first day full of nervous energy and sentimentality about the institution I was entering. I had convinced Mom to send me to school a year earlier than my brothers, in ninth grade, which in my area was the last year of Junior High School.

I knew some of the boys already from the summer football camp. I had watched the popular ones closely, sleuthing for social clues that I hoped would unlock the treasures of this new world. Some of the boys, the bigger, taller and stronger ones, already had a rapport with the coaches and were joking with them like old pals. They had big smiles and shouted when they talked, and even their straight, floppy hair oozed a native confidence that I wanted for myself.

 One of the coaches, meaty, late-20s with long blonde hair draping to his shoulders, shouted at us to get in line. One by one the coaches handed us helmets and shoulder pads and girdles and knee pads, assessing us like cattle.

"Jones what have you been doing all summer? You look flabby!"

"I've been working out, Coach."

"Working out your jaw with all that chewing."

The coaches didn't say much to me when I walked through the line, I was only 5'9 and 130 pounds but I was stronger than I looked and so had confidence.

"What position do you play?" An assistant coach asked me.

"Linebacker."

"Linebacker? Can you hit?"

"I can hit."

"Okay go practice with the linebackers."

I walked over to the linebackers' practice, which had a series of strategically positioned cones on the field. The linebacker's coach was the one with the long blonde hair.

"Linebackers are gladiators; we don't want any pussies here, if you're a pussy you can go practice with the receivers. Are any of you pussies?"

A few of us murmured no, coach.

"I said, are any of you pussies??"

"No coach!" We all answered in unison.

"Good. Let's get to work."

We formed two lines, one line playing offense and the other defense. I started on defense. As I waited in line the smell of heated plastic floated off the astroturf and I felt sweat drip down my forehead. My turn came and I ran at the runner and launched at him like a missile, knocking him down.

"Don't leave your feet when you tackle, a real running back will embarrass you!" The coach screamed.

"Here's how you do it."

He shoved the ball in my hands and had me act as the running back. I tried to stutter step him but he lowered his shoulder and barreled into me. I landed on my ass, and fell on top of me, his hot breath pouring through my facemask.

"That's how you tackle boys!" He bellowed.

He grabbed my hand and helped me up, giving me a pat on the butt as I headed back to the line.

A couple girls walked up to the sideline. One had on ripped jean shorts and a yellow tube top and my blood began to boil. They were like fairies. I stuck out my hollow chest to try to look good for them. During a water break I stood near the girls, awed by their giggling aura. Another ninth grader went up to them and started talking to them, they smiled and laughed. My throat grew sandy at the prospect of talking to them.

"You gotta remember," our linebacker coach told us after practice, "that these are the best years of your life. You better enjoy them!"

I didn't believe him. I knew that a gulf existed between the raging sentiments and emotions within me and the pallid, almost lifeless outward expression I was able to give them. The next four years was my chance to merge this gap, and in this merging, my real life would begin.

As I walked into my first day of school I felt a desire to do in a single year what my peers had done in six. The honors classes were already full and so I was put in the "regular" classes, which I didn't mind. It meant less homework and more time to look at girls. History was third period, and the teacher looked about a hundred years old. He had long white hair which went down to his shoulders and a bushy grey beard and mustache. He had a great gut and oversized jeans held up with dark brown suspenders over a blue and yellow plaid shirt. He wore the same thing every day. Our in-class assignment, likewise unchanging, was to hand copy newspaper headlines upper-case (minus five points for using lowercase), including the date, the location, and the publication along with a five-sentence summary. He never assigned homework.

I was busy copying headlines when I felt a nudge. It was the boy sitting next to me, Ali. He had his penis out and was wiggling it with his hand. I stared at it for a few seconds, it looked like a thick brown earthworm waving back and forth.

"Take yours out," he whispered.

"I can't, the teacher will see me."

"Come on."

"I can't."

He scowled and put his dick away.

Finally, I got to sixth period, Geometry. We sat down, and the teacher passed around a seating chart and asked us to fill in our names. I put mine down, Dean Patrick, and passed it on to one of the football boys, Spencer, a receiver, who giggled as he filled his name in. Spencer turned to me and whispered, "Ellie's so hot," pointing at a Brunette girl who had just stood up to sharpen her pencil. I hadn't noticed her before.

"She's got a great ass," he continued.

"Yeah, she does," I answered.

I had never once considered a girl's butt; it might as well have been an inert object. But the way he had whispered, "Ellie has a great ass," was the exact way I had imagined the clandestine world of public school, full of essential secrets of real life, would be imparted to me, and so I took special note of this comment, resolving to study girls' asses and use my whispered opinion of them as a binding mechanism connecting me irrevocably with the world of the cool boys.

Finally, the seating chart reached the teacher who read out the names.

"Is there a Bean Patrick here?"

"Uh, it's *Dean* Patrick."

"Oh okay sorry about that."

Spencer roared with laughter and even the teacher couldn't stifle a giggle. But my embarrassment disappeared when Spencer slapped my back and said "You're a good sport, buddy." I was in.

CHAPTER TEN – JUNE, 2017

By the time I got to New York, cocaine, the lawyer, and bad trades left me with $1,800 in cash. My remaining assets included $1,000 in cocaine, a baggie of 30mg Adderall XRs, a few dozen 2mg Xanax bars, a Macbook air, a $500 navy-blue Ted Baker sports coat and 4.8 $ETH. But my spirits were good, I had my health.

Before arriving, I had found a summer sublet for $750/month in StuyTown and an internship at EtherMosaic, a blockchain venture studio in Williamsburg founded by early crypto pioneer John Larrabee. Pythia had been incubated out of EtherMosaic and apart from paying $22/hour, it offered an inside track to top-tier ICOs.

StuyTown (for its part), is an old red-brick residential complex opened in the mid-40s for veterans that looks like a cluster of bear shit from the sky. On my first day of work, I rose at six and ran along the East River, pumping my legs up and down and sweating in the late-June Manhattan heat. I took in the high rises and imagined the eating and shitting that went on in New York every day. Piles of food and shit the size of the Empire State Building flooded through millions of bodies each day, in and out, like a giant industrial machine.

I laughed at the thought. Sweating and laughing and pumping my legs up and down to Seaport and back, over seven miles, feeling like a real person when I got in the shower. It had been four days without using and my brain was primed for a binge. I stashed a two-gram bag in my pocket and walked to the subway.

I got off the subway and followed Google Maps to the street address. The office was in Williamsburg, Brooklyn's hipster mecca and the headquarters of Vice Media. Every other door a speakeasy façade, and the rest entryways to former warehouses turned startup headquarters. But even amidst Williamsburg's superficial dilapidation, the entrance to EtherMosaic's headquarters stood out–cross-hatched with so many stickers and graffiti. It was dive bar bathroom meets Post-Malone's face.

The HR director, a woman in her mid-30s named Samantha, welcomed me with a breathless hug and smile and took me into the office. Ethereum's price had surged from $10 in January to over $300 by the time I arrived and EtherMosaic, funded entirely by Larrabee's war chest of seven million ETH, now had nearly $2 billion at its disposal.

Inside EtherMosaic HQ, assigned desks were eliminated to maximize spontaneous interactions, and all employees shared an expansive room with Larrabee. The kitchen had a keg of cold brew coffee and shelves of craft beers, wine and liquor. I kept sneaking side glances at Larrabee during Samantha's tour.

Physically he was nondescript, balding black hair, with a slight stoop, as if years of hunching over keyboards had subtly collapsed his frame. He wore an understated black t-shirt and baggy blue jeans. An alpha nerd whose presence, despite his total lack of mainstream cultural coolness, caused my adrenaline to surge like a high schooler at the homecoming dance.

The office was filled with the sounds of shuffling chairs, clicking keyboards and murmuring conversations that occasionally burst out into heated professional shouts–the undulating soundtrack of a hundred mostly twenty-somethings packed into one room and armed with the fervent conviction that they were changing the world. EtherMosaic had "no bosses," Samantha explained, but it was obvious what she meant. Power was determined by proximity to Larrabee. The seats closest to him were competitive items, staked out early in the day and fiercely guarded. His grip on power was solidified by his being among the oldest at a company where being 25 made you an elder statesman. When I was first hired, I was told that I would be one of fifteen interns. But on my first day, Samantha told me they had ended up hiring fifty.

"John told me to hire anyone who seemed qualified!" said Samantha cheerily. Because many full-time employees worked from home or at offices overseas, almost half the summer bodies were interns.

The whole world was waking up to crypto that summer, and the person I was told to "ask if I could help" (again, no bosses) was William Kenney–one of the key figures profiting from crypto's rise. I later learned he was EtherMosaic's fourth hire and their "head of business development," who reportedly held a multimillion-dollar crypto position that was doubling weekly.

"Samantha told me to ask you if there are projects I can help out with," I said, taking a seat across from William.

"Are you an engineer?" he replied, glancing up at me and narrowing his eyes, apparently wary of any more non-technical interns being foisted on him.

"No, I'm majoring in Economics."

"Ask around; I only need engineers right now."

"Sure thing."

"Want to help me on a real estate project?"

I turned and saw the question came from a smiling, bearded man, probably in his late 20s, sitting next to William.

"I'm Gary. What's your name?"

"I'm Dean. But I don't know anything about real estate."

"That's a good thing."

The EtherMosaic business model involved giving $200,000 to anyone with a plan to decentralize a major industry. Gary's idea was to put all real estate titles and transfer documents on the blockchain, cutting out real estate agents and slashing closing costs.

It sounded boring to me. But Gary told me he could benefit from someone "with a fresh perspective."

"What did you do before this?" I asked Gary.

"I worked at Goldman Sachs."

I did a bump in the bathroom and came back with a sudden interest in decentralized real estate. He asked me to go through his pitch deck and try to think of anything he had missed. I went through the deck, but I didn't understand it.

"It looks good to me," I told him.

One thing I had learned in my relatively short life was that success had very little to do with knowing things. It had very much to do with getting the right people to think you knew things.

"That's great. Now, what we need is a real estate company to develop a proof of concept with us. Can you do some outreach and set up meetings?"

"Okay."

I set to work but quickly grew bored. What interested me was learning who in the room was working on the next Pythia.

Pythia was the biggest company EtherMosaic had incubated thus far, and its June market cap of $2 billion *exceeded* Ethereum's market cap in January. I assumed everyone wanted to launch their own Pythia, and I wanted to invest in them. After lunch, I made the rounds of the office. I first went up to a man, around 25, and the only person in the office wearing a suit and tie.

"Hey, I'm Dean. I'm an intern this summer, and I'm curious about what you're working on."

"Glad you asked, Dean! I'm Joe, I'm working on a permanent co-living community that uses blockchain to radically reinvent power structures."

"How do you define power?"

"Have you read Foucault?"

"No."

"Well, anyway, you know money is power. And money, from the standpoint of labor, is equal to time. Time is the ultimate scarce asset, the ultimate currency. Think about how much time a billionaire can buy: it amounts to the lifespans of tens of thousands of people. That disparity is the foundation of inequality in our society."

"Yeah, like how Larrabee is buying all of our time."

Joe frowned. "So what we're doing is creating an egalitarian society where time *is* the formal currency. Everyone in the community is allocated twenty-four 'TIME' coins each day, and they can trade them for anyone else's 'TIME' coins, one-for-one."

"But what if I want to take a day off?"

"That's fine. You can take your TIME coins off the market, but you can't purchase anyone else's that day."

"And what happens if Einstein is in your community and he keeps having to stop working on special relativity to mow someone's lawn?"

"Then Einstein will mow the lawn," Joe said, smiling mischievously.

"What did you do before this?"

"I was at McKinsey."

"And where is this community?"

"We're looking to buy property somewhere in the desert, Nevada or California."

"Thanks for taking the time to share your vision; I guess I owe you one of my TIME tokens now."

He laughed and shook my hand. I liked him; he had a dream that wasn't just about getting rich. I envied him, even though I thought his idea was stupid. The next founder I spoke to wanted to put all global water rights on the blockchain, and another was doing something vaguely related to the music industry, but when he mentioned they had no plans for an ICO, I stopped paying attention.

Most of the founders were in their mid-to-late 20s, with backgrounds at elite consultancies and banks. The interns, not having the confidence or freedom to make a multi-year commitment to a startup, made up the rank-and-file staff of these fledgling businesses.

It was clear to me that most of these projects lacked the multi-billion dollar potential of a Pythia. They were quixotic, like the Burning Man idea, or simply orthogonal to financial speculation, like the water rights startup. Even Gary's real estate startup lacked the flair to attract the army of retail investors to make it a Pythia-level success.

It was now late afternoon, and I was starting to grow ornery. The coke was leaving my system, so I went to the bathroom and refreshed myself. On emerging, I saw a vibrant-looking man with a well-cropped beard dressed in a black cotton T-shirt and cargo shorts standing behind a desk smiling in my direction. I went up to him and introduced myself, asking him what he was working on.

"My name is Alejandro," he responded. "I just founded a company called Liquid Freedom with Amalia." He gestured to a woman in all black, probably in her early 40s, bent over a laptop. "We have another founder, David, our CTO, who lives in South Africa."

"What is Liquid Freedom?"

"Well, we're still trying to figure that out. But what unites us is we have all been disenfranchised by the traditional financial system. I'm Venezuelan."

"Enough said," I interjected.

"David lost access to his money for months due to a banking error. So now he doesn't have a bank account, he uses Bitcoin exclusively. And Amalia is an activist, she used to work at JP Morgan..."

Amalia broke in.

"The system is totally fucked. It was the Occupy Wall Street movement that stole my heart and re-ignited my activist flame." She spoke with a thick German accent and her speech had a lyrical quality, like she was performing Shakespeare. "I've always been an activist you see," she continued, "ever since I was a little girl. But EtherMosaic has given me an outlet to pursue it as a career. We want to bank the unbanked, and franchise the un-enfranchised."

"But what are you actually building?" I asked.

"A decentralized exchange," Alejandro answered. "David has found a way to facilitate crypto transactions without an intermediary. What we want is to build the ultimate censorship-resistant platform. A platform which no government can shut down, accessible to anyone, anywhere in the world without fear of retribution."

"Power to the powerless!" Amalia shouted out, raising a fist and then throwing her head back in laughter.

Amalia's comment touched my heart. It reminded me that my first interest in blockchain arose from a genuine feeling that this technology could help the most vulnerable people—a feeling I had chosen to bury. But now I had a chance to marry my financial dreams with my neglected idealism.

"Can I join you?" I asked.

I explained my credentials. A decentralized exchange could use an economics major, someone with at least a cursory knowledge of financial markets and incentives. They agreed.

I went back to Gary and told him I was leaving his startup.

"That's okay man! That's what this place is about, following your heart!"

The next day I traded in my coke for the more stable boost of Adderall. I began the morning with two 30mg XRs washed down with coffee before showing up at EtherMosaic to take my seat at one of the communal wooden tables next to Alejandro and Amalia.

On Friday morning, after four days of work, I decided I would take a long weekend at home. The job was optionally remote, so I settled into bed with the baggie, sniffing coke, and turning my attention once again to the fund. The legal registration had been dragging on for several weeks so I sent several encouraging emails to my lawyer.

Before I knew it it was Sunday afternoon and the bag that was supposed to last me two weeks was empty. I went online and ordered another half-ounce, but it would take days to arrive and so I began a frantic search around the room for any spilled coke in a desperate effort to continue the binge. Just hours earlier I had been careless, like a euphoric drunk ordering shots for the entire bar. In the frenzy I had dumped piles of powder on my phone, spilling little bits onto the floor and the bed, encouraged into reckless profligacy by the size of my remaining stash. But now, with the coke gone, every white speck lost in the carpet was like bits of red meat to a starving dog.

I ran my finger along every smooth surface where I had made lines and sniffed the residue off my fingers, grimacing when I invariably tasted dirt or lint.

The promise of finding The Big Rock somewhere sustained me in my search. A big chunk of coke that would keep me going for a few more hours. After an hour of desperate searching, I gave up. Reclining in bed to face withdrawal. I was still wired, but all the euphoria was gone.

The shadows around my room became freakish, menacing figures. But they did not bother me like they had before. I had learned my lesson–they were merely withdrawal's cheerleaders. I popped a Xanax and put on YouTube clips of The Howard Stern Show. Six hours later, around 4 am, I fell into a fitful sleep. Waking at 9:30, I dragged myself to the shower and steamed off. One of my roommates came by, another EtherMosaic intern.

"Hey man, haven't seen you at work. You good?"

"Yeah I'm good, I'm actually launching a hedge fund right now, I've been so busy."

"A hedge fund?" He raised his eyebrows in surprise, "How old are you again?"

"Twenty-one."

"A hedge fund at twenty-one, that's incredibly impressive." He forgot all about my appearance and stared at me in awe.

"Thanks man, we'll see how it goes, haven't made any money yet." Despite my attempt at humility I grinned broadly, pleased with his reaction.

I felt a wave of nausea and said, "See you later," before ducking into my room. My whole body was aching, but it didn't matter; I was a winner.

CHAPTER ELEVEN - 2011

Ninth grade ended with a field day. We all filed out onto the football field for three-legged races and capture the flag. A year had gone by and I had no solid friendships. Spencer had too many actual close friends to consider me in his inner circle.

Two months earlier I was in the back of Spencer's Mom's Ford Explorer driving to the park when Spencer, with three of his close friends also sharing the car, handed me a plastic water bottle and said, "have some wine." I had never drunk before and grabbed it greedily. The others had been drinking before Spencer picked me up, and I was desperate to merge with the exuberant familiarity of the group, punctuated by roars of laughter from inside jokes whose meaning escaped me like the spurts of my affected laughter. I unscrewed the top and took a big swig. It was warm and had a mute, almost sour taste. I had no idea what wine tasted like, so I shrugged and took a longer pull. Taking a half swallow and spitting out the rest. The wine was so revolting to my system I just couldn't put it down. Then Spencer laughed and shouted, "you're not actually drinking that are you?"

"Uhh what do you mean?"

"That's my piss bro."

Acquaintances on the sports teams would wave at me in the halls, but I had not managed to enter into their private social world. The football boys, who I was ostensibly one of, and their cadre of attractive girls and hangers-on, talked in a wide circle at lunch with effortless energy and confidence. Nice clothes, little acne and powerful bodies. Their seemingly innate confidence confused and humbled me.

I passed my lunch breaks with Kian. He was Iranian, short and squat with mess of straight black hair shooting halfway down his neck. He followed me around with the persistence of someone who sensed another being as lonely as him. Of course I considered myself too good for him and would act dismissively, crossing my arms and leaning on a wall away from him when popular guys walked by. But his attention flattered me, and I was grateful to have someone with whom to pass the agonizing lunch breaks.

During field day I was surprised to see Luke, the leader of the football clique, approaching me.

"Hey Dean, we're doing a body-boxing tournament in the boys' locker room after school. You interested?"

"Yeah definitely."

"Okay meet there at 2:45."

When I arrived, the locker room was full of forty or more guys and almost as many girls. A match was underway. Ali, my history classmate, was pounding away on a scrawny kid who I had never met but who was taking the beating nobly. Ali's punches swung wide and connected continuously with his side body and chest, the scrawny kid had his elbows dug into his sides protecting himself and he grimaced, exhaling at each punch. The circle was collapsing and reforming to make way for the fighters as they moved around the locker room. Ali backed his opponent into a corner and began swinging faster, going for the knockout, but his breathing grew heavy and his punches slowed. The scrawny kid wound up and dug a series of hard uppercuts into Ali's stomach. He gasped, bending over, "I'm out!"

There was an eruption of applause and shouts. The scrawny kid threw his hands up in the air before hugging it out with Ali.

"Dean you want next?" Luke asked me.

"Sure."

"Okay you take Sam."

Sam was one of the most popular football players, he played receiver and was tall, fast and skinny. He had freckles and an attractive face that the girls constantly fawned over. There was no one who felt more socially distant than Sam. But in this fight I knew he didn't stand a chance. I had wrestled in the winter season and had built up some stamina and muscle and had a sense of how to fight.

The locker room grew quiet as we squared up, Luke gave the signal to start and we began circling each other, feeling it out. Sam's face was tense and he was standing straight up. I got into my stance, knees bent, upper body slightly forward, right foot in front of left. I moved in on him and landed a sinker into his right side, he groaned and threw a right but it had no juice. I knew I had him. I let out a blizzard of hard jabs, and Sam gave out. He put up his hands to stop the fight.

"He sucker punched me in the balls!" Sam shouted.

"No I didn't, It was a fair fight."

Luke hesitated, "did anyone see any sucker punches?" he asked.

"It was a fair fight," Ali interjected.

Apparently satisfied, Luke let it pass but Sam continued spreading the rumor, "Dean's a dirty ball puncher."

I waited my turn for the next bout, the semi-finals. Luke stepped in and cleaned up his first opponent, Joey, a lineman who fought tough but gave in after a minute or two to Luke's cannon punches. Everyone said Luke was the favorite, he hit harder than anyone, kept his head and knew when to make his move. I wanted Luke in the final.

My second match was more challenging, against the captain of our wrestling team, David. He was part-Samoan and built like a bulldog. But I had seen him get pinned several times in wrestling matches and knew he wasn't invincible.

We squared up and this time I waited for David to make the first move. He felt me out with a few light jabs, before winding up for a hard right, I bent into the swing and absorbed it. Then he went left, same thing happened. I circled around eyeing him, noticing a twinkle of doubt in his eyes.

I moved in, plowing a cross into his chest with my right and then digging an uppercut to his belly with my left. David absorbed it with a grimace and took two steps back, the circle opened to let us move and I pressed the advantage, cracking him with another left-right combo before doubling over from an uppercut to my stomach. Sensing his opportunity, David let out a barrage of punches and I stumbled back, but he was slow to move forward, giving me precious time to recover my breath. Finally he came at me but I had recovered enough that his punches lacked knockout power. He lost his breath from effort and I went on the offensive, pressing forward with a wild series of crosses, left-right, left-right, straight down the track. He began an all-out retreat to the corner, genuine fear now shining in his eyes. I kept pounding away, my breathing grew heavy but I redoubled my efforts and he finally surrendered. I was in the finals.

I had entered ninth grade with high hopes of being whisked away in a whirl of pleasure and enthralling drama, but the reality consisted of keeping my head down and praying for a swift end to the day. But I had learned to survive in the social wilderness, mostly by not saying much and accepting the adolescent suffering of being a social outsider.

I had also embraced the minor injustices of a bureaucratic system. An anti-drug policy limited us to carrying only the books we needed for our next class. I had two classes back to back on the far end of the school away from the lockers, and I simply did not have enough time to walk to the lockers and back in time for my next class. For the first month of school I ran to make it on time.

But after a while I got tired of running and started to walk. Every day I would get to class exactly 60 seconds late for fourth period. After my second tardy the teacher gave me a pink slip for lunch detention. I taped each pink slip to the inside of my locker and counted forty-seven by the end of the school year. I didn't mind really; it just meant that I had to eat lunch with the detention teacher at a special table in the middle of the cafeteria, which saved me from having to sit with the other kids.

One day I was taking my usual time in the lunch line, cutting continuously to the back so as to reduce how long I had to sit at the detention table, when I overheard one of the girls talking about college.

"My dream school is Stanford!" She told her friend, "it's the best college on the West Coast, maybe even the whole country."

It was the first time I had heard kids my age talking about college. I figured I would go to the University of Washington, where my parents had gone, but I hadn't given it much thought.

Luke took the scrawny kid for his semi-final match and dispatched with him after just half a dozen hard punches. It was time for the final. The crowd in the locker room was now overflowing into the hallway, it seemed like half the school was there and the energy had reached such a pitch that Luke and the others had to continuously quiet the crowd for fear of attracting a teacher reprisal.

I overheard one of the popular girls whispering to her friend, "Dean stands no chance against Luke, unless he goes for the balls like he did with Sam." I reddened with embarrassment.

A special effort was made to create enough space for a small ring in the center. Luke and I both took off our shirts and squared up. There was a series of bets and commentary coming from the crowd. "Dean's a pussy!" Sam shouted, "he only wins with sucker punches!" At Sam's words, just moments before the final was to begin, a terrible anger that had been locked away in a seal of loneliness and fear exploded into a rage that burned my insides like battery acid. My peripheral vision blurred and I felt myself transform into a wild animal, I rushed at Sam with a feral scream, tackling him to the ground. The moment our bodies hit the floor the anger evaporated off me like steam, and arms, which had flown around me in an effort to restrain any further assault, retracted in recognition that the outburst was over.

I stood up and looked around, the whole school was staring in shock at me and I knew I had done something terrible. There was a brief discussion on how to proceed, and it was decided that the final should continue because Sam was unhurt. I wanted to run away and cry, but I steadied myself to fight.

Although I was five inches shorter and at least thirty pounds lighter than Luke, I cut an intimidating figure. A year of athletics and my first genuine sprouting of adolescent development had left me with a toned, almost ripped body. Luke eyed me curiously and I even sensed a glimmer of worry in his eyes after my assault on Sam.

The fight started and he immediately went on the offensive, landing a series of hard combos straight into my stomach, I flexed and took the beating. His punches had a special force to them and I knew I couldn't hold out long. I came at him, swinging wildly and backing him up slowly. But his body was firm and I could tell my punches did not have the effect they had had on my previous opponents. He swiveled around me and landed a hard series to my right side which sent icicles of pain shooting through my torso. I took a deep breath and channeled every ounce of available energy into a torrent of left-right crosses into his chest and stomach. Luke went into an all out retreat to the corner. He was so strong, my punches, which would have put away almost any other opponent, did their damage but were not quite enough. I saw fear flicker in his eyes and I unloaded my most powerful combo yet in a last burst of energy, but it was not enough. I had exhausted myself, as well as my best chance to win the final. I stumbled back, trying to buy precious time to recover my breath, but Luke, savvy fighter that he was, didn't give me the chance. He came at me with almost the same speed as I had at him but with even more force. Against my smaller body his punches sent an unbearable pain exploding through me and, still gasping for air from my own all-out assault, I surrendered.

The crowd erupted in cheers and Luke raised his arms in triumph. "Wasn't even close!" He shouted, "wasn't even close."

"I almost had you," I said, heaving.

He smiled at me and shook his head.

"I destroyed you."

CHAPTER TWELVE – JULY 2017

In early July I got the news that the fund was registered and the $1 million arrived a week later. Then, after finishing his post-grad vacation in the Maldives, George arrived in New York.

"I just rented a place in Midtown," he texted me, "Come meet me tonight."

For the past couple weeks I had been reconsidering my partnership with George. In theory I didn't need him or even like him but I was lonely and craved companionship. That night, I took the R train to Midtown, rose up into the wriggling mass of cell phone photographers in Times Square, and headed north. There's no worse place for a lonely person to go than Times Square, it's too anonymous. The billboards gave way to a gauntlet of Duane Reades and McDonald's, and the tourists morphed into haggard-looking business types and fast walking well-built women who I stole greedy looks at in anticipation of my coming fortune.

George shouted as he opened the door, "Dean Machine has arrived!"

He was swishing a whiskey on the rocks in his left hand as we came together in a bro hug.

I grinned broadly, "what's up man? You look tan and refreshed."

"I am man. I'm fucking ready to go! Crypto is booming man, it couldn't be a better time."

The room had oak flooring and a full kitchen opening into a small hallway leading to a sprawling living room with access to two separate balconies.

"What are you drinking?"

"I'll have what you're having."

"Let's go outside; the view is unbelievable."

As we stepped out onto the balcony I really couldn't believe how beautiful it was–man-made stars reflecting off an ocean of glass. Before taking a drink I was already intoxicated. Feeling a sense of pride I hadn't anticipated, I straightened up and felt my chest expand.

"Listen man," I began, " we got a million in the bank and with the way crypto's going we can have ten million before the year is out. Twenty percent of that is two million, four-hundred-thousand of which is yours."

"Fuck yeah man. I'll drink to that."

We clinked glasses.

"So," George continued, "when are you moving in?"

"What?"

"Yeah. I'm taking the master, but the other room is yours."

"How much is it?"

"$3,500 a month each. Good deal right?"

My drug habit took most of my EtherMosaic salary and with just $20,000 a year in management fees from our $1 million fund, I had already mentally prepared myself to move under the Queensborough bridge to make the finances work.

A rush of conflicting emotions went through me, moving in with George meant welding my life to his schemes and unscrupulousness. But being with him, and in this apartment, made me feel like I had already arrived in the world I was trying so desperately to enter.

"Great deal. I'll move in at the end of the month, I have to give notice at my place in Stuy Town."

"Stuy Town?" George asked, with a hint of disgust in his voice, "just move in, I'll cover the rent for now."

"You're a good guy, man," I said, feeling a surge of genuine affection for him.

I moved in the following week. To satisfy his Dad, George took a job as an analyst at Fortress Group, a large asset management company, while I stayed at home, sniffed coke and touched myself while doing my best to promote G2H2 to entrepreneurs and media.

A few days later I convinced a reporter at Business Insider to interview me for a feature story on crypto. His office was two miles away and I decided I could use a walk. I put on my sports coat and slacks and headed out. The sun was sticky and hot and the heat came off the pavement like a slow roaster. I plugged my ears as I walked by a reversing garbage truck going "beep beep beep," and then two women walking by shrieked with laughter and I started. I checked the time and saw I was going to be late. I took off my sport coat and began to run. The sweat soaked through my armpits and ran down my white dress shirt like racing stripes. After seeing a pretty girl walk by, I put the coat back on, trying to ignore the blisters forming on my feet as they rubbed against my dress shoes. Finally I made it to the office, three minutes late. I checked my phone and saw a text from the reporter.

"Something just hit my desk, have to cancel."

As I walked home a homeless man asked me for money and I gave him $160. He stared at me in shock before shouting "thanks man!"

When I got home I stripped naked and sat down on the couch. I did an enormous line and opened my laptop. I began to check my email before sighing and clicking over to PornHub. I reached down my pants and got to work. The coke made it hard to finish, which wasn't a problem. It felt good, and I wanted it to last– opening one porn tab after another. Soon I had dozens of videos open and I flicked between them continuously, trying to find the perfect shot. A sommelier of porn, I tasted hundreds of options but didn't allow myself to get drunk. Two hours passed. I went into my room in case George walked in. Eventually he came home and knocked on my door.

"Dean Machine, you in there?"

"I'm busy! Working right now."

"Cool. Want to come get drinks with some of my coworkers?"

"I'm good man! Enjoy." I shouted back.

More hours passed, and then the sun set. I only took breaks to sniff coke and go to the bathroom. As time wore on, an awful feeling creeping around the edges of my awareness grew harder to ignore. The porn and the coke acted as a dam keeping a flood of pain at bay.

My eyes were achingly dry and I had to switch to my left hand after my right began to cramp. I had to go to the bathroom but didn't want to get up so I grabbed a cup at my bedside and pissed until it started to overflow, some of it sloshed over as I set it on the floor.

Then I heard the birds outside my window trumpeting the arrival of first light. Cars honked and pedestrians shouted and I imagined the many thousands of earnest New Yorkers on their way to work, and here I was, wacking away in the early morning hours, having done nothing but dry out my eyes watching porn for twelve hours. Finally I couldn't take any longer, I finished and was at first assaulted by disgust. But to my surprise I also felt incredibly relieved. It was finally over, and now I could get on with my life. I walked out of my room to use the bathroom and to try to score some Xanax from George. He had his suit on, about to go to work, and he looked me up and down.

"What the hell have you been up to?"

"Working."

"That's good, glad to see my partner has a work ethic. But how about a shower?"

"Sure thing. Can I get some Xanax?"

"It's 7 am?"

"Yeah I'm just trying to crash."

He went into his room and came out to give me the stuff. I mumbled thanks and went back into my room, turning on comedy tapes in a desperate bid to stave off the avalanche of self-loathing.

I woke in the late afternoon and went for a walk in Central Park to clear my head. The porn seared into my mind, sexual iconography appearing everywhere. I gazed at the clouds only to find that they had morphed into round breasts with nipples. I closed my eyes, shook my head and opened them again to find the tree leaves shimmering with images of men and women fucking. I turned to the sidewalk and was repulsed by a vagina pulsating in the cracks.

When I got home I checked my email and found a message from a Russian founder named Ilya. He had just launched an ICO and was coming to New York to raise funding. I found his idea intriguing, a crowdsourced cloud mining network for gamers called PlayCrux. PlayCrux was launching a "utility token," which users would be required to purchase to pay for the service. PlayCrux's idea was intriguing, but the bonuses they were giving out to "pre-ICO" investors like myself sealed it.

Here's how the ICO game worked: two months before ICOs listed on exchanges, they conducted a private "pre-sale" limited to accredited investors with some cachet. A public sale would commence one month before listing at roughly twice the price of the private sale. If the ICO was good, the main sale, variably capped between ten and two hundred million dollars, would sell out. Once the token listed on an exchange, it was hockey stick time.

PlayCrux would sell their tokens to me and other large investors for thirty-five cents apiece. Then, a month later, they would charge the small investors one dollar before finally listing on a public exchange for all of us to dump. It was crude and unfair, but at least it was more open than the even cruder game played by Wall Street firms to squeeze all the profit out of an IPO listing before the public could invest.

Ilya and I met at the Hard Rock in Times Square. It was his suggestion. It was his first time in New York and he probably assumed the Hard Rock in Times Square was where all important business was carried out. He looked only a few years older than me and he seemed overwhelmed. His eyes flitted around and he was visibly sweating.

Meanwhile, I was sober and since my nervous system was blown out from the coke, I spoke slowly and deliberately, like a monk. Ilya's plan was good. He knew the crypto game, wanting to list the token quickly. That was more important than anything: if you had a way to get to the critical exchanges and influencers you couldn't miss.

We signed the paperwork and I wired him $100,000. A week later I received 285,714 PlayCrux tokens. PlayCrux raised $10.5 million in total, $3.5 million from large investors at 35 cents, and $7 million from "retail" at $1. When they listed on exchange, the token shot up to almost $3. I moved to sell immediately. Careful not to overwhelm the liquidity, I sold in drips, taking almost a week to offload my investment. The largest investors, who had purchased as much as $1 million in tokens, were forced to sit on the sideline to wait for more liquidity to appear. Six weeks after investing, the fund had its first half-million-dollar profit.

CHAPTER THIRTEEN - 2011

Like most middle-class men, the bulk of my father's life was devoted to securing the money to feed his family, afford a home, and max out his IRA. And since the emotive and loving part of himself had been turned to ash in the cruel bonfire of the market, it was our job to comb through the wreckage for evidence of his love.

Some men shoulder their burdens inwardly, and while Dad did his best, even a small trigger could ignite his incipient flame. I didn't know exactly what he did at work each day, but in the theater of my imagination he stormed the beaches of Normandy every morning before returning at night battered and bruised and sensitive as a live wire.

A nature lover who spent his free evenings reading the biographies of great war heroes and explorers, my Dad felt stifled in his suburban sales job. Love was missing, so he demanded respect. Respect for freedom lost.

Like most men of his generation, he didn't cry, and even joy— laughter or a reckless smile, would dissolve into a severe expression accompanied by the statement, "Okay, time to get back to work." As a child, I felt bad for him, even as I feared him, wishing he could just relax and let loose at home as he seemed able to do when camping or hiking. Throughout my childhood, my father leaned on stress until it collapsed into anger. His thumb and index finger would mash in agitation, and he flitted around the house with tensed shoulders. Neurotic by nature, three young boys and a job selling CD replication services in the early 2000s frequently tested his limits.

By high school, I took all his stress and pain and anger and distilled their source down to a single cause: money.

Money hovered over everything, could we afford it? The mantra of our lives. Money was the same as security, happiness.

With my parents away from home one day, I walked into their bedroom and sat down on their bed. I opened my father's high school yearbook and read the notes from his classmates.

"See you next summer you little shrimp."

"You're a nice guy but smaller than a mouse."

"Hit the gym faggot."

I felt sad and closed the book.

But that summer, an event shook the foundations of our family identity and changed how we saw ourselves in the world. Tyler got into West Point. The previous summer Tyler had received a packet from the Army inviting him to apply for a summer visit to West Point. Our family was in a state of ecstasy, *West Point,* we had all read books about the great Military Academy. We knew the generals who had graduated from it, and my Dad, more than anyone else, was taken in by a sense of soaring pride that one of his boys would step onto the same path taken by the great American heroes whose stories filled our bookshelves.

The news that Tyler was entering West Point also changed me. Tyler was my brother. Yes he was probably smarter and more capable than me, but I also knew his flaws and recognized that it was not perfection that this famous institution had looked for in him, but promise. And even though I was no match for Tyler, I too had promise.

And so when I entered the tenth grade at Inglemoor High School, where Evan was now a senior, I did so, for the first time in my life, with a foreign feeling of fledgling confidence. *I have an older brother at West Point.* But it was through athletics, with an unlikely coach and in an even more unlikely sport, that my fundamentally nervous energy transformed into the first solid self-confidence of my life.

CHAPTER FOURTEEN – SEPTEMBER 2017

One day, while working together in the living room, George stood up and walked to the kitchen, returning with a carton of eggs.

"Wanna toss some eggs off the balcony?"

"Won't people get hurt?"

"Nah the shells are soft. They'll just shatter on impact—like getting a pat on the head!"

He shoved one into my hands and ran out to the balcony, hurling two eggs with one hand over the 350-foot ledge. I leaped up and caught the tail end of the carving route the eggs took—the leading egg exploded on top of a yellow cab that lurched forward in response to the impact. The other egg disappeared into a sidewalk drain.

We took a few moments to recover from our doubled-over laughter before George shouted: "Throw yours!"

I scanned for a target and noticed a man talking on the phone in front of a floor-to-ceiling window of an apartment across the street, about ten stories below us. I wound up and launched in his direction–the egg shattered on the window. He gave a start and shuttered his blinds. George and I erupted.

Then George began, as if playing a basketball arcade game, to toss the eggs as fast as he could over the balcony. Most splattered harmlessly against pavement but one egg splattered through the gelled hair of a businessman and oozed down onto his shoulder pad. He yelled and began shaking his fist at George and me.

We ran back inside and decided to call it quits for the day.

A few minutes later we heard a knock on the door.

It was the building manager, Sam.

"Fuck that entitled motherfucker," Sam said, walking in the room and sitting down on the couch.

"If you see him again, pelt him as hard as possible."

George was an expert in NYC building management politics, befriending employees with hundred-dollar bills to avoid packages getting "lost" and maintenance requests "not going through." George had taken special care to befriend Sam by supplying him with a steady stream of free Xanax.

"What happened?" I asked.

"The guy you hit came into the lobby yelling saying he got hit in the head with an egg by two hooligans on the top floor. He was threatening to sue, what a bunch of bullshit. I told him to fuck off if he didn't want any more trouble."

Almost every day, I encountered Sam at various stages of ossification: slumped over in the elevator or pelting obscenities at passersby while standing on the street outside the lobby. One day, while out for his lunch break, Sam stumbled across a parking garage exit when a departing car apparently got too close to him. He turned and pounded the hood, howling slurred vituperations until the driver, his ego stoked to the point of rage, emerged from his car with both arms swinging. The brawl was officiated by an NYPD cop who had "never seen two kikes fight before" (in Sam's telling), before giving them both a court date for disturbing the peace.

After having a drink, Sam joined us on the balcony and tossed a few eggs over the side.

After Sam left, George shook his head in exasperation, "That guy is fucked up."

CHAPTER FIFTEEN – SUMMER 2012

"Nationals duz not know a ubermensch iz comen!" Karol, my Slovakian kayak coach, bellowed as I approached the dock paddling an eighteen-inch rocket boat.

My delight at staying upright, avoiding Karol's now familiar refrain that "Kayak is not submarine!" spread across my face in a wide grin.

I was sixteen years old and had been training in sprint kayaking for exactly six weeks, earning a spot at US nationals by sheer chance. Thanks to Karol's influence, I joined the club hosting the event that year and was given a spot gratis.

Until now, a week before nationals, I had never successfully paddled one of the fast but unstable fiberglass racing boats, so Karol had secured a plastic boat with a three-foot hull, "the tub" in his parlance, the equivalent to training for NASCAR in a minivan.

A few months after entering tenth grade I had signed up for the kayak leg of a ten-event relay race my Boy Scout troop was competing in called "Ski to Sea." Karol, a Slovakian immigrant who attended the church hosting our troop meetings, was an eccentric sixty-something Soviet dissident and a former world champion kayaker. It didn't take long for him to project a wild love for his adopted country onto me. He was five-foot-eight with a healthy-looking belly and an "outie" belly button so large it looked like a thumb. He had a broad, ruddy face with a big nose and narrow eyes framed by white, closely cropped hair. He would turn on Estelle's "American Boy" as we drove to practice and shout, "Urv meh Ahmaricahn boi!" while gruffly smacking me on the shoulder.

Our relationship blossomed throughout the *Karate Kid*-style training regimen he'd crafted. Between devastating workouts, he would check my stool to ensure I was eating properly.

"Yur pop look lick mush! Et more banana!"

Our training consisted of intervals where Karol would point with his paddle at a bridge, buoy, or weeping willow. "We race until finish line," he would say, nodding gravely before counting down to three.

The race would start with a torrent of grunts and slaps of the paddles catching the water. After a few moments, Karol would pull ahead, blasting my boat with his wake.

But as I climbed toward life's physical peak, Karol descended. A month into our training, his face gleamed with sweat and his breath quickened in time with my rising pace. One day, while charging toward a willow, my body's parts, once awkwardly independent, moved as one. As the nose of my boat punched ahead of his for the first time, I heard a "Hooray!" rise up behind me. I glanced behind me to catch the pride gleaming in his eyes before my body screamed for air and I doubled over, gasping.

Karol was born amid a bloody theater of war featuring the Red Army and the Nazis. The trauma of the conflict had caused Karol's mother to dry up.

"I seckled frum eh got."

"From a goat?" I clarified.

"A got! Fer tree months I nursed frum gots tit!"

He ultimately escaped the Soviets in the early eighties by swimming across the Danube to Austria while bullets tore up the water around him. Needless to say, his psyche was deeply scarred even as his body escaped harm.

"Gypies ar scum," he declared, "but Ressians er evn verse."

In the dark pall of the Soviet bloc, Karol found his way on the water. Kayaking was his light, his literature, his music, and his freedom. At their best, sprint kayakers look like dancers—rhythmically flipping their hips t0 transfer the power from their twisting torsos into the blade. Each stroke is punctuated with a pause, "the catch," to glide swan-like through the water. While kayaking, Karol was as free as the fish and the birds—emancipated from politics, oppression, surveillance, and the totalitarianism that weighed him down on land.

On the water, he laughed and glided and pulsed his body in tune with the wind and the waves. He wove himself into the thread of nature that evaporated human derangements like dew in the morning sun. Coming to America gave Karol the feeling of kayaking all the time. It made sense he would want to share with me what probably felt to him like the most American of sports.

After nationals, Karol reached out to his contacts in Slovakia and secured me a spot at the Olympic training center in Trenčín. I would miss a semester of high school, which was all the convincing I needed. The experience included the dorm master calling me a "filthy American" and waking me up at 5 a.m. by dumping a bucket of water on me while demanding—in Slovak—that I clean my room. I was the first American to attend the local school, and my grades defaulted to all "As" since I couldn't understand anything happening in class.

After training for six months abroad, I returned to win a silver medal at the national championships, which is not as impressive as it sounds. Winning a medal in sprint kayaking in the US is like winning a regional bowling tournament. There are only a few hundred teenagers nationally who train regularly.

But it was dream material for college essays, and the news that Evan had gotten into Stanford before my return from Slovakia affirmed my potential. A great future was set before me on a platter; all that remained was to reach out and take it.

CHAPTER SIXTEEN – SUMMER 2017

Satoshi Nakamoto is dead. But the wife of Bitcoin's pseudonymous creator would say he's just hibernating, his body suspended in time and space in a vat of liquid nitrogen.

Hal Finney is also dead. And while nobody knows if Hal is actually Satoshi, he was probably the only person on the cypherpunks' mailing list not to roll his eyes when Satoshi shared his creation with the list on Halloween night, 2008. Finney was on the receiving end of the first Bitcoin transaction, and he apparently worked closely with Satoshi (a clever guise for Finney should he turn out to be the true creator) on Bitcoin's rough early software. When Lou Gehrig's disease evicted Finney from his first flesh-and-blood home in 2014, a cryogenics team was standing by, and the moment Finney was declared legally dead, they vampired his blood, setting his body on a cooling course to 320 degrees below zero.

Cypherpunks, whose legendary mailing list peaked in the '90s when they appeared, masked and holding a wrinkled American flag, on the cover of *Wired* magazine, were known for their resistance to government surveillance and essential contributions to digital privacy. But cypherpunks are fundamentally futurists who embrace the unknown with their entire beings, submitting themselves to a cryogenic fate in the hopes of being resurrected in the impending age of immortality, when they can again drink greedily from the elixir of youth.

So what led the cypherpunks to develop Bitcoin, a defiant monetary foil to the US dollar that has grayed the hairs of regulators the world over? To answer that, we have to understand the flaws the cypherpunks saw in both the debt and discounting principles embedded in the financial system.

Discounting is the single most important concept in finance and possibly economics. It's the idea that money is less valuable tomorrow than today. The reason is quite existential: our impending death. Better to spend now than to never enjoy the fruits of your labor. The related inexorable march of inflation also ensures money is less valuable over time. The USA's central bank, the Federal Reserve, has two goals: ensure the dollar can buy 2 percent less stuff a year from now, and keep the unemployment rate as low as possible. In other words, because we are all going to die and because the greatest economic minds on the planet are dedicated to ensuring every dollar is worth 2 percent less every year, we have a "discount rate" that roughly equals the rate of inflation plus the average level of existential angst in society.

But Finney, if not Bitcoin's actual creator then its primary early sponsor, believed that one way or another, he would live forever. Inventing digital money with a fixed number of total coins (i.e., no inflation) was critical to ensuring bodily resurrection would resurrect a similar level of economic security to that enjoyed at the moment of freezing. (Cypherpunks do not use the word "death.")

Belief in immortality, however, played no role in my interest in digital currencies. In fact, they were a means to make my life, in the face of my glaring mortality, meaningful. Ironically, it was the enormous volatility of cryptocurrencies that gave me the faith that in a few months I could accumulate many lifetimes of wealth and enjoy all of life's pleasures before time ran out.

Bitcoin is insulated from the corrosive forces of inflation; one Bitcoin today is at least as valuable as one Bitcoin tomorrow—or so the theory goes. For this reason, the cypherpunks rejected one of the tenets of modern financial theory: death is optional, and therefore money is no longer worth more today than it is tomorrow. A monetary system based on steady inflation to stimulate hot-potato spending—even if it lubricates the gears of the economic machine— is unethical in light of immortality.

The cypherpunks believed they would live forever, and so built a monetary system instantiating this philosophy. Bitcoin is god money. This is one reason why it can be hard for those of us still resigned to mortality to embrace Bitcoin fully. Bitcoin is built on a philosophical foundation as different from the mainstream one as Mars is from Earth. Understanding this underlying design philosophy is critical to understanding the confusion many feel in reconciling the world of Bitcoin with the world of stocks and bonds.

But it wasn't just discounting that the cypherpunks rejected; it was the notion of debt itself. Satoshi embedded "The Times 03/ Jan/2009 'Chancellor on brink of second bailout for banks'" into the Bitcoin genesis block. Financial tomfoolery was not to be tolerated in Bitcoin. What you see is what you get, transparency, code, blockchain.

But as the summer of 2017 melted into fall, the absurdity of the ICOs that were emerging all over the globe stung in their contrast to Satoshi Nakamoto's pure vision. An exchange built on the debt principle, "Bancor" raised $100 million in the early summer of 2017 in an ICO that should have caused Finney to thaw with rage.

The many extant Bitcoin purists, including David, my co-worker at Liquid Freedom, did fume against ICOs like Bancor as "selling shit-coins to idiots." But their voices were drowned by the hype. The Ethereum subreddit exploded from less than 10,000 subscribers to over one million in 2017 as moderators played whack-a-mole with posts promoting dubious ICOs.

The ICO pitches I received, which began the moment I listed "ICO investor" on my LinkedIn profile and accelerated after Coindesk announced G2H2's PlayCrux investment, grew in absurdity by the day—from "BananaCoin" decentralizing the fruit industry to $SEX, a cryptocurrency incentivizing prostitutes to get regular STD tests. One day I received a pitch that caused me to laugh and then grow intrigued. An entrepreneur named Sergio was repackaging his brick-and-mortar tax filing franchise (competing with Liberty Tax's sign-swinging army) into an ICO.

Sergio's hazy vision was to build a blockchain-based tax preparation platform called LedgerTax that would "put TurboTax out of business."

I met Sergio at a small café in the East Village. He was 6' 2" and built like a retired linebacker, with a pot belly that sagged over his hulking frame. He looked like an overgrown school child on the little metal cafe chair and the sweat poured down his face in thick lines resembling translucent earthworms.

"Listen," Sergio began, "I'm a hard worker. There's nothing I won't sacrifice for this company. I'm already working 140 hours a week."

"140 hours?"

"140 hours."

"How much do you sleep?"

"Maybe two hours a night."

I stared at him for a few seconds in disbelief mixed with admiration.

"So how long do you think this will take?"

"Well, I already have a team in Romania working on the proof of concept. It should be ready in the next few weeks."

"And how much money are you raising?"

"As much as we can. We want to capitalize on the hot market and launch our token before Christmas."

"The guy's full of shit," George said, after I told him about the meeting. "And what he said about working 140 hours is nonsense; these guys always lie about how much they work."

Despite George's skepticism, I was excited by the prospect of being the first investor in an ICO. Our profits would be ten or even a hundred times greater than later investors. George and I scheduled a time to meet Sergio again with his partner, Roy. I asked for 3.5 percent of the ICO proceeds in exchange for a $50,000 investment. Sergio agreed to the terms on the substantial condition that I serve as CTO for an additional 1.5 percent.

George was unhappy about how much time the CTO role would take up. But Roy, a former Citibank executive in his 50s who talked about his connection with Donald Trump, sold me. As far as I could tell, he was a serious businessman, and he laid out the value I would have to their brand as a 21-year-old Stanford dropout.

"It'll give our boring Tax business a little sex appeal if you don't mind me saying." I didn't mind him saying.

Our third meeting was set for two days later at a diner in White Plains just north of the city, near Roy's house. I got on the train wearing a navy suit and carrying a black briefcase I had purchased on Amazon for $19. I was self-conscious that wearing a backpack would lead people to mistake me for a student. In the movies, businessmen carried briefcases.

"The waitress is a smoke show," Roy commented as we sat down for lunch, "I bet you could get her."

"I don't know about that."

Roy ordered three drinks and pushed one towards me.

"You got a girlfriend?" he asked.

"Yeah long distance, she's still in school."

"Do you love her?"

"I think so. Although we've only been together a few months."

"Don't even think about getting married. You're young, you're good-looking, you got the world by the balls. What I would give to be in your shoes, man. Listen. You wouldn't believe how many fucking trivialities women pull you into—the rug, the wallpaper, all this bullshit. Then they stop fucking you and you're stuck, and if you want another woman they leave with half your money plus the house. I didn't even have kids with my ex-wife and that was the deal. That shits worse than rape."

"That's crazy."

"Here's my advice: wait until you're about 45 or 50 and marry someone half your age; they won't be jaded, they'll look up to, and they'll treat you right. My friends with younger wives are a thousand times happier I promise you."

"But what if I fall in love?"

"If you do, don't marry right away. Wait. Wait long enough to see past all the chemical shields blocking you from seeing who she really is, and if you still like what you see, maybe, maybe go for it. But think long and hard. Personally, I would recommend against it."

"There's nothing more pitiful than an unhappy married man," said Sergio shaking his head, "they suck the energy out right out of a room."

"And what about happy married men?"

"Never heard of one," said Sergio. Roy and Sergio both started laughing.

"Listen," Sergio said, recovering himself, "I have an exciting update for you."

"Yeah?"

"Roy and I have been talking and we think you would make a better CEO than me. I want to focus on our brick-and-mortar business and you can focus on the crypto business."

"You mean you want me to do this thing on my own?"

"Listen," Sergio said, "this is a big step up in responsibility, I know. But we're here to support you as advisors, anything you need you can just call us."

"So you're saying that I give you $50,000, build the entire business and run the ICO and in exchange I get 5 percent?"

Roy and Sergio sat silent for a few moments. Finally Roy spoke.

"We'll give you ten percent."

"Listen I have a fund to manage, and I'm not sure I can take this on. Let me think about it and I'll get back to you."

We shook hands and I left. On the train I texted them and told them I was out. George had been right. They were using me for a cash grab. Sending me out to shill their shitcoin to investors while keeping most of the profits for themselves.

I immediately got a text back from Roy.

"This is a god damned betrayal, I thought you were a Boy Scout."

I didn't respond.

I got an email from Roy later that day cc'ing my lawyer saying he was going to sue me.

I told George when he got home from work.

"Fuck those losers!" He bellowed, "let's get them back."

That night George created a Grindr account with Roy's face and put his phone number in the bio asking for dick pics to be texted directly to him. We had a good laugh and closed the app, I never heard from either of them again.

The following week Boris, George's father, visited and we all went out to dinner.

"In the 90s in Latin America governments were throwing money at different businesses to try to stimulate the economy," Boris said at dinner, "basically anyone who set up a business, legitimate or not, could get millions of dollars if they played the game right. That was how I got my first start in business, and there's a lot of similarity between that and these ICOs you guys are involved in."

"What do you mean exactly?" I asked. Boris was vague in his reply and then changed the subject.

"I have to have a serious conversation with you," George whispered to me as we left dinner.

"Listen," he began when we got back to the apartment, "we need to do what my Dad said."

"What do you mean, what did he say?" I asked.

"Well he didn't want to say it explicitly for obvious reasons but you were able to read between the lines right?"

"I have no idea what you're talking about."

"Don't be dumb I'm talking about setting up fake ICOs and ripping off retail investors. That's what he was saying about LATAM and setting up shell companies to steal the government's money."

"Are you joking?"

"Dude, I'm not joking. You know how many fucking scam ICOs there are out there? These guys are making millions, what are we doing over here if not trying to make money?"

"I'm not running a scam dude."

"Well, just tell me some of your legitimate ideas then."

"You mean ICO ideas?"

"Yeah."

"Well there was one idea I had for a decentralized exchange..."

"How much money could we raise?" George asked.

"I don't know. There are a lot of factors. We would have to hire a team to build a proof of concept, market it, see what level of interest we receive…"

"We won't actually build the product though. All we need is a landing page and a white paper. Then we raise the money and run off with it," George cackled.

"You mean steal the money?"

"Not stealing. It's not illegal. These things are unregulated."

George's face suddenly looked very punchable.

"Just because it isn't illegal doesn't mean it isn't wrong!" I yelled.

"Okay, okay. Calm down. We don't have to do it."

I stormed off to my room and slammed the door. I reached into my desk drawer for the only thing I knew would make me feel better. But this time my greatest friend and ally, my precious cocaine, was about to turn on me.

CHAPTER SEVENTEEN – OCTOBER 2013

At the start of Senior year, just after returning from Slovakia, I found out that Eva liked me. My eighteenth birthday was just two months away and I still had not had my first kiss. Joey, one of the guys on the wrestling team, told me he had had sex with eight girls already.

Eva was popular and beautiful. She had jet-black hair and was half-English, half-Somoan. She was about 5' 3" and had great wide dark eyes and a broad ear-to-ear smile that lit up her little round face, and, to top it off, she was the captain of the soccer team with college offers. She had a bubbly personality with her friends that would retreat into a shy, coquettishness with acquaintances that occasionally erupted into an infectious laugh that would spread so much joy into everyone that heard it that you couldn't help but fall a little bit in love with her.

Several times I passed her in the halls and caught her eyes smiling softly at me and I diverted my gaze in shyness. She was so friendly and kind that I assumed that was how she looked at everyone. But what I didn't realize was that to her, I had a special attraction not because of who I was but because of who I wasn't. I had been absent from school for nearly a year and was therefore *mysterious*. My European adventures, which were unusual, almost fantastical to high schoolers, increased my myth. I was shy, had no definite reputation, and, most importantly, had never been with another girl. The blankest of canvases, in other words, to paint her romantic fantasies.

When whispers of her attraction reached me I downplayed them but there was a secret hope kindling in my heart. In the end it took her best friend, Amy, telling me that Eva definitely, one hundred percent liked me to finally convince me. When Amy told me I blushed and felt my whole body seize up in anxious ecstasy, I didn't realize how physical and all-encompassing my attraction to her was until I found out it had a hope of becoming reality.

"What should I do?" I asked Amy.

"Ask her for her number, stupid."

"Can't you just give it to me?"

"Don't be silly."

Every muscle contracted in defiance but I managed to approach Eva after school. If there had been even the slightest dimming of her smile, which was so inviting and affirming, I would have turned and sped-walked in the opposite direction. But even the most self-defeating thoughts wilted in the light of her obvious attraction. I approached her in the open courtyard; she was standing with Amy who was all but beckoning me on with her arms.

"Hey Eva."

Amy slipped away to a nearby circle.

"Hey Dean! How are your classes going?"

"Good."

"That's awesome! I was watching you in the football game last week, you're so good!"

"Thanks! I can't wait to watch you play soccer."

She smiled and was about to say something before I blushed and mumbled, "can I get your number?" I recovered and added, "I would love to talk to you more after school."

"Absolutely!" She beamed, putting her number in my phone.

At practice that afternoon I played soft. "Pick up the intensity Patrick!" The linebacker coach shouted when I half-assed a tackle. He didn't know I had Eva's number.

Things went well at first. We set a date at her house that Wednesday night. I drove with a pounding heart up a long driveway lined with old-growth pine trees to a secluded three-story modern home.

I rang the doorbell and was greeted by her Dad. A great big Somoan man.

"So you're Dean, huh?"

"Yes, I'm here to see Eva."

"I heard, she's in the living room."

"Dean!" I heard Eva shout and then footsteps, and then her arms were around me.

"He didn't scare you away, did he?" She asked, nodding at her Dad.

"No." I smiled.

We walked into her living room and sat on the couch on opposite ends, making small talk as her Dad milled around behind us.

"Hey Dean, you know "The Rock?" Her Dad shouted.

"Yeah, I know The Rock. He's a big movie star."

"You like him?"

"Yeah, he's good."

"I like you already! Did you know The Rock and I are cousins?"

Eva rolled her eyes. "Every Somoan calls every other Somoan a 'cousin,'" she whispered.

I acted impressed for Eva's dad's sake and then got back to Eva. The conversation turned flirtatious and I grew more comfortable. Her Dad disappeared and we turned on a show. I shifted towards her and put my arm around her and she snuggled into me. The show all but disappeared for me. My mind and body were ablaze with pep talks and visualizations of kissing her. I imagined the kiss going awry, *what if I accidentally kiss her chin by mistake and blow the whole thing?*

Before long, Eva yawned.

"I have to go to bed now but I'll walk you to the door," she said.

Outside I hugged her and then, in the greatest summoning of sheer will in my life, I leaned down and kissed her. I landed just a little to the right, but it was okay, I had gotten about eighty percent lip. Spasms of excitement shot through me.

"Bye Eva!" I said, as I straightened up.

She smiled, "bye Dean!"

The next step was to ask her to homecoming. I got the school administration to make a PA announcement at lunch asking Eva to come to the courtyard. There I organized a line of football guys to hold signs spelling out "E-V-A HO-M-E-C-O-M-I-N-G-?" A big crowd gathered after the PA announcement and when she came into the courtyard, I handed her a bouquet of pink roses and made my ask. She said yes, we hugged, the crowd cheered.

A couple of weeks later the day arrived and the homecoming group gathered at a huge modern home in the Woodinville hills. It was all windows and sparkling clean with furniture that looked unused. None of my friends were there. It went without saying that we would go with Eva's friend group, which included all the most popular kids. I felt like an extra at an A-list party and trouble started right away. As soon as I got out of the car I caught sight of Eva. She was dressed in a sparkling pink gown with immaculate hair and makeup, posing in the driveway for pictures. I approached her with the corsage box, my hands shaking as I extracted it, dropping it on the ground.

"Oh I'm so sorry, so sorry," I said.

Eva didn't say anything, a new anxiety appeared in her eyes as I picked it up and put it on her wrist. She held herself with an elegance and seriousness that made me so nervous I barely spoke as we took pictures. Eva made the rounds and I followed behind her, watching her hug her friends and exchange small talk.

"That's such a nice suit; where did you get it?" One of her friends asked.

"Oh this? The jacket and slacks are my Dad's and I borrowed the shirt from my older brother." Eva looked annoyed and her friend changed the subject.

On the party bus the guys passed around a bottle but as it went around it never seemed to make it to me. "I got us a bottle for the after-party," Eva whispered. But I needed that bottle now.

I tried several times to inject myself into the conversation but my comments fell flat and Eva flashed a look that I perceived as disgust. The guys started talking about how Matt, the apparent group leader, had recently tweeted at a Dallas Cowboys receiver that "the only thing he blew more than games was guys." And the player had responded, "suck a dick." The exchange ended up on Barstool Sports. I had never been on Twitter and had never heard of Barstool. After a few minutes, Eva went to sit with her friends and I sat by myself on the bus until we got to dinner.

At dinner, Matt gave a toast and the table roared with laughter and Eva reached over and stroked his arm in delight. She was paying less and less attention to me. I didn't really care what anyone but Eva thought, but it was clear that what she thought depended a lot on what everyone else thought. Eva ignored me on the bus ride to the dance, so when we arrived, I made straight for my friends.

"Got any alcohol?" I asked Spencer.

"Sure I got a flask." I took a long hit of straight Vodka, choking and spluttering but I got it down.

I felt better after that. Eva was still mine.

When it was time to leave one of the guys from our group grabbed me and said, "Eva is pissed that you ditched her!"

I tried to patch things up as we returned to the bus.

"I'm really happy I'm here with you," I said to Eva. She didn't respond.

"Are you cold?"

"A little."

I gave her my jacket, but she gave it back to me.

On the bus everyone started grinding with their dates and so Eva grinded on me but I could tell she wasn't into it. I couldn't see her face, but one of the guys whispered in my ear, "dude Eva looks miserable right now. What did you do?"

When we got to Matt's house for the afterparty, Eva immediately went to the bottle. When I asked her for some she said it was empty. I went to the bathroom and when I returned I saw Eva standing in the middle of the living room turned dance floor, cradling Matt's head with her outstretched arms and pressing her lips together with his in a passionate, obscene make-out. An unbearable sorrow, fear and rage mingled together in a violent stew in my stomach and chest–"What the fuck Matt!" I screamed over the music, interrupting their kiss, my first definitive statement of the night. Matt looked at me with fear in his eyes.

"Hey man, she came up to me, what was I going to do?" Eva looked at me with a sinister expression but didn't say anything.

"I'll kick your ass," I said. Matt took off and Eva ran after him. I let them get a lead and then followed them, pretending to stalk him down. I didn't want to fight, I wanted to trade places with Matt. I watched them disappear into a bedroom and I approached the door. I was about to bang on it but I thought better of it and returned to the living room.

Ellie, Matt's date, seemed much more blasée about losing her date and started grinding on me. I will never forget Ellie; she took some of the pain away.

The party ended and I went home. I laid in bed and asked myself how things had gone so horribly wrong. But the final dagger in the heart came the next day. I still held on to the fact that I had actually *gone* to homecoming with Eva. That counted for a lot in the parochial high school world. But then the all-important Instagram posts came out. Eva's post was captioned. "A night spent around close friends is never wasted." I was nowhere to be found. She had erased all the social proof that I had been there at all.

For six months, I did not recover. As far as I was concerned, the world of women was completely closed to me. I had taken one real risk asking a girl and had been stomped on. I would go my own way.

CHAPTER EIGHTEEN – FALL 2017

The same day Boris came to visit I had found a surprise in my mailbox. A deep web dealer had sent me a few grams of black tar heroin as a "gift," along with my usual cocaine order. He'd included a note: "Try this with the coke, it'll blow your mind." I had dismissed it initially, but tonight, after my fight with George, I craved numbing more than stimulation. I sat in bed in my usual posture; knees pulled up with my laptop resting on them, head propped up on a pile of pillows, the posture in which it was easiest to forget I had a body.

I started with coke of course, sniffing a couple of lines to begin my transformation. Then I googled "how to take heroin," taking it out of the bag to examine it. It was a dark-brown goo that looked like dried molasses. I took a spoon and dipped out a flea's worth, adding in water and mixing it with my pinky until it was viscous enough to snort. Then I plugged my left nostril and sucked the liquid through the right. The intake burned only a little and I was pleased at my success. After a few moments it felt like a heated blanket had been wrapped around my insides. But the blanket started to itch, and so like a dog with fleas I scratched and scratched, dragging my nails along my arms and thighs in a counterproductive bid for relief. Before long I began to bleed, and the blood mixed with sweat, and I started running brown like heroin itself was leaking out of me.

I did some more coke to feel better. But the combination of cocaine and black tar heroin, colloquially referred to as a "speedball," made my heart beat powerfully and irregularly. I became fixated on my heartbeat, continuously reassuring myself of its existence by plunging my right index finger into the soft skin where my jaw met my neck. But fixation bred paranoia, and I googled "complications from speedballs." Every result warned of the risk of cardiac arrest.

I tried to relax but everything brought me right back to my heartbeat. Each beat would bring relaxation and each space between beats would bring panic. Over time the relief lessened and the panic grew into a complete obsession.

Suddenly my hands and feet grew numb and I started gasping for air. My rising panic broke into grandiose hysteria— *I'm too young to die... I'm only 21. I have not yet climbed to the heights from which a true tragedy plunges.* The tightness in my chest was horrifying—a terrible pain that radiated throughout my body—terror of death.

I reached for my phone and texted my parents: "I love you." Using drugs whenever I felt anxious was so ingrained that I reached for my coke bag before retracting at the sickening numbness in my arms. I was against the wall. The one thing that could always be relied upon to make me feel better had turned on me. After a few moments I couldn't take it and sniffed some coke only to instantly regret it. I was in a sickening spiral and I had to stop or I would die. For the first time in my addiction I faced the horrifying yet hopeful reality of how much life I still had left to live. To die now, I realized, would be to die without ever having really existed.

George had left for the night and I was so alone. Unable to breathe properly I crawled into the living room to look for some aspirin that would hopefully relieve my blood pressure.

With an immense effort I pulled myself up to the medicine cabinet in the bathroom and spilled bottles on the floor until I found the aspirin. I took four pills and returned to my room where I searched YouTube for "how to stop a heart attack."

I found a video of a monk teaching a breathing technique. He said to breathe slowly through my nose, six counts, hold at the top, six counts, and exhale through the mouth, six counts.

I followed his instructions and after twenty minutes, the feeling had crept back into my hands. After forty-five minutes I had recovered enough to crawl into bed and lay there drenched in sweat for many hours before finally drifting off into a fitful sleep.

The next day I received another unusual package in the mail. It was a care package from Sarah, complete with my favorite snacks and, since I had shared with her my desire to buy a sports car, a toy Maserati with a note that read, "I bought you this to save you some money 😊."

"I love you so much; your package was a gift from heaven," I texted her. When you're truly lonely even the smallest gesture can feel like the difference between life and death.

I had shared some of my struggles with Sarah, which I'd described as "depression," but had left out the extent of my drug use, fearful she would leave me if she knew the truth. But there was only so much I could hide, and in our conversations, she must have sensed how much I was struggling. The note she'd left in the package included a quote from Albert Camus:

"In the depths of winter, I found within me there lay an invincible summer."

It was the first time I had seen articulated how inside despair lay the seeds of redemption. I had felt it firsthand. In the blissful feeling of rebirth that I sometimes felt after emerging from a binge. But now I sensed that what lay ahead was not just a short recovery interval to prepare for my next binge, but a radical reconstruction of my psyche to allow me to function free of drugs.

I read Camus' words over and over, and by the tenth time I was in tears and by the fiftieth, I had resolved to kick my drug habit and reconnect with my better self. I would get sober, move in with Evan in San Francisco and get back on my feet.

But over the next few days, out of the gaping hole of my drug abstinence emerged a deeper loneliness that enveloped me like a black fog. Sarah's care package had reminded me how good human connection felt, but it had also left me choking with desire for the touch of a woman. With Sarah 3,000 miles away, I was getting desperate.

Then I was faced with the first great test of my new sobriety. The arrival of a drug package which I had ordered a week earlier. I opened it up and extracted the ounce of cocaine it contained. I had rehearsed in my head ten thousand times the act of flushing it down the toilet. But as I cut open the bag and held it over the toilet about to tip it in, a thought grabbed me, the same thought that has ruined addicts from time immemorial— *just try one little line, it couldn't hurt right?*

I did a line, and then another. Then, I got the idea to go on Craigslist. Never having done this before, I texted the first number I found under "personals" that advertised "late-night companionship."

"Hey I'm in midtown, can you get someone here tonight?"

An hour later my doorbell rang, and I hustled to answer it. Unsure what to expect, I opened the door to find a middle-aged Asian woman wearing a white dress.

"Show me your room!" she commanded.

I shrugged and led her inside. She was in good shape, and despite her age I found her elegantly pretty. As we sat down on my bed, she reached for my pants and started tugging at them like a parent changing a toddler. I reached to pull off her dress and then looked down to find I already had a condom on.

"What are you, a magician?" I joked.

She ignored me and started going down on me before I stopped her and asked, "Look, you're great at that, but can we just have sex?"

"Sex?" she asked, seemingly offended. She thought for a moment and then spat, "That will be $700 more!"

I gladly paid.

"You have a nice body," she commented as she pulled my shirt off.

Taking this as a sign of affection, I leaned in to kiss her.

"No kissing!" she hissed, putting her hand over my face.

"Alright, alright," I responded.

As she lay beneath me, she looked at me like a parent waiting for their child to finish using the bathroom, arms folded and impatient.

"You finish?" she demanded the moment she heard me grunt.

"Yeah," I responded, a little sheepishly.

"See you again," she said, brusquely snatching up her purse and throwing her dress back on before speed-walking out the door.

"See you," I called softly after her.

After she left, I reached for my laptop, logged onto the deep web, and ordered another ounce of fish-scale cocaine before collapsing into bed and falling into a deep sleep.

CHAPTER NINETEEN – SEPTEMBER 2014

"DAD! I GOT INTO STANFORD!"

"WHAAT?" he gasped as he ran toward me for a double high-five. I had never seen him so excited. Evan had gotten into Stanford two years earlier, but he was a better student. The best way to impress your parents is to set the bar low.

That summer, I got a job at a WhatsUP Kayak and Surf at Bothell Landing, just five minutes from our house. It was a little taco-truck-style stand on the Sammamish River, a slow-moving thing less than twenty feet at its widest in the summer that wound its way alongside miles of tree-lined bike paths and mobile homes.

Every day I set up the stand, hauling heavy plastic kayaks and stand-up paddle boards out of a corrugated steel storage unit and carrying them 100 feet to the bank of the river. Then I would wait in the stand and people would come by and ask about them and sometimes I would rent to them. It was a simple job. I took people's money, had them sign a release, helped them into the water, and helped them out. Then I would wipe down the boats and that was it. I made $10 an hour.

Sometimes, customers would kayak to a brewery a few miles up the river and return hammered. Something about seeing them drunk, rolling around in the grass as they came out of the water, disgusted me. They seemed like animals.

That summer lasted a long time but then the future came. I waited until the last moment to pack, rushing into the kitchen, grabbing a handful of forty-gallon black trash bags from under the kitchen sink, and returning to my room to pile drive clothes into them. When I finished I was sweating, the early September sun had risen high and was now beating hard on my window.

My parents drove me down in their Toyota Sienna minivan, stopping at Clear Lake in Northern California. We set up the tent, and my Dad made small talk with the people walking by.

"We're taking my son to Stanford!" He shared, beaming with pride.

"Wow, very impressive!" An elderly couple responded.

"I just wish I was eighteen again so I could start the journey all over!"

I knew he had meant to be encouraging, but I couldn't help but wonder. What had the journey been for if he just wanted to start it over again?

We pulled into Stanford and up to my freshman dorm. "You're in Twain! That's a great dorm!" I was told by a bright-eyed Sophomore girl at the check-in. I smiled at her and took a key card and a printed copy of the orientation week schedule.

I noticed there were a lot of immaculate and expensive-looking cars around. The people inside them looked scrubbed and fit not in an athletic way but in a way that indicated they had expensive trainers and good doctors.

One man, who stood about six two with salt and pepper hair wearing a purple dress shirt with three buttons undone with Ray-Ban's sitting on his high forehead, was walking around with his wife and two blonde daughters. "That was my old dorm; what I would give to go back in time and move in again!" He shouted, gesturing at Twain. There it was again. What was it about being eighteen again that seemed so appealing? To be anxious and feel incompetent again? Surely by that time you would feel secure in the world and what a relief that must be.

My heart pounded as I stepped out of the Sienna and approached the entrance to Twain. I got tunnel vision, trying my best to project a sense of cool confidence. The sun was so bright and the swishing sounds of the palm trees stunned me for a moment, but I gripped my trash bags and walked up the steps, flanked by my parents, to check in. I didn't care who these people were, I told myself. I was just going to be me—these trash bags were me, my face was me, my personality me. But as we got in line I grew confused. I wanted so badly to have a good reason to be here. To explain to everyone "I'm here because of xyz" and to have everyone nod and say "that makes sense." "Stanford makes no mistakes," they had said in the admissions letter, "you *belong* here."

The people who checked us into the dorm were also Sophomores, they told us. Their eyes were bright and their voices cheerful, I read on their faces a definitive statement: "we belong here."

"Do you need help moving in?" My Mom asked.

"I got it Mom, no worries. You guys just take a walk around campus, go enjoy yourselves."

"Okay love you, honey. We'll meet up for dinner tonight."

I walked into my dorm. My room was on the first floor, and the hallway smelled of carpet cleaner and sunshine. My roommate had already moved in. I learned his name was Sal, and he was from Chicago and interested in math and economics. He was short, wore a backwards hat and a Bulls jersey, and asked me if I played any sports. I said I was considering joining the rugby team, and he thought that was cool. He told me he had met the newest Stanford quarterback recruit and that they were going out later. I said I thought that that was cool.

For reasons I could not comprehend, Sal had managed to arrive at Stanford with a built-in friend group of half a dozen other freshman guys. During orientation week, he would come home at night and describe with awe the venture capitalist father of a student or the size of the trust fund of another. I didn't know what a venture capitalist was or why it was considered impressive. But I took mental notes of everything Sal said and did my best to react according to what I thought he felt was appropriate.

Sal seemed to sense that I was out of it, despite my best intentions to prove that I wasn't, and so he didn't invite me out with his friends.

One day one of Sal's friends, Brad, came into our room and immediately walked over to my bed and jumped on it. I was sitting by my desk pretending to work while I listened in on them. Brad was thinner than me but around my height, wearing salmon chubbies, a faded cap and a too-large green cotton T-shirt that said "Pebble Beach." His shorts pulled back and his long hairy legs sprawled on my mattress as he leaned back against the wall. He hadn't asked permission to go up on my bed, which wouldn't have been so bad if it hadn't been for his disgusting spider legs. I sat there, watching his legs and hating everything about him. I had a strong urge to punch Brad in the face but in the end I didn't do anything. The conversation turned to one of their other friends, Joe.

"Joe's Dad is a Sequoia partner," Brad said.

"Yeah he's got his name on one of the fountains," Sal responded.

"What's Sequoia?" I asked.

Brad yawned, ignoring me.

"It's one of the biggest VC firms in the world," Sal responded tartly.

"What are you guys thinking of majoring in?" I asked.

They both looked at each other.

"I was thinking about economics," Sal said, finally.

"Same," said Brad.

"Yeah, me too." I lied.

Since Brad and Sal were studying economics I decided to look into it. I figured "economics" meant the theory of making money. Since there wasn't much else I felt drawn to I decided I might as well learn how to get rich.

On the first day of "Introduction to Economics," I arrived early and sat down in the middle of a large theater. At nine the professor walked in and addressed the packed crowd of over five hundred students. I shifted in my chair excitedly, I was going to learn the secret of making money.

"Today I'm going to talk about coffee," the professor said to murmured laughter. She was an elegant-looking woman in her late 40s wearing a black pantsuit and her voice came out high and sharp with a light German accent.

"You wake up early in the morning to come to class, and you stop at Coupa cafe for a cup of coffee. You pay $3 for a cup of coffee, by show of hands how many of you get more than $10 of value out of that coffee?"

Most of the hands went up.

"Now keep your hand raised if you still get $10 of value out of a second cup of coffee?"

Almost all the hands dropped.

"And a third cup?"

The rest of the hands dropped.

"That is the law of diminishing marginal return. The first cup will always be worth more than the second cup, and the second will be worth more than the third and so on."

I didn't understand exactly what this had to do with making money, but I figured that would come later.

But throughout the two-hour lecture the professor never explained any money making secrets. She drew a lot of graphs, which everyone around me was copying into their notebooks, so I copied them too. By the end of class I had learned that the intersection of supply and demand was called the "equilibrium price." It was pretty boring stuff but I figured we had to understand the basics first.

Later that week I was sitting at lunch with some dorm mates. The conversation turned to "what we did to get into Stanford."

Sid, a short Jewish boy from Palo Alto said he had worked in an oncology lab and been an author on a paper that had significantly advanced the treatment of melanoma.

"It's not as impressive as it sounds," he said, "the research just kind of did itself."

Allison, a Chinese girl from South Florida said she had published a children's book that became a New York Times Bestseller.

"I've always been fascinated by children's literature, it's like writing poetry!"

It was my turn.

"I was a sprint kayaker, I won a silver medal at nationals."

"Wow!" Allison said, "So are you kayaking here at Stanford?"

"Uh no there's no team here. And frankly I don't really have a passion for it anymore. I'm not really sure what I want to do."

They nodded and the conversation moved on.

I noticed that Sal's friend group had a certain uniform. Ray Ban's, boat shoes and bright colored shorts. I knew I shouldn't transform overnight, for fear of being too obvious, so I decided to start with the sunglasses. I looked on the Ray Ban website and saw their entry level sunglasses were over $200. Thankfully I found a knock-off version on a Chinese website that was $12.99, so I ordered a pair.

By the end of my first quarter I found myself grappling, for the first time in my life, with genuine loneliness and disillusionment. Stanford in many ways is a utopia of self-development. But after eighteen years of relative unconcern with my status in the world, Stanford triggered a cascade of self-analysis that transformed into self-loathing when my own humble estimation was compared with what I imagined to be the perfection of the people around me.

The economics professor had kept on drawing graphs with equilibriums and local optimums and other things that didn't seem to have any practical relevance to making money.

I had also taken the habit of entering the dining hall, piling food on my plate and returning to my room. "Studying?" Allison had asked me one day, as she saw me approaching my room with a plate of food, "yeah."

At night I would sometimes stand in front of the bathroom mirror, flexing my abs and telling myself, "it's okay, I'm at Stanford, it's okay, I'm at Stanford. I'm smart, I'm attractive, and I will be okay."

Then I took the mantra out of the bathroom and throughout campus. Whenever the feeling of loneliness and fear would creep in I would say to myself, "it's okay I'm at Stanford, I have a good body, I'm smart."

A part of me was satisfied by the mantra but the other part was still afraid. Why was I so afraid? A journal entry from several years later conveyed how I felt beneath the surface, reflecting on my experience two years into Stanford:

Stanford's meticulous landscaping and sweeping mission-adobe architecture morphed into a subtle suffocation in a vacuum-sealed temple to sanitized beauty. Perhaps overly cynical, I saw Stanford as an attempt at utopia through architecture that mocked the failure of the individual. As if to say, "Stanford has done all it can to make your experience perfect; any failure is your own." Subconsciously, I was prepared to take everything personally. To embed my experience with stories that revolved around me and to become neurotic in light of them.

To my mind, the whole place seemed to announce money. Domed and temperature controlled, like the Truman Show. It smelled like freshly trimmed bushes. Its manicured, crafted nature reflected the scientific desire to control our environment. To make man god. Even the squirrels and birds seemed to know their place. They never begged, rushing to get out of sight to let the very important humans focus on their work. At Stanford, I saw smoothed surfaces to eliminate obstacles to trip and fall on. Stucco walls that looked like each dot were hand-placed. The picnic benches perfectly smooth, you could slide a quarter cleanly across them. The whole campus was like an enormous room full of expensive furniture and houseplants.

The constant sun splash diffused through trees and buildings gave the grounds a somewhat layered appearance. Only the community boards were allowed to become unruly, as if to say, "Only humans are allowed to make a mess," or, "We are so overflowing with culture it cannot be contained."

Everything looked freshly swept and washed. Smooth circular concrete tables appeared like flying saucers in front of the student union. There were few shouts, or loud noises generally. The space was so open you were constantly aware of the presence of others, like living in a panopticon where you could be observed at any time by friends or acquaintances. As a result it was essential, to my mind, to never show weakness. To plaster a smile on my face that projected a brilliant confidence.

Great masses of parked bikes, everywhere. The grass, always green, freshly cut, contributed to the suburban aroma. The fountains padded the atmosphere in a soft white noise, mixing with the patter of bike tires on smooth concrete paths completed the beautiful perfectionism that I, again, in my fantastic ability to manufacture personal unhappiness, managed to take personally. Why wasn't I this perfect, my subconscious seemed to nudge.

The ideal, unchanging weather and lack of seasons contributed to the sense of human dominion. The neuroticism of students matched only by the administrators themselves. A 97 % graduation rate jealously guarded, and lorded over college ranking agencies alongside a $30 billion endowment.

Even "Greek Row," usually a broth of dishevelment featuring scattered beer cans and broken tables, looked like an Atherton cul-de-sac.

Fit grad students with sinuous legs ran by, chattering on AirPods with dyed-blonde ponytails swinging. Or if they were male, wearing tight-fitting shirts and boasting shapely calves. The grounds of Stanford were perfect for bikers, smooth as sheet metal with no incline. New bikers beamed as they felt the power of their movements.

The week before finals I walked into my dorm and Sal was talking to James, one of his buddies who lived across the hall from us.

They stopped talking as soon as they saw me.

"Don't worry," Sal said, "Dean's cool."

A warm feeling percolated into my stomach at being called "cool."

"Cool," James said, "I was just saying to Sal I got a great Adderall hookup. With finals coming up I was just making the rounds to let the guys know in case anyone wants some."

"I'm fine myself," Sal said, "but maybe Dean wants some?"

It was a rare moment, feeling included in a conversation between James and Sal, and despite never having tried Adderall or having any particular interest in it I found myself saying: "I would love some. How much?"

"Ten bucks a pill."

"I'll take five."

I forgot about our agreement until three days later James knocked on my door.

"Hey man, here with the stuff."

"Oh right here you go." I handed him the $50 and I got a little ziplock with five orange pills in it.

James left and I sat looking at the pills. They seemed to have an aura about them. *The famous Adderall,* I thought, *why not give it a shot.* I popped one in my mouth and washed it down with a swig of black coffee.

For a while, nothing happened.

But after an hour I started to feel a warm tingling in my stomach. It was like when Sal had called me cool a few days earlier, but stronger and more stable. The best part was that I became incredibly interested in studying for my Econ final. I clicked over to Wikipedia to look up "price elasticity of demand" and realized twenty minutes later that I had just read the entire article.

Sal came into the room and asked me how I was doing.

"Great!" I practically yelled back.

"Studying?"

"Yeah dude I'm gonna crush this final I can feel it!"

Sal looked at me, impressed.

"Got any plans later tonight?" He asked.

"Hell yeah dude I'm getting fucked up."

Sal laughed. "Haven't heard that from you before. Let me know if you want to pregame with me and some of the guys over in Wilbur." I knew then that I had found something that was going to help me for a very long time.

CHAPTER TWENTY - FALL 2017

In late September I went on a Liquid Freedom team retreat in Beacon, New York. I had managed to stay sober for a few days before the retreat and so when I met Amalia, David and Alejandro at Grand Central I had the unusual sense that I was just a normal human being boarding a train.

"How's the fund going?" Alejandro asked, taking the seat across from me.

I compulsively pushed the armrest up and down as I contemplated an answer.

"Not bad. We've only had one investment so far, but I'm working on a few deals that I think will be big."

"Have you heard of Bloom? I think that team went to Stanford as well."

I had heard of Bloom, they were all over the crypto media and I had been trying for weeks to get a hold of Jesse Leimgruber, their 24-year-old founder who, along with his two co-founders, had been dubbed "The Stanford Bitcoin Mafia" by Forbes[3], each reportedly worth many millions of dollars thanks to early Ethereum and Bitcoin investments. They were launching Bloom as an ICO to replace FICO scores with a transparent, blockchain-based system.

"Yeah I have, do you have a contact?"

"I don't, but Amalia does."

Amalia texted Jesse who told her he would call me the following day.

We arrived in Beacon and the next day visited the Dia:Beacon museum, a sprawling warehouse filled with large, experimental art pieces. As the rest of the team walked around admiring the art I was buried in my phone, researching Bloom.

"Hey Dean, what do you think of this one?" Alejandro called out to me, with a wide grin on his face.

I looked up and saw a pile of sand lying on the floor in the shape of a large-breasted naked woman encircled by a velvet rope.

"Yeah not a bad one honestly, beats most of the pieces in here."

"How much would you pay for it?"

"If I get this Bloom deal and it goes 100x I'll buy a beach and make a hundred of those things."

---

3   In a Forbes article from 2018, written by my Freshman hallmate Rahul Singreddy, Singreddy bestows the mafia moniker onto Jesse and friends while including this quote from Jesse [Bloom's founder]:
"I've got friends who were sleeping on couches a year ago. Many didn't join crypto for the money but have now found themselves with five, ten, twenty million dollars worth of crypto," Leimgruber said. "It's really shaken up the space in a crazy way, because Silicon Valley has always had a young culture, but crypto is a new level. You go to any conference, almost everyone is 30 or under. And there are now tons of young people who have found themselves rich, with millions in capital to invest early and fund projects. This is why we see projects raising Series B, Series C levels from the get-go. Million-dollar deals are getting done on handshakes over dinner all the time."

Alejandro laughed and walked away. I reached over the rope and pinched off a nipple and stuck the sand in my pocket. Then I got the call.

"Hey man it's Jesse, from Bloom, I heard from Amalia you have a crypto fund and are interested in investing."

My heart rate increased at the sound of Jesse's voice, and I began tucking my shirt in and out unconsciously. I instinctively went to the bathroom as we exchanged formalities, snorting a bump off the metal top of the toilet paper holder.

"How is the raise going so far?" I asked, with a sudden energy in my voice.

I punched the mute button and flushed the toilet, holding the speaker close to my ear to listen to his response.

"Honestly we're oversubscribed. We aimed for $5 million in the presale and have over 2x that committed."

"Could you make any room for a fellow Cardinal?"

I walked out of the bathroom without washing my hands and stood swaying side to side in front of giant piles of twisted metal that used to be cars.

Jesse laughed. "I could make a little room, how much you thinking?"

"How about $200k?"

"I could do $100k at the most, does that work for you?

"It would work. But would you mind if I asked you a few questions first?"

"Why?"

"Well I just want to do some diligence on you before I write a check."

Jesse laughed again. "You're the first investor that has wanted to ask us anything to tell you the truth!"

I asked Jesse several questions about the data science behind their FICO algorithm, but as we hung up the phone I realized it made no difference.

The profitability of any ICO investment depended on one factor only: *public narrative*. Because most ICOs went public before they had any products or revenue, no concrete metrics were available to value a token rationally. All that mattered was whether people thought the project had potential. It was for this reason that Warren Buffett called Bitcoin and all cryptocurrencies "rat poison squared.[4]" Bloom's public narrative was whipped into a frenzy thanks to its all-star team and market potential; there was no reason to ask any other questions.

Two weeks later Bloom announced they raised over $30 million in the public sale. But over the next few weeks, the first signs of weakness in crypto's seemingly impenetrable bubble began to form. The market grew queasy after a raft of questionable ICOs had gone belly up and crypto prices began experiencing sharp, periodic drops followed by partial rebounds.

When Bloom launched on exchanges, the price stagnated. I realized with alarm that the ICO market might be in trouble, but I had an ace to play with Bloom.

Jesse had messed up his accounting and accidentally sent me double the tokens. I informed them of the mistake and promised to return half. But now, with the market tanking, I seized on an idea.

---

4   https://www.cnbc.com/2018/05/05/warren-buffett-says-bitcoin-is-probably-rat-poison-squared.html

By selling my double share now, I could lock in a return and wait a few weeks for the price to drop more, buying back the extra tokens for cheap and sending them back to Jesse like nothing happened.

I sold the tokens and waited. Within weeks, the price dropped almost 75 percent, so I bought back the half share I owed Jesse and pocketed an extra $75k for the fund.

But I would need more than $75k to get me a house on St. Marks. And even as many ICOs plunged in value, Ethereum had embarked on an epic rally from less than $300 in September to close to $1,000 by January. Despite my investments so far more than doubling the fund's value, I wasn't satisfied. And I knew my investors weren't either. With many expecting the ICO market to recover in the late winter, I saw this as my last chance to throw everything I had into a market that had made so many of my generation rich beyond their imaginations. I was not planning on missing out.

CHAPTER TWENTY-ONE - 2015

At the start of spring quarter all the attention of Sal and the guys had turned to rushing frats. There were over a dozen frats on campus but only two that mattered:

"Kappa Alpha and Kappa Sigma," Sal said, "those are the two I'm rushing."

James and Brad and the rest of the guys came to our dorm for a pre-game before the first rush event.

"The first two events are open," James was saying, "then, if they like you, they'll send you an invitation to the third event."

"So tonight is huge," Brad said, "it's our first impression with the guys."

"Not for you," Sal said, smiling at Brad, "I heard you were making out with some chick at a KA party last weekend."

"Yeah," James said, "turns out it's one of the Senior guy's girlfriends, probably best if you don't show your face there."

"I like Kappa Sig better anyway," Brad said.

I ducked into the bathroom and popped two 30mg pills of Adderall, returning to the room to swish a mouthful of Coca-Cola in my mouth before taking a quick pull from a handle of McCormick

Vodka and swallowing the mixture in a giant gulp. I knew where I was headed first: Kappa Alpha.

KA was the athlete frat, and I had an in. I started playing rugby in the fall, and several of the older guys on the team took a liking to me and asked me to rush. Most of Sal's group had a slight preference for Kappa Sigma and so that was where they were headed first.

"I'll see you guys later," I said, taking one final, long pull from the handle, "I'm going to KA first and then I'll swing by Kappa Sig." None of the guys paid any attention as I left.

Outside the night air refreshed me and I began to ruminate on the one-mile walk up the hill to Lake Lagunita where the KA house stood. Everything was riding on getting a bid. It was the difference between social annihilation and standing at the vanguard of all that was cool.

I approached the steps of the house with a pounding heart. There was a thump of bass and what sounded like heavy furniture being shifted and boys shouting. The KA mansion had string lights hung around the gutters and great torch lights on its corners radiating a web of light that shuddered at each bass thump.

I walked inside to find a mass of guys filling seemingly every available space in the great hallways and open rooms that made up the first floor. The Adderall had started to hit and a warm glow pervaded my body.

"Dean!" It was Roger, one of the Rugby guys. "So fucking glad you're here man! Come upstairs, we got beer up there."

On the way upstairs I heard another shout, this one decidedly less friendly.

"What is that motherfucker doing here!" A six-foot-six giant of a man was standing on the top of the stairwell, swaying from intoxication and pointing down at me.

"Uh…" I said, turning to Roger, who shrugged.

"That motherfucker made out with my girlfriend at our party last weekend, I've been looking for you."

"I think you have the wrong guy," I said, "I've never been to a party here."

"Yeah you got the wrong guy!" Roger rejoined.

Ignoring us, he launched down the stairs at me and tackled me to the bottom of the stairwell. His gigantic body was suffocating me. Then he pulled his torso back and swung at my jaw from above which connected and sent spasms of pain shooting down my neck. By then Roger and a half-dozen guys had managed to pull us apart.

"What the fuck is going on!" Roger shouted, "why did you attack Dean?"

The six-foot-six guy stared at me with a glassy-eyed expression.

"Dean? I thought your name was Brad."

"I'm Dean."

He looked at me more closely and then his expression softened.

"Oh fuck I fucked up. I'm so sorry dude I thought you were someone else."

"Jesus Christ Jeremy," Roger said, "you're going to get us sued. What the fuck is your problem."

"Dude I'm so sorry," Jeremy said, now almost in tears, "come on give this guy an automatic bid!" He lunged at me and I braced myself before discovering that he had enveloped me in a giant bear hug.

"It's all good man," I said, "honest mistake," after he pulled away several long seconds later.

"Come upstairs with me," Jeremy said, "I'm going to make it up to you."

I followed Jeremy upstairs to his room, full of half-a-dozen other guys all at least six-foot-four.

"Why is everyone so tall?" I asked.

"We're athletes," Jeremy said, then he shouted to his friends, "hey mother fuckers this guy here is a legend! His name is..." he turned to me, "what's your name again?"

"Dean."

"Dean! And he's getting an automatic bid."

There was a murmur of greetings.

"Now everyone get out! I want to talk to Dean alone." The other guys shuffled out and Jeremy shut the door behind them.

"Listen man," Jeremy began, "I'm really fucking sorry about what happened and I really do want to make it up to you. You seem like a cool guy and I promise you I'll do what I can to get you a bid."

"I appreciate that man but don't worry about it, seriously."

"You're a cool guy. Now listen, do you need any party favors?"

"Like beer?"

"Dude I got it all, molly, coke, beer anything you need. You do drugs?"

"Not too many, I mean I like Adderall."

"Adderall's shit man. If you like Adderall you're really going to like this stuff." He reached into a drawer and pulled out a baggy with some white powder in it.

"Ever try coke?"

"No I haven't."

"You want to?"

"Yeah I do."

He spilled some out on a table in the center of the room and handed me a cut up straw.

"I just suck it up through the straw?" I asked.

"Yeah like this." He demonstrated, bending over the table and lightly sucking up a small pencil-lead thin line.

I put my nose to the straw and leaned over the table, plunging the straw into the heart of the pile and sucking as hard as I could. A giant clot of coke lodged into my throat and my whole body exploded with light and energy.

"Holy shit!" I said, sitting up.

"Holy shit is right you damn near sucked up the whole table!"

"God damn that stuff is good," I said, shouting, "can I get a little for the road?"

"I'll get a little baggy for you but don't tell anyone I gave this shit to you, okay?"

"I won't!"

Once I got outside I started sprinting down the hill toward my dorm howling with laughter. For the first time in my life I finally felt like I had always imagined I should feel. Every insecurity, every fear had vanished and Stanford seemed almost too small for me. I was *alive*.

CHAPTER TWENTY-TWO – JANUARY 2018

There are lots of reasons people become addicts. The one most often described by the media, or witnessed in the streets, is the lost soul, the one who never found his or her place and so turned to drugs to numb the pain of loneliness or mental illness or a life of toil that failed to offer a better life. This is an addiction of lost hope.

Addiction also stems from poverty (although just as often, it causes it). If life is miserable and characterized by privation, despotic bosses, and endless bills, addiction is an escape: the addict's life philosophy. And those who have a lot to escape from are most prone to addiction. The more you use, the more you need to escape, so the cycle goes.

There is also a third class of addicts: the young who start using substances for group acceptance, and then dependency follows into adulthood and their bonds of chemical slavery grow nearly unbreakable. But while closer than the first two reasons, this was not the total explanation for my addiction.

Yet another class: Outwardly successful addicts, like doctors or lawyers, or financiers, those with stable families and a good social circle but who, relatively late in life, come to realize they have not found their true calling, and simply fulfilled the wishes of their parents, who strove only in response to social expectation. They turn to drugs to numb the pain of living someone else's life. Stuck in responsibilities that they are convinced prevent them from changing course.

My addiction was a mix of some of these categories. But it included another core characteristic: the desire to rise to the absolute heights of human experience, to chemically blow the mind wide open to heaven, to use my divine perch to stake my place at the helm of society. To become God. To experience all there is to feel in life. A wild craziness, a boundless energy that seems too great for my body and that is hard to channel; physical exercise helps, but the boundless energy is matched most readily through the use of powerful stimulants that endow me temporarily with the endless confidence to pursue what seems worthy of this quaking, limitless wildness. I believe there are actually a great number of addicts like this.

After Christmas, Bitcoin broke $20,000, a new all time high; and despite their recent losses, ICOs would go on to raise $2.4 billion in the month of January alone, their highest monthly total yet.

All my discussions with investors, peer funds, and cryptocurrency insiders at networking events concluded that the party would end, but not yet. The crash was always "six months out." John Larrabee declared that Ethereum would hit $10,000 by the end of 2018 and had tripled his workforce in anticipation.

My investors believed I had a small but not insignificant chance to make them ten or even one hundred times their money. I had heard it straight from their mouths. The exponential growth in the market meant returning investor money now could leave an additional 1,000 percent return or more on the table. I imagined the terrifying pain of facing my family, myself, or my investors if I missed out.

So I went all in. In the first two weeks of January I invested the entire fund in a half-a-dozen promising ICOs.

But by late January it became clear that all the industry's high hopes were on the verge of being crushed against the harsh boulders of reality. Bitcoin and Ethereum had retreated over 30 percent from their all-time highs earlier in the month and the rest of the market was in free fall. My enthusiasm was descending into despair.

Then George went away for a week, leaving me alone. That was the crucial thing. A roommate, even one you're fighting with, exerts a check on behavior—they say hi in the morning and cast a spell of interpersonal consciousness, a constant, if barebones reminder of basic social responsibilities. A mirror that will turn a disgusted face if your room gets too messy, or if you are still awake, furiously typing away at 4 am, your nose dripping blood.

With George gone and with no capital left to make new investments, I turned to cocaine. But as I lay in bed, scraping the bottom of the dopamine pale for the thousandth time for one last boost of good feeling, I realized that the end was near for my addiction too.

After close to a year of compulsive use, a year in which I had spent well north of $100,000 on cocaine, my ability to get high was dying, and with it, my will to live was dying too. Even the first hit after two or three days off, formerly a glorious feeling that made me the master of the universe for a few short hours, now passed straight into the nasty shaking anxiety that had previously characterized the second or even third night of a binge.

Even after the psych ward, the heart attack scare, all the hellish nights of prickling, aching anxious terror I had not given up on coke as my final savior. But this time, after the first hit did nothing but cause me to shake in fear at the sight of shadows, the full force of this terrible realization hit me. I had nothing left. Even if the crypto market did rebound, and I made millions, I would not be able to get high.

I got out of bed and walked out onto the balcony of my apartment, gazing down at the honking Manhattan traffic. Pressing both hands onto the waist-high railing I swung my right leg over, straddling the last barrier between me and the sea of asphalt a football field below.

CHAPTER TWENTY-THREE – JANUARY 2016

During the winter of my sophomore year, Tyler came to visit me at KA. He had graduated from West Point the summer before and he showed up with his cropped military hair and camo duffle bag. I laughed at him but was also proud. My brother, the serious and powerful army officer.

"You ready to party?" I asked him.

"Yeah definitely, can't wait."

"Listen, feel free to hit on any girl you want except for Grace and Sarah. Those are the two girls I'm seeing right now and they don't know about each other. I'll point them out to you."

"Grace and Sarah," Tyler repeated, "got it."

At the pregame Tyler and I sat together on a grassy knoll overlooking Lake Lagunita's dry bed in front of the KA house. I was pulling out clumps of grass as we talked and unconsciously depositing them in a pile next to me. Beer-soaked shouts and bellows of laughter floated up as the Palo Alto sunshine glinted off smiles almost psychotically wide.

"Look, Ethereum's gonna be huge," I said, turning to Tyler. "We're talking about the next dot-com here."

Tyler was swaying slightly after his third "Natty," or Natural Light, the drink of choice in the wealthy but body-conscious frat scene.

"Do you think I should put $20K in?" he asked.

I began pulling up larger clumps as I fought to steady my voice.

"Yeah, sure. Probably a good idea. It's trading for around $15 right now, so I can get you around thirteen hundred tokens."

My attention flickered to the half-a-dozen drinking games underway on the lawn below. Teams of two stood on either side of long wooden tables, all shirtless; zero knees and only a few self-conscious thighs were covered. Whenever a faculty member walked by on the popular Lake Lagunita trail, someone would tear-ass after them with a can of Natty outstretched like a sprinting beer zombie. If caught in the right mood, the professor would accept, transforming into a fraternal caricature: speed-chugging the upturned can to the roaring delight of the guys.

Only completely blacked out did I ever achieve the full inhibition release of the beer zombies, relying on the assurances of others the following morning that I had been "so fun" or "a complete fool."

"Okay, I'll schedule a wire transfer for tomorrow," said Tyler. When he said that I felt fear, but the fear was also excitement.

I hadn't realized how much fear I felt in my day-to-day life until I had tried cocaine. Sober, I was afraid of other people, afraid of my homework, and afraid of cars, bikes, and girls. Fear was like a prison and I didn't want to be in prison. I also wanted to be more than not afraid. I wanted to be powerful, confident, dominant.

I had first learned of Ethereum a few months earlier, when I had chosen "blockchain" as my topic for a rhetoric class. I discovered that blockchain had a lot more to do with fighting the financial and internet establishment than it had to do with nerdy internet money. It appealed to my desire to carve out my own cultural and technological real estate rather than just live on the land others had already built on.

But my conviction in it was sealed only a few weeks earlier, when Vitalik Buterin stepped out in front of the several dozen of us gathered at the Hacker Dojo in Mountain View, California. Vitalik had become something of a hero to me, he was socially awkward and was stick-thin with a physique that many referred to (with affection) as "alien-like." He represented an alternative life path: one where with sheer originality and creative genius you could ignore everything you'd been told about how the world runs and build a new system entirely. A life in other words, lived without fear.

Vitalik was still just twenty-two, but he had only been a late adolescent when, stuttering and fidgeting, he'd introduced Ethereum at the Miami Bitcoin conference in early 2014. A year after Miami, Ethereum launched and had now been running more or less smoothly for nine months, prompting a global speaking tour to discuss what came next.

We levitated back and forth on our tech-issue Aerons in front of glossy white tables while Vitalik tested the clicker with deliberate, jerky motions—like Heath Ledger's Joker finishing off Gotham General.

Ethereum, if you're unfamiliar, is the first general-purpose world computer. "Turing complete" in computer science parlance is another way of saying that it can run any code recognizable by a computer. But Ethereum is the democracy to your MacBook's dictatorship. On Ethereum, you're just one of thousands determining the next action the computer should take. This means Ethereum's processing speed is glacial, prompting the question: Why build the world's slowest MacBook?

One word: trust. You see, Ethereum isn't just a computer; it is also a web. A web-computer hybrid. Today, the web is a series of walled gardens forever under siege: Google, Chase Bank, Cloudflare, the US Government—all have built byzantine walls of encryption and threat detection. All have been hacked. Ethereum eschewed walls in favor of consensus, requiring total agreement before executing any process.

Web 1—mostly text and images published on self-hosted websites—reigned from 1993 until roughly 2000. "Surfing the web" meant jumping from wave to wave, where a "wave" was an independent server and "jumping" meant clicking hyperlinks. As Web 2.0 began replacing Web 1.0, everyone more or less joined the same wave—or the same few waves, specifically Facebook, Amazon, Netflix, and Google, collectively referred to as "FANG."

In short, web 1 was decentralized, whereas web 2 is centralized. The companies that make up FANG benefit from network effects and corral financial returns, enabling them to hire tens of thousands of software engineers to make their platforms better and more addicting. This started out great for everyday users. But the relationship has turned toxic as users are now dependent on these platforms, a process Cory Doctorow refers to as "enshittification."

By 2016 it was clear to me that the Web 2 world had become saturated and monopolistic. No one with a genuine desire to change the world could work for Facebook or Google. Ethereum was the blockchain industry's leading light, representing my chance to get in on the ground floor of the next great tech revolution.

Ethereum and its acolytes called this new world "Web 3." Where all the control and profit of global technology platforms would be redistributed back to users. By early 2016, Ethereum's early adopters were already launching new tech platforms run with tokens issued in ICOs on Ethereum that ostensibly gave most of the power and profits to the little guy. What none of us realized in the hacker dojo that day was that ICOs would kick off a multi-billion dollar speculative frenzy. A frenzy that would come close to bringing down the hammer of regulation with such force that it would threaten the very existence of crypto and the Web 3 dream.

"Okay," said Vitalik, having gotten the clicker working. "Let's get started."

I straightened up in my chair and beamed.

"That's Grace," I whispered to Tyler, pointing at a bleach blonde girl wearing a tight-fitting black T-shirt, fishnet stockings and a black skirt with Birkenstocks who had just walked onto the lawn, "we've been seeing each other for a few weeks." Tyler nodded and threw a thumbs up, "got it." Grace spotted me and smiled and waved.

Grace wore dark eyeliner and sat in the lecture hall of one of my economics classes with a serious, studied expression that intimidated me. She was always dressed in elaborate fishnets and skirts and black or green blouses. I was drunk when I spotted her at a KA party and made my approach. Apparently (she filled me in later on the details I was hazy on) I grabbed her and declared that I had been obsessed with her since I laid eyes on her in class. Luckily this was charming to her and we spent the night dancing and after the night ended I sent her a text message declaring that "against all the wishes of the other knights of the order of Kappa Alpha I am making known throughout the halls my total and untainted ardor for you!"

We had seen each other several times since and I had learned she grew up in LA and her father made documentaries and her mother had died when she was very young. I had grown to like her, but remained puzzled by the strength of my blacked-out passion for her.

A few days earlier Grace and I had been in bed together and I was just preparing to leave when she had wrapped her arms around me and declared "I'm your girlfriend!" A bolt of nerves shot through me and my mouth dried up. I had never had a girlfriend before and didn't particularly want one. I was terrified of disappointing anyone who was affectionate or kind to me and the look in her eyes was so pure that I couldn't bear to let her down. I decided I would think things over and tell her where I stood the next time I saw her.

This wouldn't have been a problem except for Sarah. Grace was in Kappa and Sarah was in Theta and as far as I knew they had never once spoken to each other. I had met Sarah at another KA mixer and I liked her better.

"That's Sarah," I told Tyler, pointing to my strawberry-blonde future girlfriend standing in a large group of her many friends.

"Your Girlfriend?"

"Well, sort of. Grace is kind of my girlfriend too."

Tyler nodded solemnly and staggered off to get more beer.

Xander, one of my frat brothers approached me. "Hey man you got the stuff?"

The son of a successful Hollywood actor, Xander had asked me if I could get some GHB for us to do together at the party. "It's liquid orgasms," he told me, "you gotta try it." I had never heard of GHB before but I found some on the Deep Web and it had arrived just in time.

"Yeah I got it," I said, "follow me."

We walked into my room and I produced a vial filled with a viscous clear liquid out of my desk drawer.

"Mm," Xander said, "this doesn't look like the stuff I took in high school, you sure it's the right stuff?"

"Pretty sure," I said.

Xander shrugged, unscrewed the cap, and took a swig, handing it to me. I killed the rest of it and we walked out.

"It should hit us in about an hour," Xander said, grinning and smacking me on the back, "enjoy yourself!"

As I walked outside I ran into Sarah, "hey Dean!" she said brightly, throwing her arms around me.

"Hey Sarah! So good to see you." As we hugged I glanced over her shoulder and was relieved to see Grace wasn't around.

"Listen," I said, "my older brother Tyler is here, let me introduce you."

Tyler had joined a circle of girls next to the lake bed and was flirting with a natty in each hand. He was swaying so much I was afraid he would lose his balance.

"Tyler, this is Sarah," I said, introducing them. They shook hands and I nodded and winked at Tyler, "I told you about Sarah."

"Hey Sarer," Tyler said with a slight slur, "nice to meet yer."

I went inside to use the bathroom. As I was washing my hands I felt annoyed at myself that I had led on both Grace and Sarah when it was inevitable they would find out about each other. It was cruel, really, this greed of mine.

I walked outside again to find Tyler speaking with Grace, touching her arm and laughing with animated gestures, his clumsy mating ritual I recognized at once. "I'm telling you," Tyler was saying loudly to Grace, whose face was contorted in a pained expression, "Sarah is Dean's girlfriend!" "But I'm telling you, I'm Dean's girlfriend!" Grace said. "No Sarah is!"

Grace saw me approaching and burst into tears, "you cheated on me!" she shouted as she saw me approach, "no, no what!" I said, lost in confusion and turning to Tyler who just shrugged. Grace ran off and I went at Tyler. "What the fuck! I told you not to talk to Grace." "Sorry I didn't realize."

"Give me that, I need it more than you!" I said, snatching his beer out of his hand and draining it. I ran into the house and pulled out a handle of Vodka from our liquor supply and downed two huge gulps. The warm feeling of the liquor calmed my nerves and I walked outside with a warm glow in my stomach. The GHB must have been kicking in too. *I'll deal with Grace tomorrow*, I thought.

Outside, Xander's voice came over the loudspeaker. "Gimme a P! Gimme a U! Gimme a S! Gimme a S! Gimme a Y! What's that spell?! PUSSY!" I started cracking up, and ran towards the stage as the music started back up and began to dance. I felt like my body had disappeared and I was a cloud of pleasure floating through space. Tyler came over and started dancing next to me. "Hey!" I shouted, "don't worry about what happened, I forgive you."

"What happened?"

"Forget it."

I roped my arm around my older brother's shoulder and together we stumbled around kegs and pockets of merriment, typified by a 100-foot slip-n-slide and food trucks that turned the sprawling K.A.

lawn into a demented child's birthday party. A symbol of where we all were in life. Caught somewhere in between having play dates at our parents' houses and living as adults in the so-called real world.

The DJ finished his set and most of the partygoers were making their way home. I stumbled on stage in a vague, belligerent attempt to keep the party going. But the human chemical experiment I had been running on myself had produced an unexpected reaction. As I found out later, the combination of alcohol and GHB in the body produces a roofie that paralyzes the body.

As I was holding the mic and shouting "hey hey parties not over yet fuckers," my legs gave way and I collapsed on stage, crumbling in a pathetic mass of weary regret. Tyler, who was still on the lawn, roused himself from his ossified state and staggered over to me.

"Hey you okay?"

"I don't think so," I whispered back. Every ounce of energy had left my body and I could barely speak. He grabbed me and attempted to shift my weight. The roofie had taken full effect, I was dead weight. Two other frat brothers were summoned to help move me inside. I was carried like a wounded soldier off a battlefield, arms draped over a shoulder on each side of me; my legs dragging behind me.

"I'm going to call an ambulance," someone said.

A group gathered around as I waited by the entrance to Kappa Alpha. I was lying on a bench, still unable to move. An ambulance arrived and I was taken inside where an EMT stuck an IV in my arm and began pumping something into me. By the time we pulled into the Marc and Laura Andreessen Emergency Department I was feeling much better.

As I was wheeled into the ward, I was reminded of a talk I'd attended where Marc Andreessen—multi-billionaire venture capitalist and inventor of the first internet browser—and entrepreneur and investor Balaji Srinivasan discussed their conviction that technology would untether the individual from authoritarian institutions.

"Airbnb will untether us from homes..." Balaji announced on stage at Stanford's Greene Auditorium as he karate-chopped his left index finger with his right hand. "...Uber from cars..." his middle finger was chopped next. "...Bitcoin from banks..." his ring finger gone. "Ultimately all ties holding an individual to a place or institution will be cut by technology."

Andreessen smiled and nodded as Balaji spoke.

"We will be utterly free," he agreed.

CHAPTER TWENTY-FOUR – JANUARY 2018

I felt a buzzing in my pocket; it was Sarah. I picked up.

"Hey how are you?" She asked.

"I'm good, how are you?"

"Your voice sounds strange."

"Yeah I'm just getting over a cold I think."

"Oh. Sorry to hear that."

"It's okay, I'm feeling better now." I swung my right leg back over the railing, slumping down against the sliding glass door.

"I was thinking it would probably do you good if you moved out to the Bay Area. You know how you talked about living with your brother in San Francisco? I think you should do that. I'll visit you on the weekends."

"Okay I will."

"You will?"

"Yeah."

"That was easy," she laughed, "don't change your mind and text me your plans, can't wait to see you!"

We hung up. I went inside and puked before lying down in bed.

George came home the next day. I was dreading our conversation. I imagined shouting, threats, and demands for money but knew no other way. As soon as morning came I summoned the nerve and walked out to tell George I was leaving.

"Listen, man, I have something important to say," I told him, standing at the entry to the kitchen as he was making breakfast.

"Sure, what's up?" He shut off the stove and turned to me, his palms open at his side.

"Things aren't going well."

"I know." I detected a softness in his expression that surprised me.

"The market is crashing and to be honest my mental health is at an all-time low. I'm going to San Francisco to stay with my brother and get back on my feet. There's still a chance the fund works out and we make a lot of money, but honestly I'm not holding out hope."

Wordlessly he approached me and hugged me. His response so surprised me that my eyes grew misty.

He backed away. "Dude I gotta say, I had a fucking blast working on this fund with you, and it was an honor that you included me. I learned so much about entrepreneurship and crypto and even though I'd loved to have made a shitload of money at the end of the day it's no big deal."

I smiled. "Thanks brother, I'll keep paying rent until you get another roommate, I know you have another six months on this lease."

"Don't worry about that. I can get my Mom to cover it or something, it's not a problem."

As I walked back to my room, sobriety suddenly didn't seem so terrifying.

The next week I moved into my brother's house in San Francisco. It was a sizable four-bedroom home in Glen Park; eight people lived there. I was the ninth and I was to share Evan's bed and his room with him and his roommate, Jake, an Apple engineer. It was a small room, not more than 10' x 10', and my portion of the rent was only $375, a tenth of what I had been paying in Manhattan.

I had hoped that sharing an intimate space with two people would exert a social pressure on me to stay sober. But I underestimated the power of my addiction. Within a few days of moving I ordered an ounce of fish scale online.

In the meantime I tried to keep up some kind of routine by working out of the EtherMosaic office in the Tenderloin. While Ubering to work for an early morning call, a shirtless man with blood dripping from his nose approached the car as it was stopped at a traffic light. I put my phone down and watched as he swung open the front passenger door and hurled his torso onto the passenger seat. Almost prone, he pulled out a knife and made a pass at the driver, who punched the gas, throwing him out into the street; I turned to look out of the rear view window and saw him sprinting after us before stopping to let out a blood-curdling scream while beating his chest with both fists.

"That motherfucker was definitely on drugs!" The driver shouted, heaving with excitement, "these goddamn addicts are ruining this city!"

"Drug addicts are the worst."

"You got that right my brother!"

At the office I immediately went to the bathroom and did a line of coke. Then I checked my messages and saw a text from a Stanford friend.

"Hey man I have a connection with a real financial heavyweight coming to the Bay to meet with some crypto funds. Do you want to meet with him?"

"Maybe, what's he looking to do?"

"I don't know. His name's Abdullah and he runs a giant wealth management company based in Luxembourg."

The next day I was sitting at a long table in the lobby of a First Republic Bank in the financial district with a half-dozen other twenty-somethings who either ran crypto funds or worked for Abdullah. At the head of the table sat Abdullah, the Luxembourg wealth guru who looked to be in his early fifties, he had a black beard sprinkled with gray and he was modestly overweight which gave him a dignified appearance. He was wearing a tight fighting purple turban and a black suit with an expression of sarcastic superiority on his face. "Okay let me go ahead and get started," he said. His voice was so soft it was at times difficult to hear. But I sensed an edge to him.

As he spoke I read between the lines. He had smelled easy money in the Web 3 game and had flown to the US to round up investment partners with marketing and crypto know-how to help him launch a token. The pitch: tokenize a global wealth management fund to let all the little guys in on the same investments as the rich.

"I'm thinking we start with a fifty-million dollar raise; what do you think?" He asked, turning to me.

I had stayed up the night before on cocaine and my body was in one of those strangely relaxed states after a binge. If Abdullah had spit in my face I probably would have just smiled.

"I think that's just fine, but what makes you think you can do it?"

He stared at me.

"I run one of the biggest wealth management funds in the world, what do you mean 'can I do it'?"

"You're an old school guy, if you don't mind me saying," Abdullah's smile turned serious, "the web-3 world is a different animal, you gotta be cool, you gotta market this thing right. And besides, people aren't interested in 7 percent returns, they want ten baggers."

"Ten baggers?"

"Tenfold returns."

"And how do you think we do that?"

"You're the one pitching me."

I yawned; I just wanted the conversation to end so I could go home and sleep. But Abdullah took my disinterest as the ultimate sign of competence.

His eyes, which had been lazy and downcast, were now burning with energy, "Listen," he began, his voice growing noticeably bolder, "I have to run to another meeting but I think we can do something special together. Let's meet for dinner."

"Fine with me."

I went home and napped before taking the Bart train to Berkeley to meet Abdullah. He told me he was visiting his son in grad school. I was refreshed after sleep and arrived for the meeting with a new energy.

We strolled down University Ave as he told me his life story.

"You wouldn't believe some of the projects I've worked on, billion-dollar construction projects in India and Saudi."

I nodded along, barely getting a word in.

"I own one of the largest houses in Luxembourg. It's on a huge hill and looks down on the peasants below."

I assumed he was making a joke and started to laugh.

Abdullah looked at me and seemed like he was about to ask me why I had laughed before thinking better of it.

"I ran a 10.6 100m when I was at Cambridge and I was the captain of the soccer team."

"Impressive."

"And I'm telling you, my life has been extraordinary. The hundreds of women I've been with over the last twenty years. Even my wife was beautiful but she couldn't stand how many women I was with so we ended up getting a divorce."

I stifled another laugh.

"The point is," he continued, "I've never lost once in my life. I only win. And I intend to win at launching an ICO."

I found it curious that he did not consider his divorce a "loss," but my head was starting to hurt and I didn't feel like pressing him on it.

"Let's get some dinner, I'm hungry," he said finally.

At least I'll get a nice dinner out of this, I thought.

We stopped in front of Chipotle and he turned, "this look good to you?"

"Chipotle? Sure I guess."

As we walked through the line Abdullah said, "get whatever you want; dinner's on me."

"Right, thanks."

"Listen," he began as we sat down, "tell me about your fund; what are your intentions in the long run?"

It was the first question he had asked me in over an hour.

"Well, to be honest I just made a big round of investments last month and I plan to return as much investor money as I can as soon as any money comes back."

He stared at me in shock.

"Return money?" He asked, gaping. It was like I punched him in the face. "The number one rule of investment management is you never, ever return money unless you absolutely have to."

I shrugged. "I don't know, I think I just want to go back to school and finish my degree. I'm kind of sick of this whole investing business."

He shook his head in disgust. "My friend, you are not made for this business if that is your intention."

"Fine with me."

"Let me try to convince you otherwise, come let's go to a bar."

The thought of drinking with Abdullah made my headache worse but I couldn't see a way out. I followed him to a dive bar on the Ave, and we sat down and ordered drinks.

"Listen," he began as soon as we sat down, "the number one rule in my life is to never give an inch when it comes to business." I sensed a long rant coming and I took a long drink of my IPA, wiping the foam from my mouth with my sleeve. "I have workers at my house now. I shipped them in from China, real craftsmen. I told my staff to feed them beans and rice. You know what I feed my wolf dogs?"

"What?"

"Wagyu steaks."

"That's terrible."

"Terrible? The only thing you get in this world is what you take. You can not give up money unless it is absolutely necessary."

"But isn't feeding the dogs steak a waste of money?"

He shook his head. "You simply do understand life my friend."

"I guess not."

"Listen, why don't you come with me to Luxembourg? You can live at my house and learn from me, how does that sound?"

"Uh, I mean I have a lot to do here, I'm not sure I could..."

"Think about it, don't give me an answer now."

Abdullah excused himself to go to the bathroom. I checked to make sure he was out of sight before standing up and walking out. As soon as I was outside, I began to run, and I did not stop running until I reached the bart station.

CHAPTER TWENTY-FIVE – APRIL 2017

I was preparing a line of coke at my desk when I got an email from one of the undergraduate deans. "Dean is everything all right? You're failing your classes and one of your professors said he hasn't seen you in four weeks. Please come to my office this afternoon."

As usual I was in the midst of a binge, and wouldn't have shown up had I not been afraid that someone would come looking for me. I was alert as I walked out of the dorm, and deftly ducked behind a palm tree to avoid being spotted by a wandering KA brother.

I arrived at the Dean's sun-soaked office and was directed to sit across from him in a Stanford Cardinal-branded armchair. The big open windows and ray-rich California sun punctured the air so every dust particle burst forth only to melt back into a dreamy gauze. A self-assured smile glowed on my face; it was saying to the dean "you're not real." The nonchalance of the chemical refractory period.

"I'm worried about you, Dean," the dean began. He was in his late 50s with a soft chin and a concerned expression in his eyes, magnified by his glasses with thick, wooden-looking frames.

I giggled inappropriately.

"Do you find something funny?"

"Even though my name's Dean, I don't think I'm dean material."

He smiled.

"From one dean to another, I think you're dean material if that's the route you choose in life. But tell me, what's been going on?"

I scratched the right arm of my chair.

"Well it's a long story, and while you seem like a nice guy I'm not sure I feel comfortable talking to you. You're a dean after all, you have a lot of power."

He nodded.

"I understand, how about we take a walk to a campus psychiatrist. Will you take a walk with me?"

I nodded.

"So I understand you've been going through a rough patch."

The psychiatrist was in her early thirties and wore a navy blazer with good posture and hair that looked expensive; I read her look when I sat down as wary compassion.

"Isn't that something you could say about everyone that comes in here?"

I smiled, but her expression remained frozen. A few moments passed in silence.

"Well, the truth is I haven't been sleeping," I said, filling the void. "Haven't slept at all the past two nights, actually."

I glanced around the room carelessly, then back at the psychiatrist. Her eyes were boring into me.

"So, how's your day going?" I asked.

"Good. Thank you for asking."

"I really appreciate you seeing me. I know normally there's a long waitlist for these sessions. Is there usually a long waitlist?"

She ignored the question.

"Can you tell me why you think you aren't sleeping?"

I noticed that her words were echoing. She felt pseudo-real, just like the dean.

"I've been snorting enormous quantities of cocaine. Kind of makes it hard to sleep."

I found myself speaking without a filter, not out of a desire to be honest, but because after days without sleep at the tail end of a binge it felt like there was nothing solid left of myself to defend.

I laughed. Then my nose started to bleed, and I smiled at the cinematic timing.

"See?" I said, pointing.

"So the blood, that's from the coke?"

She offered me a tissue box, and I plucked one out and wiped the underside of my nose, examining the red streaks on the tissue before tearing some off to shove into my nose and then dropping the rest into a wastebasket.

"Yes. These are usually for tears, not coke bleeds, right?" I laughed again.

"Why did you start using so much coke?"

"Well I was mostly using it socially until about three months ago. That's when I moved out of my frat and into a new dorm. Then I began using every day."

"So you mostly just use when you're in your room by yourself?"

"Well you don't have to put it so bluntly," I laughed, "but yes, mostly I'm just holed up doing coke."

"And what kind of things are you doing while you're on coke?"

"Oh all kinds of things. I've been researching cryptocurrency and masturbating. Lots of masturbating."

"I see. And how are you affording all this coke? It's quite expensive isn't it?"

I frowned.

"Well some of it comes from money I made on crypto and the rest is money I stole."

"What do you mean 'money you stole?'"

I began digging the ball of my right foot into the carpet.

"About a year ago my older brother.."

"Can you speak up, I can't hear you?"

I cleared my throat.

"About a year ago my older brother gave me $20,000 to invest in a cryptocurrency called Ethereum. And the rest of my family gave me another $10,000 or so. I got into the habit of selling some of the Ethereum to pay for drugs but I always repurchased it whenever the price dropped. That worked for a while but then the price stopped dropping. It was around $10-$15 when I originally bought it, and now it's worth around $80. That means I should be holding almost $200,000 of their money."

"And how much are you actually holding?"

"It's all gone."

"Wow."

"Yeah, wow. Anyway, that's one reason I've been using so much coke. I'm trying to figure out a way to make all that money back."

"But you do realize the coke is what got you into trouble in the first place. What makes you think it can help you get out of trouble?"

I looked at her seriously.

"I don't think you understand. With coke I can not only make this money back, I can make 100 times the amount of money I owe them."

"How do you plan on doing that?"

I waved my right hand in the air dismissively. "I'm figuring that out. But believe me, I will die before I fail."

CHAPTER TWENTY-SIX – FEBRUARY 2018

A few days after moving into my brother's house, I started getting emails from ICO companies I had invested in that said things like, "Due to adverse market conditions and US regulatory concerns, we have decided to postpone our token launch indefinitely." Then two of my investors emailed me asking for their money back.

"My hands are tied," I wrote back, "all the money has been invested in illiquid tokens; there is no cash on hand to meet redemption requests."

I slept late, long after Evan and our other roommate, Liam, had left for work. I didn't like Liam very much. He was tall and skinny and seemed to force an air of ease and jocularity that I felt was his attempt to disguise a hidden depression, one I recognized all too well in myself. But when he walked in our room, thinking I was sleeping, he would tiptoe almost silently so as not to disturb me and in those moments, I almost loved him.

I would lay in bed for many hours, too awake to fall asleep but too tired to get up and walk around. I tried my hardest not to think about my life. I went to war with my thoughts, silently screaming at them to shut up. I listened to the Joe Rogan podcast and endless hours of the Howard Stern show to drown out my thoughts. It occurred to me that I was terribly lonely. I thought about all the millions of people, many probably lonely like me, who listened to Joe Rogan's show and pretended he was their friend.

I ran out of coke within a few days of getting to Evan's house and my next shipment was delayed. But I hardly cared. I had only ordered more out of habit. Sarah had asked to hang out a few times but I kept cancelling. I guessed she was probably mad at me but I didn't want her to see me in this state.

I was lying in bed one morning, ruminating, when I felt my phone buzz. It was for a meeting I had forgotten.

"This is Dean." I propped myself up on my elbows as I spoke.

"Hey this is Francesco, is now still a good time?"

"Uh sure, now works."

"We met at Devcon last year, remember?"

"Yes I remember." I did remember him. We had spent the better part of an evening together at a conference over drinks. I recalled being perplexed by his vague and slightly creepy descriptions of what he did for a living.

"Listen, I have an exciting proposition for you."

"Okay I'm listening."

"I have one million euros sitting in the trunk of a car in Sicily. If you send me €700,000 in Bitcoin I will hand over the one million euros along with the car. All you have to do is drive it up to Switzerland and deposit it at a bank account we have set up for you. In other words, you make €300,000 for taking a nice road trip."

"What's the reason?"

"It's for taxes. The Italian government would take over half if we reported it, this way we get to keep more of it and you make money too."

"Interesting."

"So are you in or what?"

"I don't know. Let me think about it."

Francesco told me I had twenty-four hours to decide and hung up.

I got out of bed and dry-heaved in the bathroom before walking outside to clear my head.

It was a foggy day, and my head felt infested with flies. I walked past a group of young professionals on a balcony sharing drinks and laughing. They looked happy. I frowned and opened my phone, staring at it for a few moments before remembering why I pulled it out. I was going to look up flights to Sicily. I found a flight departing from SFO that night arriving the next day. But then I remembered that I needed the coke. I couldn't travel without coke.

"Hey honey, how are you?"

It was my Mom. I realized I had called her. I didn't know why I called her but here I was, talking to her.

"Not good, honestly," I felt myself say.

"Oh I'm sorry to hear that. What's been going on?"

"I think I hate what I do for a living."

"Mm.. well you're still young, you don't have to love what you're doing now."

"I know but... things are really really hard right now. I'm not sure how much longer I can keep going."

"Dean, I have to tell you something."

"Okay Mom."

"Evan said he found a package at his house addressed to you that looked really... suspicious. We're all really worried about you."

My heart dropped.

"He found the... he found a package? Did he say what was inside?"

"It doesn't matter. The point is we're here to help you. Would you be interested in going to a program?"

"What kind of program?"

"A program to help you get back on your feet. And to stop using anything that might be hurting you."

"That might be nice. Yeah, I think I could use that honestly."

"I actually have been doing a lot of research already, and I found a program nearby that I think would be really good."

"Okay."

"It's called Chi Recovery, and it's in Sonoma County. The main thing is that it's outpatient and three months long. Which apparently has a much higher success rate than the typical four-week program."

"Okay. I'm ready to go. Thank you Mom."

"Love you honey."

I tried to say "I love you too," but the words stuck in my throat.

"Okay bye."

We hung up. For a few moments I stood stunned. I felt my feet start to move again, I was going in a loop. I passed the balcony with the drinkers and laughers and looked up at them again. I felt a smile tug at my lips. I pulled out my phone and texted Francesco. "I can't do it sorry, I have some other, very important business I have to take care of in the US for the next few months." Then I pocketed my phone and walked home.

CHAPTER TWENTY-SEVEN – ONE WEEK LATER

I was packing my clothes into trash bags when Evan and Mom walked in.

"Hey Dean, how are you doing?" Mom asked.

"Not bad," I said, looking up at them.

"I just want to say I'm happy you're doing what you're doing. It's not easy."

"I'm proud of you," Evan said.

I shrugged, "thanks."

"You ready to go?" Mom asked.

"Almost yeah. Five minutes."

I found a couple Xanax bars in my backpack. The only drugs I had left. I bit off half a bar and swallowed before walking out to the car.

On the drive I was silent. Mom looked over at me anxiously for the first few minutes, trying to make small talk, and then gave up entirely. I mostly stared down at the space between my tennis shoes.

"I can't help but think of what my investors would say if they found out I was in a drug recovery program," I said, finally.

"They don't have to know."

"I know."

"I'm so happy you're doing this."

"Yeah."

"I know it's not easy."

"I know but I need to. It's out of my control at this point. I have no other choice."

"That's true."

"Yeah."

Mom flipped the indicator and pulled off the 101 into downtown Sebastopol. It was an old hippie town filled with yoga studios and apothecaries. Chi Recovery was located in a small office park on a dusty end of town, sandwiched between a Subway and a tax attorney. I was nervous as we parked; nervous that I would be slapped with the label of "addict" for the rest of my life. Yet, there was also a peculiar comfort in the idea of adopting a new identity, one that would attract sympathy and support.

We walked in and a plump older lady wearing a bright red floral moo-moo with short white hair came out to meet us. I guessed she was in her mid-60s. She introduced herself as Rose, the program founder and director.

"We're very happy you're here, Dean."

Everyone kept saying that. How "happy" they were.

My Mom and I followed her to her office upstairs. It was full of statues of Buddha and Hindu gods and there was a poster on the wall of an orange sunset with bold black lettering that said "acceptance is the key to change."

"I won't ask you directly about your drug history with your Mom here," Rose began, "we will have plenty of time to get into that over the next three months. But I want to give you an overview of the program. Are you familiar with the four quadrants model of wellbeing?"

I shook my head.

She pulled out a dry-erase marker and sketched a large square with a 't' in the middle on a whiteboard next to her desk, dividing the square into four equal sections.

"The four quadrants of well-being are one, physical," she said, writing "physical" into the upper left box, "two, emotional, three, spiritual, and four, intellectual." She then filled in the rest of the squares. "Now, a balanced person pays roughly equal attention to each of these four categories. Most people who come here are okay in one or two categories but often quite weak in the others. Can you think of which categories you might be strong in and which ones might need some work?"

"Well intellectual I'm pretty good in, I think," I said, crossing my arms and gripping my opposite elbows.

Rose and Mom both nodded.

"Physical is not bad. I mean obviously the drugs aren't very healthy but I do work out. But yeah, physical is probably my other decent one."

"Okay, and what about emotional and spiritual?"

"Those could use some work," I started to rock myself back and forth, "I don't do very well with emotions and I really have nothing going on in my life that seems very spiritual."

My Mom and Rose shared a knowing look.

"Don't worry, that's very common," Rose said.

"Okay."

"We require all of our students to attend at least twenty spiritually enriching classes during their first thirty days. This could be yoga, meditation, twelve-step, church, tai chi, anything. As long as it nourishes your spiritual growth."

"Okay. I mean frankly I'll try anything at this point."

"That's the spirit," Rose said, smiling. "Now, I want to spend a few moments talking about the financial side of things."

After meeting with Rose my Mom stayed upstairs while I went downstairs to the in-house doctor who gave me a physical with an EKG. He was tall with long gray hair and a puffy face and wore a huge bright yellow Hawaiian shirt.

"Hey brother," the doctor said, shaking my hand, "you look pretty good. You don't have the shakes or anything, a lot better than most of our intake patients."

"Thank you."

"Now are you coming off heroin or opiates?"

"Not really, I mean I did some heroin but cocaine was my drug of choice."

"Okay, that's good. Now listen brother, you already know this but cocaine really gets your nervous system jacked up and does a number on your heart. Even though you're young it wouldn't hurt to go see a cardiologist to check things out. Other than that, I just recommend you relax. The main thing for the next few weeks is to get your nervous system back into balance—Eating well, exercising, meditating, that sort of thing."

"Got it."

"And avoid stress at all costs."

"Got it."

———

"Dean, I want my money out now! As far as I'm concerned crypto is going to zero in the next six months and I'd rather see something than nothing." I was sitting at a coworking desk I'd rented in downtown Sebastopol three days after my intake. I was on the phone with one of my largest investors. *I need coke,* I thought. *God do I need coke.*

"Listen, one of the ICOs we invested in in January will be listing in the next week," I responded, "I'll sell whatever I can of that and give you your share of the fund back as soon as I can. You're at the top of the list."

I heard a sigh on the other end of the line. "Thank you. I understand the market is out of your control but Jesus Christ do I wish I had pulled out two months ago."

"You and me both."

He laughed. "Yeah I guess you're in way more shit than I am. At least most of my net worth is in real estate and stocks."

"Yeah, good thing."

We got off the phone and I went into a private room to check the Ethereum price before opening a meditation app, "Waking Up" with Sam Harris. His monotone voice vibrated through the speaker and I shut my eyes and tried to relax my shoulders and jaw. Two minutes in, I paused the meditation and rechecked Ethereum. It hadn't changed, still down 50 percent from its all-time high. I sighed and kicked myself for getting so distracted and then restarted the meditation. Three minutes later I checked again, and then once more towards the end. Finally I got through the ten minutes, stood up, and went back to my desk, opening Instagram as soon as I sat down.

———

"My name's Dean and I'm an addict."

"*Hey Dean,*" a chorus of voices responded.

"My name's Darrell and I am *definitely* an addict."

"*Hey Darrell.*"

"Thank you for attending this meeting of narcotics anonymous," Darrell continued, "let's open the meeting with the serenity prayer."

I listened as the group of thirty or so men and women broke out into a chant. "*May God grant me the serenity to accept the things I cannot change, the courage to change the things I can, and the wisdom to know the difference.*"

There was a pause before Darrell spoke again. "I want to begin by recognizing any of our brothers and sisters that are new here with a show of hands." I felt a nudge. It was Robin, one of the councilors at Chi recovery who had driven me to the meeting at a church in downtown Santa Rosa. Even though we had only known each other a few days, we had developed a friendship. She was blunt and strong, an addict herself and she wasn't afraid to say the uncomfortable things I needed to hear.

I put my hand up along with a couple others to scattered applause.

"Newcomers are the lifeblood of NA," Darrell continued, "we're happy you're here. One day at a time brothers and sisters. Now when I was asked to share at this meeting I thought about the message I needed to hear when I was new. That was in 1994, twenty-four years ago last month." Scattered applause. "Now when I first came into recovery I thought I was better than everyone else, even though I was about 95 pounds and had track marks running up my arms and neck. I looked like I had just gotten out of a concentration camp." A group of old timers cackled in the back. Darrell smiled. "I felt like I was better than everyone else. Those other people have a problem, not me. That's why denial stands for 'Don't Even Notice I Am Lying.'" Laughter. "And so I bounced in and out of NA for the better *Chi Recovery* of a decade. Getting clean from smack and then getting high on ice. I thought I was making progress, but I was just changing seats on the Titanic." Laughter. "Now as addicts we talk a lot about our 'bottoms.' I think we all know what that means. For a lot of our brothers and sisters out there in the streets that bottom may be death." There were murmurs and nods. "And in my case it was seeing my son on the nightly news. He was only seventeen and the headline read 'double homicide in Santa Rosa,' and there was a big picture of his face up there on the TV. My own son, a ruthless killer."

There was a rare silence in the crowd. Darrell choked and dabbed at his eyes with a tissue.

"You know I'm a tough guy, ex-Marine. It takes a lot for me to cry, but even now, twenty-four years later, I still get choked up—

because when I found out my boy had killed two innocent people, I was prepared to take my own life. He had joined a gang and shot two women; Rebecca was one—she had a newborn baby in the backseat—and her friend Samantha. He had never met them, but he murdered them in cold blood."

Darrell paused, inhaling audibly before continuing.

"Because it was my son, it was as if I had pulled the trigger with my own hand. I spilled that blood. And believe me when I say it would have been easier for me to take my own life than to keep going. But enough blood had already been spilled. And more importantly, I realized that my addiction was not about me. It was about all the people in my life who I had hurt. I think I speak for a lot of addicts in the room when I say that if it was just about us we would gladly accept the suffering and pain that comes with our addiction if it meant we could continue to use. But our disease doesn't just affect us, does it?" An old timer in the back cupped his hands to his mouth and shouted "no it doesn't!" Darrell nodded, "no it doesn't. And I take a lot of responsibility for my son's actions because I wasn't there for him as a father. And that is a wound that will never heal. But that's okay. Some wounds aren't meant to heal, they shouldn't. Because they remind us why we're all here."

I looked over and saw Robin had tears in her eyes. I felt like I should cry too but I felt very little, except for a murmur of fear in my heart.

CHAPTER TWENTY-EIGHT - SIX-WEEKS LATER

The hardest part of recovery was going to bed. I was okay when I was active, but as darkness fell and it was time to face my pillow I felt afraid. When I lay down my disappointed investors—Tyler whose money I had stolen—my frat brothers and Sarah appeared before me, howling every transgression I had ever committed in a pitiless witch trial.

I got some twisted comfort from the thought of pulling the trigger of a massive handgun, visualizing the bullet entering my brain and ripping the engine of my painful thoughts apart, silencing them forever. I was afraid of death, but it was a comfort to know that the often terrible experience of being alive could be shut off in an instant.

I sat up in bed, and reached for my phone. It was easier to have some other voice at least partially drown out my own—the only way I could fall asleep in those days. Finally, with the sound of Norm Macdonald interviews on YouTube droning away just inches from my head, I managed to fall asleep.

At 7:30 in the morning, I crowbarred myself out of bed, grabbed my phone, and clicked the side button to silence the alarm. After using the bathroom I slumped down against my bed frame and set the dial of my phone timer to 20 minutes before crossing my legs and beginning my meditation. My face twitched and I clenched and unclenched my hands before finally settling them palm down on my knees. I clenched my jaw and shifted my body from left to right, fighting to keep my body still. After what felt like hours, the timer rang, and I sprang up, pulled on some shorts, headed out for a two-mile run, and then drove to Sebastopol for my weekly meeting with Robin.

"So you have a girlfriend huh?"

"Yeah," I took a sip from a limoncello-flavored LaCroix that Robin had given me.

"What's her name?"

"Sarah."

"And do you plan on staying together after recovery?"

"I guess so. I mean we've been through so much together, she's stayed with me through my addiction."

"That's no reason to stay with someone."

"What do you mean?"

"I have clients who come in after years of active addiction, and they say things like 'my girlfriend has been with me through everything, I *owe* it to her to stay.'"

"And what's wrong with that?"

"You don't owe anyone anything. This is your one life, a relationship cannot be sustained by a debt."

My index finger and thumb dug into the top of the LaCroix, leaving finger-sized indents in the aluminum.

After leaving Robin's office I checked my phone and saw an email from EtherMosaic legal, telling me I had a mandatory meeting with them in one hour. When I flipped open my laptop and clicked open Zoom I was confronted with four very serious lawyers sitting at a table together, presumably at EtherMosaic HQ. All were women in pantsuits, the leader of whom, I guessed, was the one sitting closest to the camera with her thumbs and index fingers pressed together on top of the desk in a triangle.

"Dean, thank you for joining this meeting on such short notice," the leader said.

"Thanks for having me."

"My name is Gina and I am in charge of EtherMosaic's legal department."

"I would say it's nice to meet you but I'm assuming you're about to tell me something very unpleasant."

"I'm afraid we do have to have a difficult conversation today. We recently discovered that you run a fund, G2H2 Capital, that invests in ICOs, is that correct?"

"Yes, that's correct. Although there haven't been any new investments the past few months."

"Unfortunately, because you have access to potential insider information on ICOs, we have to terminate you immediately."

"What? But the entire EtherMosaic leadership is far more invested in early-stage ICOs than I am, and I've never invested in a EtherMosaic ICO since I joined the company."

"I'm sorry, because you manage an institutional vehicle—no matter the size—we must terminate you. Thank you for your time."

She hung up. I tried logging into Slack and was locked out. My EtherMosaic email had been shut off, and I had no access to the invoice platform. In an instant, all of EtherMosaic was blocked by an impenetrable wall.

That afternoon I took my seat in a dimly lit room at the Chi recovery office for my second therapy session of the day. Dan, my primary therapist, leaned forward in his dark green leather armchair and opened the session, "Good to see you, Dean."

"Good to see you too, Dan." Dan was a thin man in his late forties with a scratchy-looking brown beard and soft chin and bright blue eyes. His voice was soft and he had a habit of closing his eyes and sighing deeply whenever I said something from the heart. In those moments I felt deeply connected with him.

"So," I began, by now comfortable enough with Dan to skip any preliminary small talk, "I've been reflecting on the meaning of life." I cracked a smile at the grandiosity of my statement and Dan let out a soft laugh.

"Oh?" Dan asked, "and what conclusion have you arrived at?"

"The meaning of life is... to be happy." I smiled again, "very original, right?"

I was expecting Dan to laugh again but he studied me gravely.

"What do you mean by 'happy,' exactly?"

"Right... that is the obvious question. I guess to have a life where my positive emotions far outweigh the negative ones."

Dan nodded slowly. "That's a very clinical way to look at happiness."

"I suppose it is. I mean, obviously, the devil is in the details."

"Well, let's talk details. When do you feel most happy?"

"Right after I take a hit of cocaine." I smiled again but my eyes felt heavy.

"You're not joking, are you?"

I met his gaze and frowned. "I'm not joking. I mean, obviously, I know that's an unhealthy mindset. Because what goes up chemically must come down. Not to mention that it's terrible for me. But sometimes I feel like life wouldn't be worth living without cocaine. For example, right now there's a part of me that thinks I'm just saving up dopamine for my next binge."

"Mm.." Dan frowned and gripped his chin with his thumb and index finger. I waited a few moments before taking a deep breath and continuing. "The truth is, I have a pretty dark view of what a sober life is like. It's full of unpleasantness, if not outright suffering. Waiting in checkout lines, traffic, hunger, pain, sexual urges—even just feeling desire is uncomfortable."

I paused again to let Dan speak, but he didn't. Then I picked a spot on the wall just behind his head and stared at it as I spoke. "The first time I snorted coke it was like I had discovered the really positive side of life for the first time. I felt ecstatic. Before trying coke I felt like I was just trying to get through life. Afterwards I finally had something to live for."

Dan closed his eyes and leaned back, sighing deeply. "How do you feel when I offer the statement that your desire to use coke is just your heart longing to return to rest?"

I snorted. Then grew serious, looking down to study the curls in the shag carpet.

"My initial reaction is that you're crazy. But when I think about it, it sort of makes sense. I'm usually in a lot of discomfort right before I use, and really what I'm looking forward to is quieting that feeling of wanting to use."

Dan nodded. "That's a great insight."

I shifted in my chair. "I mean it was your insight. I'm just agreeing with you."

"We arrived there together."

"Can you share more of what you mean?"

"There's a metaphor that comes to mind. Imagine you are wandering lost in the desert, suffering from thirst. In that state, you'd think, 'If I could only take a deep drink of water, I would be happy!' Do you agree this is how you would think about it?"

"Sure. I mean all I could think about would be drinking water."

"But in reality," Dan continued, "once you drink that water, you will only be at baseline. What you are doing when you use cocaine is drinking water after a period of dehydration. So the experience of the water hitting your throat—cocaine—feels like happiness. What you need to figure out is how to leave the desert."

"So in this metaphor the desert is my environment, and you're saying that I need to change my environment to one that doesn't make me thirsty all the time?"

"That's the problem with metaphors, they are abstract by nature. Let me try to say it more concretely. Your cocaine use is a stress response. Initially it drowned out your stress. In other words, it worked. But over time it's become the very thing creating your stress."

"That's true."

"And what's the opposite of stress?"

"Relaxation."

"Exactly."

"That sounds so simple."

"To truly learn how to relax is both the simplest and hardest thing in the world."

"And using Xanax doesn't count, right?" I laughed but stopped when I noticed that Dan wasn't smiling.

CHAPTER TWENTY-NINE
- MAY, 2018

"When I was nineteen, the summer after my Sophomore year, I interned at a lighting warehouse run by my old Boy Scout master," I told Dan in one of our first sessions. "The work was tough for me—I had to get up at 5:30 every morning and commute an hour and a half each way on the bus, putting in nine-hour days stacking lighting equipment in a warehouse. Of course, my Dad got up an hour before I did and was at the office by 6:00. Growing up, he would often spend the first twenty minutes of dinner talking about everything he did that day—how much he was working, how hard it was, on and on. Then, he would go around the table, one by one, and ask us 'what did you do today?' I always felt like I had to give a good answer or else I would be in trouble. Anyway, that summer, I came home from work one day, and at dinner, he asked me how my day was, just like he always did. And I mentioned how difficult my job was. He grew really serious, and as I was talking, I noticed he was muttering under his breath things like 'yeah well that's how work is. It's hard.' I didn't mean to complain but I guess it came across that way. Anyway, I said back to him, 'well you complain about your job every day, why can't I complain about mine?'

When I said that, it was like I had set off a bomb. His face flushed red, and he rose from his seat, plate in hand. He smashed it down onto the table with such force that it shattered, sending shards flying along with salmon, broccoli, and mashed potatoes, knocking over water glasses and everything. I jumped under the table to try to protect myself. By the time I looked up he was gone and all I heard was the sound of his bedroom door slamming shut."

When the program ended my family flew in to visit me. Dan suggested that we use the opportunity to do family therapy.

"Your Dad is the one I'm most interested in," Dan said, "let's set up a session just with the three of us."

"Dad almost didn't come, you know," my mom said the day they arrived, "he thought he was going to be blamed for this whole thing."

My heart was thumping like I was on stimulants again as my Dad and I took our seats on the couch across from Dan. Dan was sitting cross-legged in his green chair, chewing on the end of his pen.

"Great to see you, Steve," Dan said, nodding at my dad.

"Good to be here," he answered gruffly.

"I first want to say," Dan continued, "that you both are very brave to be here. And I'm honored to facilitate such an important and vulnerable conversation between you. Dean, is there anything you would like to say to your dad to begin the conversation?"

I thought about all the painful memories of my father growing up that Dan and I had talked about. The time in high school when my Dad and I got into such a terrible fight that he threw a metal water bottle at me and sprained my arm. My Mom had made me swear to tell the doctor it was a skateboard accident. But despite all the bad blood between us, what came out now was not anger, but gratitude.

"Dad," I began, my voice shaking, "I want to say thank you. Thank you for standing by me through my addiction and for being here now."

He uncrossed his arms and relaxed his shoulders, turning his gaze downwards, "I'm just happy you're getting better."

Throughout the session I told Dad that I took full responsibility for my addiction, and I appreciated how hard he had worked to support us financially. But it would be dishonest to leave out the impact his anger, which at times burned like acid through our family, had had on me. "I used to dream of beating you up as revenge for your outbursts."

"I never knew that," he whispered.

"Now, Steve, is there anything else you'd like to say to Dean?" asked Dan as the session was ending. My father, now approaching sixty and with the old fire in his eyes reduced to a soft sparkle, opened his heart.

"Look, we've had our differences," he said, struggling with his emotions. "And I know I've made mistakes as a father, but I love him very much." He turned to me, "I love you very much."

"I love you too, Dad," I responded, tears glowing in my eyes.

We walked out of Dan's office and Dad texted Mom to come pick us up.

"You know," Dad said, "I never told you this but I've had some mental issues in my life too."

"What do you mean?"

"Well not the drug stuff like you had, but I went through a tough time after your Mom and I got married and I went on some pills that were supposed to help."

"Did they?"

"I don't know. But they did make it difficult to..." he pointed at his groin.

"I understand. Yeah they'll do that."

We both laughed and then Mom pulled up and we got in the car.

PART 2

Home after three months in Chi Recovery. My body and mind are in a precarious state. I have every intention to try to stay sober, but my mind is full of furies, telling me I am a failure. I have to rewire my brain and adopt an entirely new attitude towards this life. I believed for the past year that I would die by thirty. I imagined myself as an Alexander the Great, conquering the world and going out in a blaze of glory before the sun set on my youth. But here I am. A twenty-two year old drug addict with a broken college transcript and a failed hedge fund who can barely write an email without craving a hit of coke. But I won't give up. I will graduate from Stanford—at least I have that—and search for peace in mediocrity. Mediocrity. That word scares me more than any other. I can't bear the idea that my life will be just like the tired quaking masses of out-of-shape, neurotic middle-class nine-to-fivers with bad marriages and kids that loathe them. I know I sound like an asshole when I say that, but there it is. That feels like a sentence worse than death. My limited faculties feel like a cage that coke helped me break out of. But now I have to look at the bars that surround me and learn to say to myself 'this is my life, and it is worth living.'

CHAPTER THIRTY – SUMMER 2018

That summer, all but two of the ICOs issued their tokens which I sold at a steep loss, sending about $500,000 back to my investors. After paying all my legal and administrative fees, I had only $30,000 left. I had clung so tightly to the identity of the financial prodigy that the thought of the fund's failure sent a painful shock through my system—I would wince in real pain. And then there was the money I had stolen. With the market crashing, the size of my heist of the family's money had nominally decreased. I prayed that a total collapse would allow me to buy it back. Then Tyler called, "Do you think it's time to sell?"

"Look, I've been too ashamed to tell you this, but the money is gone. It was hacked a month ago; it's all gone." I was surprised at how easily the lie rolled off my tongue. I had so fully avoided the thought of it that I hadn't planned anything to say.

To my surprise, Tyler forgave me instantly; without a single discernible change in his voice he said, "It's okay. It never felt real anyway, like monopoly money." He actually laughed. The thing that had wracked me with guilt and self-loathing for the better part of a year had been nothing to him. And when my parents learned of it, they brushed it off. Their response astounded me, especially Tyler's. Did he really care so little for money, when I had nearly killed myself for far less than the seemingly vast sum which had been robbed from him? I imagined the despair and rage I would feel if I learned that what should have been over half a million dollars had been stolen from me. After the surprise wore off I felt gratitude for Tyler and then anger at myself for lying. In the end I was relieved that I didn't have to think about it anymore.

Sarah graduated and took a job in Boston. She had been texting me and calling me and I was slow to respond. I guess by then she knew that it was over. "I have to go back to school and you're in Boston," I told her. She wasn't happy, but she understood.

"I still love you."

"I love you too."

I promised her that I would come visit her.

"Don't be surprised if I have another boyfriend by then."

"I won't."

"Okay then you can come."

It struck me how easily all my life's seemingly intractable entanglements had simply dissolved the moment they were brought into the light. Perhaps it was old-fashioned kindness; the people in my life gave me a pass now that they knew I was getting better.

At home, the gauntness of months of deprivation gave way to indulgence. In recovery, the twenty-five pounds I had lost had been slow to return. At home, they roared back with a vengeance.

In my free time I read. It had been over a year since I had read a book, and I picked the most intimidating titles on my parents' shelves to try to reverse the literary atrophy. I started with *Crime and Punishment*.

I had studied Russian in my freshman year and my time in Slovakia left me fascinated by Slavic culture. As I read through Dostoevsky's tale of the young student Raskolnikov robbing and then murdering a nasty pawnbroker for a relatively paltry sum, I was tortured by a creepy comparison with my own life. Raskolnikov, an atheist, justified his actions by telling himself he needed the pawnbroker's money to accomplish great things. Yet, even though she was a hateful woman, loved by none, he could not escape the event horizon of his own conscience, ultimately falling into despair. In the end, the story of Raksolnikov shows that we can not get away with anything. That no matter how solid our logical justification for bad behavior, our psycho-spiritual chickens will come home to roost. I realized that in the years since I had left the church, I had found no other morality or meaning in my life to replace organized religion. The only guiding light, the only ethic, had been to grab as much pleasure and money as possible before all experience was extinguished by inevitable death. The thought of Christianity revolted me, but so many other atheists seemed to live happy and apparently moral lives; I resolved to discover what it was they knew.

The gym was my refuge. I discovered that pushing myself physically allowed me to replicate the rush of cocaine. Especially after an hour or so of hard cardio, my mind was euphoric and clean, but I often lowered the intensity when I felt my heart palpitating too much. The fear of a heart attack came rushing back whenever my chest grew tight. I tried to meditate, but without the structure of the program, I gave it up entirely.

When I wasn't reading or at the gym, I went for long walks in the neighborhood while my parents were at work, and occasionally hung out with old high school friends. The hardest part was being alone with my thoughts. I found myself reaching desperately for some identity structure or grandiose plan for the future to quiet my fear of being a failure—Stanford, hedge fund at twenty-one, crypto prodigy. I still had a good story to spin, a way to impress the people around me that made everything okay.

I traded the Howard Stern show for Sam Harris—a vociferous atheist with a strong background in philosophy and Eastern spirituality. He spoke of "the moral landscape," a kind of hierarchy of well-being that was self-evident in its "goodness" or "badness." There were some versions of human life that were objectively worse than others based on experienced levels of "well-being." For instance, a person on the edge of starvation, constantly beaten or raped has a far lower level of well-being than someone well-educated and safe with constant access to food and stimulation. Given this fact, our moral obligation as a society and as individuals is to elevate the well-being of all, independent of religious doctrine. I adopted this philosophy greedily, espousing it at the dinner table to my parents with unabashed confidence. It didn't occur to me that in my freshman year at Stanford I had read *Atlas Shrugged* and had accepted the doctrine of self-sufficiency and self-perfection with the same ferocity that I now embraced Sam Harris's moral landscape.

Finally the summer ended and it was time to go back to school. I decided to take a hard course load. *I need to make up for lost time,* I thought.

I drove to school in the same 2007 Toyota Sienna minivan that my parents had dropped me off in three years earlier. I moved into a two-room double with a stranger in a co-ed house across the lake from KA. On the way to class I would walk almost half a mile out of the way to lower the odds of meeting any KAs. What would they think of me now—the failed hedge fund manager. Some of them had fathers who invested in my fund. There was no doubt that word of its failure had gotten out.

In my room, I put up a couple of abstract paintings I had drawn over the summer, a poster of Van Gogh's *Starry Night*, and a series of handwritten quotes from Sam Harris and Dostoevsky. I stood back and looked at my room with pride. It was the first time I had ever put any intention into my space. For the first time in a long time I felt a strange warmth in my heart, I realized with awe that it was hope.

CHAPTER THIRTY-ONE
- FALL 2018

"Never call a painting 'pretty' again! Engage with it. Delve into its depths!"

I was sitting in Bishop Auditorium at Stanford watching the director of the Art History department, Alexander Nemerov, strut across the stage in a light blue dress shirt and tight-fitting slacks wielding his clicker like a sword and stabbing it at the massive projector screen displaying early Renaissance art for the three-hundred or so students in the audience of "Art History 1."

With the energy of a much younger man, Nemerov, wiry and taut with pure white hair, was in his late 50s and pulsated with passion as he spoke. His gaze drilled into each one of us, challenging our superficial perspectives.

I was enthralled. Never before had I looked at art as anything other than a petty waste of time, something to be curtly acknowledged and, when dragged by family or friends to a museum, to be endured. But Nemerov had opened a portal to a different view, and I looked forward to coming to a lecture for the first time in a very long time.

Three hours with one painting. No breaks (except the bathroom), no distractions (especially cell phones). These were the instructions for our first assignment and I arrived at the Cantor Art Museum with visions of ecstatic engagement and profound insight. I consciously walked past the featured exhibitions and wall-spanning Rothco's for an understated landscape from the Hudson River School. After five minutes, I was convinced that I had already seen everything the painting had to offer. I fidgeted continuously and willingly gave my attention to anyone who passed in my periphery. After forty-five minutes I was ready to give up. But I visualized Nemerov standing behind me, scoffing in disgust as I walked away. I redoubled my attention and studied the painting with feigned intensity. By accident, I noticed some sheep appearing out of a layer of mist in the valley of the landscape. I was surprised that it had taken me almost an hour to see them.

For the next forty minutes I battled red-hot boredom and a torrent of mental complaints. By the ninety-minute mark I was preparing to leave. But just as I decided to walk away the intensity of my emotions broke. Like an egg cracking over my head and dripping down to my feet, my nervous system relaxed and I felt suddenly at peace. The colors on the canvas grew more vivid, and I discovered with excitement that this was my first time looking at the painting with total attention. A pleasant warmth kindled in my belly and a subtle smile played on my lips. *This is why people go to art museums,* I thought. The next hour flew by as I picked out increasingly subtle details–a tiny bird resting on a distant tree branch–and the almost microscopic splatter of white paint in the fog. The three hours ended and I walked outside feeling strangely high. I couldn't believe you could catch a buzz staring at a painting but as I walked back to my room I was amazed at the vividness of the natural world—the soft sheen of the tree leaves flowing effortlessly with the wind and the layers of blue in the sky. *Who knew the sky had more than one shade of blue!*

I remembered a line from Dostoevsky, "without beauty, science would not produce a single nail."

CHAPTER THIRTY-TWO – OCTOBER, 2018

"Hey I'm a Sophomore journalism major writing a story on crypto and I was asking around campus for people to interview and your name came up. Would you be open to an interview?

—Serena****@stanford.edu"

I had never met Serena but I was flattered when I got her email invitation, and I showed up at coupa cafe to find myself sitting across from a well-dressed brunette girl with light makeup and dimples. Her skirt was hiked up so I could see most of her thighs and my mind went blank when I took my seat.

"I'm Serena, it's nice to meet you." She extended a hand and I took it.

"Hey."

"I really appreciate you doing this. Would you mind if I asked you a few questions?"

"Absolutely! I'm an open book."

I smiled, but her expression remained serious, like a real journalist, and so mine grew serious too.

I told her about my experience running the fund, the ICO era, EtherMosaic, and the origins of Bitcoin and Ethereum as I understood them. For the first few minutes she was rapt and eager to learn more. But after a few minutes her gaze went from me to the space behind me and she began to shift restlessly. I feared I was boring her so I wrapped up the conversation and said goodbye. As we shook hands again I looked at her face and her smile had a warmth to it that I spent the next two nights thinking about almost constantly.

On Friday I got drunk and messaged her on Facebook "can I take you out on a date?"

"Yes!" She responded with an emoji of a sparking heart with an arrow through the middle of it. I guessed that was a good thing.

A few nights later we met outside the Theta sorority where she lived and I drove her in the Sienna to a Georgian restaurant that I found on Reddit in a seemingly paradoxical list of "top affordable date restaurants in Palo Alto."

She wore a tight fighting black dress and heels and her makeup seemed professionally applied. I ordered us appetizers and drinks, pretending like I didn't notice the menu prices. I calculated in my head that with any luck the meal would cost me under $90.

"I tried mushrooms for the first time last week," Serena shared, when I asked her if she had tried anything for the first time recently.

"How did you feel?"

"Kind of silly, I didn't like the feeling too much to be honest, I ended up just getting drunk to try to get rid of it. Have you tried mushrooms?"

"Not mushrooms, but a lot of other drugs," I said, smiling.

"Oh really? What have you tried?"

"Oh cocaine, black tar heroin, Xanax."

Her eyes widened and I was disturbed by her expression of apparent fear and suspicion.

"Black tar heroin? I.. I can't believe you tried that. What was it like?"

It felt like all the romantic energy had been sucked out of the restaurant. I wished that I hadn't said that.

"Oh really it's not a big deal, it just kind of made me tired."

I tried to move the conversation on but she wouldn't let it go.

"What made you try heroin, I just can't imagine?"

"I just have an open mind, I don't know. It's not like I'd ever do it again."

The flirtatious energy never returned, but as the date ended and we drove back to Theta I resolved to kiss her and invite her out again.

When we got out of the car we hugged and I leaned down to kiss her, she turned her face away from me and I lightly brushed my lips against her cheek, pulling back abruptly in embarrassment.

"Oh I'm sorry, I thought we had a good date, I didn't realize..."

"No no!" She said, throwing her hands up, "it's not that... it's just... I can't get over the fact that you did heroin. I don't think... Well I just don't want to be with someone who did something like that, I'm sorry. I do like you though."

I nodded.

"Okay well I had fun, see you around."

When I got back to the dorm I lay in bed for a while staring at the ceiling. I looked around my room at the paintings and quotes and felt disgust. What good was all my attempts at a better future if my past was just going to follow me around?

I couldn't sleep so I went over to my laptop and loaded my latest computer science assignment. As part of my ambitious course load I signed up for two challenging computer science classes. I approached the work with dread. I never had a knack for it and what talented students could do in an hour would take me ten. I had been stuck on the same part of the assignment all week, and now, as I looked at the code, I felt a wave of despair. I put my head in my hands and where tears should have fallen there was only coldness. Where was Sam Harris and my precious Dostoevsky now? The only thing left to do was to go back to the one thing that had always been there for me.

I logged onto the deep web and ordered a half-ounce of fish scale cocaine, paying an extra $50 for express shipping. When I finished I felt a rush of anticipation. I imagined how good I would feel after taking my first hit in six months. My assignment was due in four days but I knew with the coke I could get it done in less than a day so the next two days were free days. Such was my twisted drug logic.

I planned ahead, canceling any appointments two days after the projected arrival of the package and I prepared my body by eating heavily and exercising as much as I could. As I waited for the package it was as if my conscious mind had a wall of excitement that was blocking the wave of fear and self-loathing rumbling beneath the surface. When the package finally arrived in the afternoon I was ready. My room was stocked with empty pee bottles, water and protein shakes. I ripped open the package and greedily examined the contents. Wasting no time in depositing a large line on my phone and rolling a straw out of a five-dollar bill before bending over and ripping it into my nostrils. The ritual executed itself so naturally it was as if I had not been sober for more than a few days.

But as I sat up after the first line I knew instantly that I had been wrong. Six months had not been enough to reset the system. The coke high, while good, had a nastier edge than it should have for the first hit. The coke was high quality, but the blissfulness of the first hit, which I had imagined ten thousand times while waiting for the package, did not arrive. I knew beyond a shadow of a doubt that I would never experience it again. But I was in for the binge, and I instinctively sensed that my window of opportunity to do any real work would be little more than an hour or two.

I set to work on the assignment, refreshing myself every twenty minutes with a new line. I punched out code, but the creative blocks that stood in my way were unresolved. After a couple of hours my mind was turning dark, and in a last desperate effort I punched together a finicky version of the assignment full of bugs, sending it off with a mixed feeling of relief and foreboding. I hoped it would be enough to get a passing grade. Then I logged onto Facebook and sent hundreds of messages to old friends and acquaintances excitedly asking them about their projects and ideas. Then, when that was exhausted, I turned to porn. But even now, in the midst of the binge, there was a new awareness that I didn't recognize from the old times. An awareness that what I was doing was utterly futile, and that in the end all it led to was a mountain of pain.

CHAPTER THIRTY-THREE – TWO DAYS LATER

Forty-eight hours later, I awoke to a banging on my door. I lived in the inner room of a two-room double. Meaning I walked through my roommate's room to reach mine, granting me a higher degree of the dangerous privacy I had made such destructive use of.

"Dude what the hell is that smell?"

I recognized my roommate's voice and, still half-asleep, blinked open my eyes to take in the scene–posters torn from the wall and pee-filled bottles scattered on the floor. Then the smell hit me. I felt mustard gassed and began to dry heave as tears streamed from my eyes. Wetness below me. I pulled back my covers to discover a bodily crime scene, an enormous mess of dark coloration from explosive diarrhea soaking the sheets and mattress. I leaped out of bed, and shouted back to my roommate, "I don't know man, but it smells like shit! Let me try to figure it out."

"Okay I'm going to go work in the cafeteria, it's unbearable!"

"Sounds good!"

I threw open the windows and grabbed a bottle of Febreze, depressing the lever with one hand and using the other to fill several trash bags with soiled sheets, my comforter and pee bottles, synching the bags up one by one as they reached capacity and depositing them in a pile next to the bed.

After a few minutes the smell had been mostly overpowered by the Frebreze so I ran the trash bags outside, tossing them over my head into the gaping mouth of the commercial dumpster in the parking lot, before running back to my room to pocket the rest of the coke. That done, I grabbed my mattress and dragged it outside to join the pee bottles and bedding. By the time the vibration of the mattress thudding into the metal dumpster disappeared into the soft Palo Alto breeze, my mind was made up. I was done with coke. With righteous enthusiasm I buried my right hand into my pocket, pulled out the coke bag, and threw it in.

"Yeah man I think a rat died and started to rot," I told my roommate when he came back, "I threw out all my bedding to try to get rid of the smell."

He accepted the explanation without further comment. I guess he was just happy the smell was gone. Later that day I bought new bedding and a fresh mattress. When I returned to my dorm I checked my email and found that I had failed my CS assignment.

That night I couldn't sleep. After hours of being tossed around in bed by the depressing winds of a bad conscience, I froze. An ambient subconscious disturbance had broken out in the open and an idea seized me–the coke was still out there. The solution to all my problems was sitting in that dumpster. My limbs moved of their own volition, in a moment I had left my room and was clambering into the dumpster and dropping myself down into its cavernous mouth. I got down on all fours and pawed at a couple packages and trash bags before the despairing realization hit me. The dumpster had been emptied that afternoon. Gone–the mattress, my pee bottles, and the coke. I climbed out of the dumpster and felt my nervous system relax with a fresh lightness. *Thank god*, I thought. Laughing out loud in wild relief as I walked back to my room, falling asleep almost as soon as my head hit the pillow.

Two weeks later I learned Karol had shot himself. I was driving to the gym when my mom called to break the news. I put my hazards on as I pulled over and let my head fall into my hands. I hadn't seen or spoken to Karol since the previous Christmas when I had practically ignored him because I'd been so high. My first few years at Stanford I had stayed in near-constant touch with him, maintaining an email thread where I shared my observations on Stanford.

My second father, one of the most important people in my life, had killed himself, and I had squandered my last chance to spend time with him. I later learned he had suffered a seizure that drove him insane in the weeks before his suicide. Our own brains are so quick to betray us.

CHAPTER THIRTY-FOUR
- JUNE 2019

Seven-months sober. Karol's death and my relapse led to a dumpster fire of a fall quarter. Two failed classes and a miserable Thanksgiving at home holed up in my room popping Adderall had finally snapped me back to sobriety. It was so evident that nothing good, save the briefest good feeling followed by weeks of hell, came from stimulant use.

By June, we were in the depths of "crypto winter," a two-year stretch when the valuations of top cryptocurrencies fell 95 percent from their early 2018 highs. (The Ethereum price, for example, bottomed out around $88 from a high of $1,200).

The frenzied panic that characterized the crypto industry in the first few months of 2018 dissolved into numbed melancholy before finally descending into outright indifference. In early 2018, for every hundred conversations overheard in a San Francisco cafe thirty might have been about crypto. By the summer of 2019 I estimated that closer to three out of a hundred touched on the troubled industry. The fund was still alive, with three investments promising an ICO listing once the market improved, but my investors had gone quiet. They had given up.

My money was gone. I had walked in graduation, but had an entire quarter of coursework left. My financial aid was exhausted with no clear path to covering the $15,000-a-quarter tuition. I applied to part-time tech and finance jobs and was universally rejected. No money and no work was like having the icy breath of death on my neck. The anxious voice in my head changed its obsession from analyzing my social status as a Stanford student to questioning whether I possessed the fundamental capacity to survive as a human being.

Crypto, despite its calamitous year and a half, was still my best professional option. In a final act of desperation, I asked Liquid Freedom if they would take me back. Despite my draconian termination a year earlier, I knew that EtherMosaic was sufficiently disorganized that they wouldn't notice if I quietly slipped back onto the payroll. I just needed Alejandro to cover me.

When I spoke to Alejandro, I told him the truth. I was broke, I needed a gig. The fund would never again invest in a new ICO, I told him, there was no chance of my acting on any insider information. He agreed to bring me back on. "You just can't show your face at the office in Wlliamsburg or on camera at any all-hands meetings."

He invited me to join the team in Puerto Rico for an offsite retreat the following week. Puerto Rico was and remains a popular tax haven for crypto elites to enjoy the privileges of living in the United States without the burden of paying taxes.

I arrived in Puerto Rico and took an Uber to the mansion our team AirBnb'd for the week in old town San Juan.

"What up, Dean!" Alejandro said, greeting me with a bear hug, "so glad to have you back!"

"Woah, this place is amazing," I remarked as I took in the huge foyer and balconies that would ours for the week. Alejandro showed me to my room, which was the size of a small apartment with an ensuite bathroom and private deck.

"Not bad for crypto winter," I said, winking at Alejandro.

"Not bad at all, EtherMosaic gives us a budget to take team trips like these twice a year."

After I dropped my bags, Alejandro ushered me into the living room where I hugged Amalia and David and shook hands with three new, early-twenty-something Liquid Freedom hires before turning my attention to a big screen projecting an all-hands EtherMosaic zoom meeting with over six hundred attendees.

"What's this?" I asked.

"They're announcing the results of a huge internal survey." Amalia said, "Since you've been gone EtherMosaic has been hiring all kinds of consultants to try to figure out why the culture is fucked up."

"Just stand to the side, away from the camera," Alejandro said, laughing, "Dean's supposed to be in exile."

Listening to the call I learned that crypto winter had humbled the once invincible EtherMosaic. Larrabee had trimmed thirteen percent of the staff to lighten the financial burden and morale had not recovered, hence the survey to diagnose the organizational dis-ease. I surmised that the main problem, apparent even in the heyday of summer 2017, was that lack of any recognizable hierarchy was not the bedrock a large company could build on without nearly unlimited resources.

As the survey results were presented, Larrabee and the head of the survey team held court around a hollow oval table with the de facto EtherMosaic executive team (although, again, this was entirely unspoken since EtherMosaic had no official hierarchy). On the virtual sidelines the EtherMosaic rank-and-file maintained a lively stream of chat box commentary over Zoom. The results, unveiled one by one in a screen-shared presentation, were not pretty.

"This company is a shit show!" said one commentator.

"Worst place I've ever worked!"

"Do these people even care about keeping their jobs?" I asked Alejandro.

"This is the culture Larrabee has built,"Alejandro said, shrugging, "he's always preached complete honesty."

EtherMosaic's commitment to an open culture cut both ways, and the side facing Larrabee was bearing down on him throughout the meeting. Every kind of organizational metric—from transparency to feelings of inclusion—was excoriated.

There was no rhetorical sweetener from the survey team to soften the troubling reality: "For mid-sized technology companies [between 500 and 1000 employees], you scored among the lowest we have ever seen in many categories."

To its credit, EtherMosaic did score high, relatively speaking, in the category related to forward-thinking vision. But outside vision and openness, in categories like leadership, transparency, and professional mobility, EtherMosaic failed miserably.

A trans person in their 60s was having a public breakdown in the chat—describing the work culture as one of the most frustrating experiences they had ever dealt with: "I'm crying right now."

Larrabee seemed genuinely baffled by the terrible score EtherMosaic had received in the leadership category. "I see leaders everywhere I look!" he said, clearly flustered.

But Larrabee had succeeded in empowering EtherMosaic employees to be unabashedly open, and watching the entire company do battle with an identity crisis so publicly was remarkable.

EtherMosaic's issues also extended to salaries. The "Chief Disruption Officer," a close friend of Larrabee's, was a man hired to keep the counter-voice elevated to something above an ambient hum. Larrabee was very sensitive to the risk of EtherMosaic getting covered in the creative fog of groupthink. The Chief Disruption Officer (CDO) roamed from meeting to meeting, injecting creativity if not outright chaos if he felt things were getting stale. The CDO's role reached its public heights during an internal spat around salary transparency in early 2018.

EtherMosaic had started out in 2015 with a strict salary cap, something in the $70,000 range, before raising it to around $120,000 in 2017. But as the bubble blew wider, Larrabee broke ranks with egalitarianism to woo industry heavy hitters who demanded ever-greater salaries, including a former executive of Deutsche Bank. EtherMosaic's vocal activist wing did not take kindly to the lack of pay transparency, fearing the emergence of a systematic overcompensation for Larrabee lookalikes. The CDO, emboldened by broad internal support, sent multiple company-wide emails lambasting Larrabee and demanding a salary reveal.

Larrabee responded finally, admonishing him for going too far: he said (in another company-wide email) that it was apparent he was more interested in chasing the dopamine hit of sending stirring emails to 1,000 people than promoting change through targeted conversations.

But the survey debacle, to Liquid Freedom, was like watching a reality show whose cast consisted of people we knew, but had little emotional attachment to, and once the meeting closed, we had a little chuckle and returned to our work. The goings-on at EtherMosaic high command were only tangentially related to our work, which is one legitimate advantage of a decentralized work culture.

That night the team headed for a local cryptocurrency meetup at a dive bar in downtown San Juan. The meetup was organized by Brock Pierce–crypto billionaire and 2020 presidential candidate. A former Disney child star born in 1980 in Minneapolis, he had become a legend during the 2017 ICO era for co-founding Tether and the EOS protocol, the latter of which quickly raised a $4 billion ICO and achieved a $20 billion market cap in 2018. Brock was probably 5' 6" with long blonde hair and looked every bit the former child actor, sporting his signature wide-brim fedora at the meetup that last I heard is a hot accessory for upper-middle-class L.A. women. In the six months prior to the meetup, Brock had been engaged in a huge media blitz promoting himself as a key figure remaking the Puerto Rican economy to empower locals and attract global investors. But he was a controversial figure, and many assumed he was just covering his desire to avoid taxes in philanthropic paint.

There were probably thirty people at the meetup, twenty of whom were clearly mainlanders on vacation or around for a few months to establish residency for tax purposes, and the rest appeared to be local bar patrons who were there by coincidence. Brock took the stage and spoke for about fifteen minutes, sharing some vague proposals for new hotels and housing complexes with lots of billion dollar numbers attached to prove just how much the Puerto Rican economy was going to benefit.

Amalia broke in as soon as Q&A started, her voice high and sharp–"anyone here who has benefited from Brock's investments in the Puerto Rican economy please raise your hand." Not one hand went up.

The next morning, after a work session, we headed to a compound where many of the EtherMosaic and crypto elite had moved after the enormous cash grab of 2017-18, including one of Brock's co-founders of the notorious Tether stablecoin. We passed through the double-gated security apparatus in our black Suburban and entered a meticulously manicured landscape with palm trees, gentle green hills, and multi-million-dollar mansions. It struck me that it looked just like Stanford.

I realized as we drove that the entire goal of running my fund had been to end up in a place like this. This was Eden for crypto winners—a dream, I realized, no different from getting into Stanford in the first place—a dream whose only goal was to continue its own access to the dream it was already living.

The Suburban dropped us off at the house of one of the EtherMosaic multimillionaires, my boss for fifteen minutes, William Kenney, EtherMosaic's fourth hire and former head of business development.

"I'm starting a new fund," he told us, "to take advantage of the bear market by buying as much ETH as possible and using strategic leverage to increase our stack. We're just getting started. We see a multi-billion dollar opportunity just with our fund alone."

"Don't you want to just relax and enjoy your wealth?" I asked, smiling.

He stared at me as if I had just killed his cat.

"If I'm not doing this, what else would I do?"

I shrugged. It occurred to me that there must really be a fundamental difference between the William's and Abdullah's of the world and me. For them it was a game, a journey, that ended only when their bodies' did. Money was not a means, but an end. It was about seeing how big they could grow their number before nature reset them to zero. I had never really thought through why I wanted to get rich in the first place. I had vaguely imagined a whirlwind of delights and respect that would make me happy forever. But seeing William made me more sad than jealous. Maybe it was just the difference between youth and early middle age. I was still only twenty-three, William in his late 30s. I was hardly competitive with him. But there was something in his eyes, and in his voice, that hinted at a desperation and fear that disturbed me. It did not accord with my old model of the world–that wealth led to happiness and inner security.

I remembered the way my heart had opened after spending three hours with the landscape painting for my art history class, and how quickly it closed with the thought that I needed to get back to work. My life was full of those moments–opening and closing, opening and closing. Like a dam that every now and then would open its floodgates ever so slightly. I didn't know exactly what that implied about the best way to live my life. On the one hand I empathized with William's drive–my relatively paltry experiences of making quick money in crypto had felt, at the time, like the greatest rush in the world. Like suddenly my own quivering mortality was not so fragile, that somehow, money expanded my being while simultaneously insulating me from the dangers of the world. Granting me privileged access to the beautiful and delightful parts of existence. But these feelings had been fleeting—and, just like cocaine, had left me with an insatiable desire for more.

But at least I knew now that there were some experiences, some ways of engaging with the world, that opened me to a higher plane of existence that did not kickstart a cycle of escalating and fundamentally unsatisfiable desire. A feeling of attunement, stability and freedom. Beyond meeting my basic needs, keeping the icy breath of destitution at bay, money had nothing to do with it.

CHAPTER THIRTY-FIVE – NOVEMBER 2019

I finished my summer job at EtherMosaic and returned to Stanford in the fall to finish my degree–three advanced economics classes was all I had left. But then there was the nasty business of finding a full-time job. Core life achievements—graduating, getting a job, and making six figures (it no longer had to be millions)—still felt, at least subconsciously, like essential prerequisites to becoming a valid human entity. The old thoughts–*my sober self is not capable of handling life*–crept in and quickly established a stranglehold on my psyche. I didn't go back to coke. But in late October I convinced a psychiatrist in Palo Alto to give me a prescription for Vyvanse, an ADHD drug.

She had just finished her residency, "$400,000 in debt," she told me, specializing in "adult ADHD." She didn't accept insurance, and my intake visit cost $900 for ninety minutes.

"I'm struggling with my classes," I told her.

"What are you studying?"

"Economics."

She screwed up her eyes and spoke in a sympathetic tone, "that sounds boring."

"Yeah it's pretty boring. But it's the easiest major that still makes your parents happy."

She laughed harder than a psychiatrist probably should have and then told me how Vyvanse was less addicting than Adderall since you couldn't snort it. I acted shocked when she said this, like the idea of snorting a prescription drug had never crossed my mind. "That's the thing," she said, "there's such a stigma around these drugs because of the small minority that abuse them."

"That's unfair to the rest of us who actually need them to function," I said. She agreed, starting me off at 20mg.

In fact, I really did plan to use it as prescribed, *this time will be different*. But as the flush of the rush from the first pill hit, I reached for more. Within an hour, I had taken the entire bottle, staying up for four days straight and finishing my assignments in just two. With the extra time, I applied to over five hundred jobs.

In the weeks that followed, with my entire prescription used up, I fell further behind in my classes until my next doctor's appointment kicked off another burst of productivity.

After class one day I drove off campus to Sweet Green in Palo Alto for lunch. I was waiting in line when I felt a tap on my shoulder. I turned, it was Sarah. She was wearing her signature floral sundress, smiling mischievously.

"Happy to see me?" She asked.

A warm excitement flooded me at the sight of her, I hadn't realized how much I missed her. "Sarah!" I shouted, giving her a hug. We stepped out of line and I felt a rush of questions bubble out, "what have you been up to? Where are you living now? I haven't spoken to you properly in almost a year."

"I know," she said smiling, "you broke up with me, remember?"

I laughed awkwardly and looked down, "true, are you mad at me then?"

"I was, for a while, but I understood it. You were going through your recovery and it really was for the best that we broke up." She was twirling a strand of hair between her pointer and middle finger, and I noticed that her eyes had a seriousness that bordered on sadness.

"Is everything alright?" I asked.

"Yeah, for the most part. I'm staying with my parents now for the next couple of months before moving to Boston in January. I got a job at the Koch Institute in Cambridge researching mRNA vaccines. It's pretty technical but fascinating."

"That's incredible, good for you, you always were one of the smartest in our class."

She looked down, smiling with embarrassment but clearly flattered. "That's not true. To be honest, I think I messed around a little too much in undergrad. It was so hard to get a job at a good research institution, I had to have one of my Dad's friends write me a recommendation. But that only gets you so far, I have to work really hard for the next two years to get into a good PhD program, and then do well enough in my PhD to get a good postdoc and hopefully do some research I'm proud of. I want to have kids by the time I'm 35, so that's a lot to pack into a short amount of time. It's really stressful to think about."

"That does sound stressful."

"Yeah, anyway how are you? Take a seat, if you want," she gestured to a table and we sat down across from each other, my heart pounding.

"I'm okay. Trying not to fail my classes so I can finally graduate."

She laughed, "you're not going to fail."

"Don't be so sure, I've done it before," I said, looking up and smiling, "at least I'm not on coke anymore so the odds of success are probably higher. But I feel you on the stress about the future. I applied to about a thousand jobs and only got a couple interviews. I assumed because I was at Stanford that getting a good job would be automatic, turns out that's not the case."

We continued talking as we got back in line and ordered, sitting down at the same table together and asking and answering questions between bites. For the next hour I told her about rehab and living at home, and relapsing in the fall, leaving out the part about the Vyvanse. She told me about her travels across the US in her car, camping and seeing national parks, and about her dreams for the future.

When she left, my heart and stomach felt warm. I got in my car and drove home, flipping on the radio and mouthing the words to pop music as I worked my way through traffic on the 101. At home I got out the week's econ assignments and found that my mind coalesced around the math and seemed to fizz and bubble with energy before arriving at a clear solution to the first problem. It felt good to exercise my brain without stimulants. *Maybe life doesn't have to be such a struggle*, I thought. *Is this feeling of happiness possible to feel all or at least most of the time?* I pulled out my phone and texted Sarah.

"It was so good to see you, would love to get lunch or dinner again before you leave." I read over the text several times adding and deleting (as friends of course) several times before finally deciding to leave it out and hitting send.

"Me too! Just let me know when you're free :)"

I saw Sarah twice more before the end of the quarter. It took until our final meeting before I found out that she was still single.

Somehow I managed to graduate, perhaps my professors just wanted me gone. I interviewed for a dozen non-crypto jobs–data analyst, consultant, banking analyst–but none of them wanted me. I wanted to branch out, to get out of crypto–the industry that had lined the pockets of its insiders with half a trillion dollars without producing a single tangible product that benefited the lives of everyday people.

But my best opportunities were all with crypto companies. And so, with Christmas approaching–I finally decided to interview for a marketing position at a small crypto company called IoTeX. I showed up at their Menlo Park office wearing slacks and a dress shirt, armored with a disillusionment built up by my own failure to get rich quick and bolstered by a general, culture-wide disgust with the industry. But when I walked into the IoTeX offices I felt myself soften. IoTeX had about a dozen, seemingly brilliant, mostly first-generation Chinese immigrants working with genuine passion and intensity on solving censorship and data privacy problems on the internet.

The founder, a man in his mid-30s named Raullen who had received his PhD from the University of Waterloo before going on to build critical products at Google and Uber and then founding IoTeX, showed me a series of physical devices he had built with his team. Real, tangible products like an internet-connected surveillance camera that secured all the data locally, and a general purpose sensor that could be used to mine environmental data and then trigger blockchain actions.

I sat in a conference room for about two hours and met with the core leadership–three co-founders and two early hires–and talked about my experience at EtherMosaic, running the fund, learning about crypto at Stanford and meeting Vitalik in 2016. I realized that I had a legitimate resume, that spanned almost four years, in the crypto industry. Something almost unheard of for a twenty-three year old. Despite all my disillusionment, I had practically grown up in crypto, and IoTeX restored my faith that good teams were still working in the industry.

I began work in January, earning $1,600 a week, and my mental health started improving, along with my finances. I stayed clean, meditated and exercised daily, and began experiencing more regularly that warm bubbling energy in the stomach and heart that I started to call happiness. Sarah moved to Boston and we continued to text and call.

"The IoTeX team is honestly so great. They even want to me to fly out to New York in May for a conference! How's work going?"

A day would go by before she would respond.

'That's so great to hear! Work is soo busy... Usually at the office till eight or nine every night but I love my PI and the research is soo fascinating. So many smart people here!"

"Free for a call this weekend?"

Another day would go by.

"Sure, can I send you a calendar invite for 6:30 on Sunday?"

"PM right ;)"

"Yes haha."

In the long gaps between her replies I found myself longing for more contact. I realized that I had never really opened my heart to her when we were together before. Now she was the first person I thought of each morning and the last person each night.

For the first time in my adult life I felt a kindling hope that a happy future with an ambitious, smart and kind partner could be possible. Sarah had been there for me in my darkest times, a candle in the fog, and I found myself reminiscing about the good times we had together. I knew she must be wary from the breakup, but I hoped I was proving to her that I had healed enough for a second chance. But we were 3,000 miles apart, so I did my best to drive the thought of getting back together out of my head. And besides, my sobriety was still so fragile, I needed more time to focus on myself.

CHAPTER THIRTY-SIX - APRIL 2020

Right now I feel like something is missing inside of me. I know I have a sickness. I know it's there. I have something that drives me to a degree that makes me almost insane. I'm not sure how it's going to end up. But I know I'm going to do some spontaneous, crazy shit. I cannot be limited by the linear career progressions laid out in front of me.

To paraphrase Checkov, I long to wield a hammer in a great factory. To drive every street, explore every crevice. To plumb the depths of our world. That is my dream. To invade the dwelling of the most intimate. To climb the highest peaks. To fly. To push through. But I do not strive for a caricature of myself. I need to listen to myself. Meditate and listen carefully. I will not suppress the building explosion inside of me as I contemplate next steps. The drug use, the pervading sense of unrest. The lack of focus on my tasks. It all points to the fact that even now, with a job I generally enjoy and the potential for a wonderful relationship, I feel something is wrong with my life. I feel a call for a life that might leave me in poverty. But I do not know what form that might take. I keep trying to rationalize a way to move away from my current work. I just need a spark.

The pandemic hit. Everything in the real world shut down, everything online exploded to life–paranoia, fear, and desperation rocked society, etc. etc. In January, when I started my job at IoTeX, I moved into a house in East Palo Alto with eight other Stanford grads. The rent for my "room" was $535 a month and consisted of a curtained-off 8' x 8' square in the corner of the living room. On March 17th, forty-eight hours before California issued its first major restrictions, I called Sarah.

"My parents have a house in Kansas they are going to stay at. My lab labeled me as a non-essential worker, so I'm going to be working from home for a while and I decided to join them."

"Since when do they have a house in Kansas?"

"I don't know, I guess for a while, I don't know about all their houses."

"How do you not know about all your parents' houses?"

"Whatever. The point is it's probably one of the safest places in the country to be. There aren't any COVID cases there yet."

"That sounds really nice."

"You can come live with me here. It's a big house, we'll have a ton of space!"

"Really? Like as friends, or?"

She laughed, "whatever you want to call it, don't worry we don't have to put a label on it."

"Okay, I'll start the drive right away."

I messaged the IoTeX team that I was driving to Kansas and would be offline for a couple days. In ninety minutes I had packed up my clothes into trash bags and hit the road by 10:30 A.M. Afraid that California would shut their borders any moment, I drove sixteen hours straight, filling almost an entire gallon jug with pee, and arrived 1,000 miles away in Grand Junction, Colorado by three in the morning. The thought of moving in with Sarah, even with her parents and brother around, was too tantalizing to risk being stopped at the eleventh hour by a travel restriction.

Late the following day I pulled in front of Sarah's house in a western suburb of Kansas City and rang the doorbell. She answered, I greeted her and her family with hugs and smiles and then Sarah grabbed my hand and led me to our room.

"You okay with sharing?" She asked, smiling.

"I think I'll survive," I answered, laughing.

I was nervous about her father–who had invested a small amount in the fund–and feared he would accuse me of squandering his money. But, to my surprise, he seemed good-humored about the whole thing.

"It's the nature of these types of investments you know, you can't expect to get rich on every wild bubble that pops up."

"I made a spreadsheet of our schedule," Sarah said after I got settled in.

"Since when do you make spreadsheets of your schedule?"

"It's the best way to get the most out of the day!"

I was apprised of the militaristic schedule I was expected to keep– 6:30 A.M. wake up, exercise for forty-five minutes followed by a twenty-minute meditation and then breakfast and then work.

For the next two weeks we lived, slept and worked side-by-side. Exercising in the morning, working in the day, and making love in the evenings. Our weekends were barbeques with her parents and brother and long bike rides in the local parks. Before long, restlessness took hold. Working from home emphasized the abstractness of my work—cutting off the tactile contact with products and teammates. And then there was my mortality, brought to the knife edge of awareness by the pandemic.

I found a national forest in north-eastern New Mexico, in the Southern Rockies, north of Taos, and proposed a camping trip to Sarah.

"It's an eleven-hour drive so we probably want to spend at least three nights to make it worthwhile."

"But that means I'll have to take two days off work."

"Yeah so what. You're working from home anyway, they even said you're a non-essential worker."

"But I can't! My boss is going to write my recommendation for my PhD applications and I don't want anything to jeopardize his opinion of me."

"Are you serious? You can't take a couple days off in the middle of a pandemic to go camping?"

Sarah looked down and I saw a tear flow out of her eyes.

"Dean this is just too much, I really can't go."

I paused, biting my lip. This was the best evidence so far of the momentous changes that had taken place in Sarah since undergrad. Gone was the carefree girl who would ace her classes and still find time to party and take off for a long weekend. A disciplined, goal-oriented scientist had emerged in her stead. I was hurt and sad, but I was also slightly in awe of her.

"Okay, I understand, I'll just go by myself then."

I chewed on indignation that I had taken time off work to drive 2,000 miles to be with her, the least she could do was join me for a camping trip. But I also recognized that she was mourning the version of herself that had the space and freedom to take time off, and that it was probably harder for her to give up the trip than it was for me to not have her along. And when my anger cooled I felt a tingling excitement at the prospect of days alone in the wilderness. A true adventure, and time to reflect.

I packed my bags and notified IoTeX that I was taking time off. I drove all day until I was about seven miles past the Red River ski town into Carson National Forest. As the last light was receding from the horizon, I pulled off the main road. After piling rocks and dirt underneath the front tires of the Sienna to regain traction after it high-centered on a rock, I pulled into a dispersed campsite next to a creek that was distended by spring snowmelt into a foaming torrent.

I set up camp, taking care to pack my food into a bear bag and hanging it in a tree, before sitting down by the river and closing my eyes to relax into the white noise of fast moving water. A rustle disturbed me, and the familiar cycle of paranoia took hold, but this time, it was rooted in reality. I dug into my backpack and pulled out bear spray, hunting around the darkness with my eyes as I clung tightly to the bottle.

Just like the virus, camping in the wilderness forces you to think urgently about physical dangers that the advances of modernity have insulated us from. Instead of worrying about what my boss thought of my last marketing plan, my focus shifted to not getting eaten by a bear. Over the next several days my priorities were straightened, kind of like how COVID straightened priorities on a global scale. We were all afraid of the bear, and that's as natural and as human as the modern world ever allows us to be.

On my third day in the wilderness I took a single tab of LSD-25 and ascended a high peak, reaching the top right as the psychedelic took hold. I had taken some canvases with me and acrylic paint with a plan to paint the alpine landscape. And as I caught my breath and leaned back against the rocky escarpment, I felt thrown into a destabilizing intimacy with the mountain that coalesced into wonder and gratitude at the preciousness of nature. After a while these insights, pulsing through my nervous system more than they were thought, finally turned to shock and indignation at our economy's desecration of the natural world. *How could we destroy such beauty?* My body too, I realized, was as much a part of nature as the trees and the rocks. And I had nearly destroyed it, treating it as an anomic vessel of economic output and financial gain. It was a painful realization, and all the things I had done to hurt other people–my investors, my family, Sarah, and most of all myself, paraded through my consciousness like watching a mental movie strapped to the chair in *A Clockwork Orange.*

Glancing down at my canvases and paints an idea gripped me–or rather a whole series of causally connected insights bubbled up and formed instantaneously into a coherent vision for my life's work. Art. That was the tool for healing the individual and by extension the nation and the world. I thought about the experience of really looking at a great landscape painting, and how it triggered a subtler form of what I felt now. It seemed obvious that creating art was the greatest contribution one could make to humanity. But I was no painter. Instead, my body seemed to scream, I was a writer! I thought of all the great healing books that turned a mirror back on myself, like *Crime and Punishment, Walden,* The Gospels, and the nearly infinite store of magnificent works throughout history and in the modern era, and how these were perhaps even more potent medicines than the great paintings.

In a rush of manic inspiration I grabbed the canvases and began to scribble my thoughts onto them. *Why should we reserve canvases for color and lines! Words belong on canvases and in art museums too!* A genuine authenticity deep within me had finally been given space to breathe in the mountain air. Independent of the great cultural forces that scream and cajole and push. The force of creation–I was going to quit my job and become a writer. It didn't matter that I had less than $5,000 to my name, it didn't matter that I had almost no professional experience as a writer, all that mattered was that I had found my path, and I was going to help others.

In the hilarity of raw inspiration, I stormed off the mountain top, notebook in hand, hungry for a subject. I stopped by the stream near my campsite and, studying it, composed a poem. The final six lines:

No conflict in this natural world. All is joined in a whirl.

When I look about life, river there is fraught with strife.

What a lesson in this creek, for all of us to stop the bleak.

I turn back to the forest, and cast my lot with the green.

For mother's teaching such lessons, who am I to call to question.

In this river today I flow, I myself begun to glow.

I wandered around the woods for several hours in a euphoric reverie, and as night fell, I sat down by the river and listened to the water without fear. I believed no bear or mountain lion would touch me now. My real life, after all, had finally begun.

CHAPTER THIRTY-SEVEN – FOUR DAYS LATER

On the drive home from the wilderness I called my mom to announce the news.

"Hey Mom, how are you?" With my left hand, I punched the speaker icon and held the phone out in front of me as I gripped the wheel with my right.

"I'm good honey, how are you?"

"Fantastic. I have some really big news actually." I could feel my heart rate pick up and my head flush warm.

"Oh yeah, and what's that?"

"I'm going to quit my job and become a writer."

There was a pause on the other end.

"Mm... wow that's quite the announcement. Well you know I'll support you in anything you want to do, I just wonder..." she trailed off.

Silence for several seconds before she continued.

"I just wonder, why do you have to quit your job? I mean it's so hard to make money writing, can't you do it as a hobby and still keep your job?"

I felt my hand clench down on the steering wheel.

"I can't Mom, I need to give it everything I have. For a few months at least, to see if I really have what it takes, and if it doesn't work and I run out of money, then I'll go back to work. But as of now, I'm a full-time writer."

"But it's so hard. I just, the life of a writer is not easy, and as a parent I'm worried about making sure you can feed yourself."

"Mom I'm not asking for advice here, I'm telling you a life update. This is what I'm doing."

There was a deep sigh on her end of the phone.

"Okay, if that's what you want, I'll support you. But it's not an easy road."

I laughed, "thanks Mom. I know. I never wanted easy."

"I know."

When I got home I told IoTeX I was leaving my job to write a book. "We don't want to lose you," my boss told me. She offered to scale my work down to just one day a week for ¼ of my salary, enough money to keep me alive while I spent the rest of the week writing. I hesitated. Not wanting to compromise on my wholehearted devotion to writing. But looking at my finances, I barely had enough money to last a month. In the end I took the offer.

Over the next week, as I outlined a plan for a book, the acid long since worn off, my old desire to be seen as a hero reasserted itself. Before leaving on the trip I had finished Antonio Garica Martinez's book

Chaos Monkeys, a memoir about his experience as an early employee at Facebook and building a Y-Combinator-backed startup. *Chaos Monkeys* had been a NYT bestseller, granting him cult status among Silicon Valley elites. I wanted to write something similar–*Chaos Monkeys* for crypto, redeeming the financial failure of the fund and healing my wounded vanity.

The day after I got back to Sarah's house we were out for a bike ride and I declared that I would finish the book in ninety days.

"I understand you're excited but maybe don't put so much pressure on it. Why don't you set a goal like nine months instead?" She was riding behind me, and her voice was tinged with concern.

"What? Are you not supportive of me? You don't believe that I can do it in ninety days?" I grimaced, slowing the bike to a stop and swinging my leg down onto the asphalt. "I can do anything I set my mind to!"

"I know, I know, but it's almost impossible to write an entire book in ninety days, especially since this is your first one."

I swung my leg back onto the bike and sped off, beating her home and waiting in our room with my arms crossed. Sarah came into the room and talked me out of the tantrum, assuring me that I had her full support.

I spent two more weeks in Kansas and then Sarah went back to Boston to work. Her lab had called her in to contribute research on a new COVID vaccine, and I went home to stay with my parents.

"I want to come live with you in Boston, after I finish the book," I told Sarah, before we said goodbye.

"I would like that," she answered, smiling.

My writing timeline, in a way, was not far off. At home, with dinners cooked for me and no rent to worry about, I wrote five or six hours a day and for the first time in my adult life woke up each morning exhilarated, leaping out of bed and, after some stretching and exercising to clear my mind, sitting down at my desk with the complete conviction that what I was doing mattered deeply. Life had suddenly become terrifyingly precious. In my walks and runs around the neighborhood I would wait nervously at crosswalks for the widest possible gap between cars, meticulously reducing the chance that some accident would keep me from my work.

Every facet of my life was put in the service of writing. I ate lightly in the morning and vegetables and lean meat in the afternoon to keep my energy up throughout the day. I refreshed any dullness in my head with heavy exercise, and slept late when fatigue had marred my productivity the previous day. After finishing the day's writing, I went to bed early, wanting to minimize the time before I could wake up and do it all over again.

By early August I had completed the first draft of God Money, just a month longer than my original estimate. The book, as it was in the late summer of 2020, might as well have been a fantasy novel. It did not mention my drug use, exaggerated the amount of money I had raised and made during the 2017 bull market by an order of magnitude, and described a person I did not recognize who deployed his prodigious technical savvy to outsmart other crypto investors.

My first draft had been an attempt to reclaim my failure, to put an evening dress on a pig, asserting a preferable reality that would restore my bruised self image. As I read over what I had put to the page, my euphoria was interrupted by a dawning fear for myself if I persisted in my lies. I recalled one of Dostoevsky's great passages in *Brothers Karamazov*, "the man who lies to himself and listens to his own lie comes to a point where he cannot distinguish the truth within him or around him and so loses all respect for himself and for others. And having no respect he ceases to love."

On a particularly dark night, in my room at my parents house I took out my journal and wrote.

As I was writing the book I was guided by a desire to turn my tale into a heroic story of a financial prodigy getting rich in the new world of finance. This was the dream I had for myself and I still can't quite let it go. To confront reality as it actually is is so difficult. I am so adverse to failure it makes me fail. I'm someone who refuses to confront who I actually am. But, I suppose, recognizing that means I am already on the road to redemption. But for now depression has taken hold. I feel lost, sitting here after four-months of work with nothing to show for it but a loose collection of anecdotes.

I worry a great deal about happiness, which of course means I am very rarely happy. Anyway, I'm worried I'm really not so good at this writing thing and that, in the end, I might never find "my thing." Tonight I downed three beers and sat down to watch Trailer Park Boys to distract myself from how shitty I'm feeling. I really do go through major ups and downs. It's pretty wild. I wish I didn't have to go through it. I feel so fucking tortured. I know that's dramatic. I know that sounds like self-indulgent self-pity, but it's the truth... I am so unhappy trying to figure it all out.

Perhaps the source of it all is that I have a nagging feeling that I am destined for greatness. And when the harsh feedback the world gives me clashes with my grandiose self-image pain results. But in part it is the world's fault. It has told me things that I am trying to live up to. My acceptance to Stanford, for example. Something has to come back into alignment. In the meantime, I suffer.

In mid-August I embarked on another road trip, this time from Seattle to Boston, to move in with Sarah. On the drive, which took me eight days, I battled the discomfort of a growing contradiction–my newfound enthusiasm for writing and despair at the faults of my first draft. But Sarah would set things right. My writing, such as it was, had given me a purpose. Sarah would give me happiness.

When I arrived in Boston it was almost 11 p.m. and pouring rain. I drove up to our new apartment, heart beating fast with excitement, driving around for almost fifteen minutes before finding a parking spot, and then running up to her door, bag in hand, face flushed with excitement.

"Sarah!" I practically shouted when she answered the door, enveloping her in a hug.

"So good to see you!" She said.

I pulled back and looked into her face, her eyes were tired and had a hint of wariness, even as her lips parted in a wide smile.

"So this is the place huh?"

"Yep! I just got here two days ago. Still a lot of unpacking to do."

She showed me around the apartment–a two-bedroom at the top of a hill on the border of Brighton and Brookline. I wanted to share a room, but Sarah said it would be better to keep separate ones.

"My sleep is the most important thing for my productivity," she had said, "and, besides, I get up before six each morning. I'm guessing you're going to want to sleep in." She wasn't wrong, but I was hurt by what I took to be her judgment.

I was hungry after the day's drive so I went into the kitchen and opened the pantry, pulling out some rice cakes and chewing on one while Sarah was in the bathroom. I smiled at her when she came back into the kitchen.

"Wait, what are you doing?" She said, almost frantic.

I frowned. "What do you mean? I'm eating a rice cake."

"You can't eat that! Those are mine and they're expensive."

I stared at her.

"You're not serious."

"Dean, I am serious, I'm on a strict budget."

"But I literally just drove 3,000 miles to be here, do you know how much that costs in gas? I can't have one rice cake?"

"I literally changed apartments to a much less convenient location so we could live together. It's not like I'm not also sacrificing things."

"But I don't understand. Why are we fighting? I just got here."

"Just ask next time, it's really not cool."

"Are you seriously getting mad at me for eating a fifty cent rice cake?"

"It's just the principle of it. I don't like people touching my stuff."

The next day Sarah left early for work and didn't get home until almost nine. This turned out to be the norm. Sarah was gone most of the day at work while I sat at home. With the city still shut down from Covid, I left only to go for walks and runs past huge, multi-million dollar Brookline homes. The sidewalks were long and painful.

Feeling like my book was not in good shape, but without a clear vision of how to improve it, I spent most of my days burying myself in books, trying to piece together my unhappiness. All the enthusiasm of the summer had drained into a ruminating depression that drove me to study German philosophy–looking to Nietzsche, Schopenhauer and Heidegger for answers. They tickled my brain and offered a temporary escape, but no matter how much I read I still felt stuck with myself.

My money was running low, kept afloat only by my $500 a week from IoTeX, and I began to believe my life had become one great failure.

While Sarah was at work, I would write things in my journal like, *No momentary lifting of the spirit from despair brings permanent peace.* I decided that to write the book I wanted, it would be useful to have the structure and formal training of an MFA. I also wanted something other than my own dream to tell me that I was in fact a writer. An institution or agent or publisher to give me a stamp of legitimacy that I could point to and say, "see! I *am* a writer!"

I applied to a dozen programs and shopped around my clunky manuscript to literary agents, hoping that one of them would accept it and spare me the pain of having to face directly the dark omitted truths in my story.

Sarah scheduled everything. We had a chore list that detailed whose turn it was to cook, clean, and grocery shop. Everything was split right down the middle: 50/50. Thursdays we would eat dinner together, and Sundays, usually Sarah's day off, we would go for a hike.

One Thursday, in mid-October, after I spent the afternoon preparing Tofu Pad Thai and a three-layer gluten and dairy free cake for our dinner (Sarah had learned two years before, thanks to a blood test, that she had a minor intolerance to gluten and dairy and had cut both out of her diet), I received a text.

"Hey sorry, have to stay late at the office, won't be home until ten."

When she got home, she thanked me profusely for making dinner, grabbed a plate of food, and shut herself in her room with the explanation "sorry, have to do some data analysis." I sat on the couch in the living room and buried my face in my hands.

What good were all my insights on the mountain now? Was the inspiration and clarity I had felt just another chemically induced brain state, only this time from LSD instead of cocaine? I thought of using drugs every day. I would often have dreams where I took Adderall or snorted cocaine, the rush of using would wake me up with a pounding heart.

 Who was I even? And Sarah. I realized I didn't even know her. She had changed so much from undergrad—a different person practically. She had always been the one suggesting things to do, parties for us to go to, and here I was, unable to get her to sit down to dinner with me.

The next day, I put up a poster with my picture on it next to the BU bookstore that read, "Be My Friend," along with a personal bio and my phone number.

Within a few minutes:

"Hey Dean! New friend here :)"

I met six new people in a week, including a doctor and a local high school principal. The principal was an inspiring man who had founded a school for low-income students outside of Boston, someone I still keep in touch with and who introduced me to a local writing group that helped me polish some of the book's early chapters. After a few days the poster was put on a popular Boston Instagram page, and I had to change my number to stop the flood of messages.

The weeks rolled by and our fights increased. My feelings of loneliness and unrequited love turned to rage. For hours at a time I would pace around the apartment burning with anger and looking for an outlet. One day I latched onto money as the root of our problems. Calculating that I paid for most of our food (forgetting to factor in that I also ate most of it). One Saturday, while she was at work, I texted her.

Dean: "I'm pretty bitter. I feel like you are not contributing financially."

Sarah: "Yes, just remember that I am not my dad. I am very fortunate to have money saved but I don't feel like I'm rolling in dough."

Sarah: "And honestly, I am really bothered by the expectation that I help out financially just because you perceive that I am wealthy."

Dean: "I know you are. But in a relationship, you should contribute financially when able."

Sarah: "Yes I have money saved. But I also need to save money bc I am not going into a lucrative career. It would be unwise not to."

Dean: "I'm not going into a lucrative career either."

Sarah: "So what exactly do you expect of me, financially?"

Dean: "I'm just becoming aware that no level of wealth will make you generous. I pay for things all the time but you rarely do and you have way more money than me. I'm concerned that you seem to see everything in our relationship as zero-sum. IDK I just haven't experienced this level of atomization in a relationship before."

Sarah: "I don't feel financially secure. I would be making an enormous sacrifice on my future if I spent money supporting your life. Sometimes it feels like this is just you wanting to drag me down."

Dean: "I'm not asking you to "support my life" I'm asking you to do the bare minimum and be as generous with me as I am with you. I guess my entire existence is dragging you down..."

Sarah: "Yes I think we see finances very differently."

Dean: "Who's asking you to support my life? That has zero to do with it."

Sarah: "I don't really understand what you're asking."

Dean: "This isn't even about 'finances' honestly. You are so focused on yourself I can't even believe it."

Sarah: "Dean I am fuming at you."

Dean: "Im trying to say that should I achieve financial success (or success of any kind) I want to feel good about sharing that in small and big ways with you. And I feel a higher form of relationship is one where we transcend selfish mine mine mine mentalities, and I guess I'm worried that that is not how you see things."

Dean: "Let's talk more when you get home."

Sarah: "Fine."

When she got home, she was in a rage and I apologized in an effort to calm her down. I told her I had been upset that she hadn't been spending enough time with me. She said that maybe that was a byproduct of my insecurities as a man having trouble being around a successful woman.

My eyes twitched at that comment, but not wanting to start another fight I just nodded, "maybe you're right."

Six weeks later, we broke up and I moved out. I flew home to my parents house and started therapy.

"I am not a happy person," I told my therapist.

"That's a story you tell yourself," he replied.

"Some stories are true."

"But that one doesn't have to be."

"I am neurotic and introverted and low in serotonin. What else can I do? I got a bad roll of the genetic dice."

"You are a good person, though."

"Can't good people be unhappy?"

"No. Not if they are good out of love instead of good out of obligation."

"Okay, fine. I guess I'm a bad person."

"No, you're not."

I told myself that I was hopelessly depressed. The drugs had masked a lot of underlying feelings, and had given me a twisted hope, evidence that euphoric states were possible with a single sniff. It was difficult to face my predicament now, without the one thing that had worked for me in the past. But over the weeks of therapy that preceded my breakup with Sarah, one major thing did change. I no longer believed that my mind was purely a chemical apparatus. I couldn't believe that anymore. My drug use arose from a philosophical lack, I now believed, not a neurochemical one. Before, the rise and fall of the drug states had kept me occupied. Focused on physical survival. But now I had no map to guide me out of this new terrain, no drug to make me whole, even for a little while. The ground had been pulled out from under me, and, in my darkest moments, I feared I might be lost for all time.

CHAPTER THIRTY-EIGHT – JANUARY 2021

At home with my parents, Sarah gone, I began to feel lighter. Like the emotional wall I had been pushing against for months had suddenly given way into open space. My creative energy returned, and I began my first rewrite of the book. Increasing my work at IoTeX to three days a week and starting a TikTok channel educating people about crypto. But my energy was tainted with an awareness that I was on unstable ground. At any moment the positive cycle could reverse course, taking me back down the familiar spiral of wallowing rumination.

Nevertheless I was optimistic–crypto was entering a new bull market as COVID stimulus checks and trillions of dollars in artificial sweeteners pumped into global markets. In mid-January my video about Satoshi Nakamoto went viral–racking up over a million views. Then sponsorship requests–"we'll pay you $400 to make a video about XYZ coin." Then a text from an old Stanford friend–"Hey man, me and some buddies are moving to South Florida, want to be our fourth roommate?"

"Of course," I said, "be there in a week." It was all happening.

Two days later I was on a flight to Boston to collect my car and belongings from the apartment. Sarah had found a subletter, a woman our age, who let me in (Sarah was at work of course, thankfully). I piled all my stuff into the back of the Sienna and drove south. The final cord cut—a new beginning.

I stopped in Richmond for the night and went on Hinge, setting my location for South Florida. Swiping through smiling faces. Spending no more than ten seconds on any given profile—applying some vague mammalian mating heuristic impossible to articulate. A few conversations began and sputtered out.

Then I matched with a twenty-one-year-old blonde girl named Emily from Boca Raton. She had pictures of herself on sailboats and in exotic, south-east Asian locales. Wealthy, it appeared, and smart—her profile said she went to Yale, at home now. A gap year. What struck me was her smile—exuberant and ear-to-ear, practically exhaling joy—so much more alive than the typical overly manicured dating app photos. Her third picture was her posing with a painting she had made of Ram Dass, a spiritual influencer and writer who I had listened to on YouTube. "I love Ram Dass," I messaged her, "do you meditate?" A paragraph of text came back, full of exclamation points and emojis.

I wrote back a paragraph in kind, describing my interest in Sam Harris, Alan Watts and the German philosophers. We made plans to meet three days later in Delray Beach.

As I waited for her, I sat on a bench next to sun-bleached palm trees and watched bald men and plastic-surgeried wives walk around. In South Florida, momentum determines the right of way: mass times speed, and pedestrians are always the last to go. None of the sure-footed Beatles-struts of Palo Alto residents who'll stare you down if you so much as poke your plate over the stripes. The people too—flamboyant and diverse. Bodies bronzed from too much sun, muscled from too much exercise, or soft and loose from too much drinking.

And so, when in the middle of these reflections Emily's bobbing, smiling face popped up in front of me, it was surprisingly, refreshingly, normal.

"Hey, so good to meet you!"

She came at me off kilter and more body-slammed me than hugged, slapping her left arm around me.

"Nice to meet you too," I replied, trying to decide if Emily's awkward hug was off-putting or charming.

I shared my observations with her as we walked down Atlantic Avenue—her laughing, leaning in and asking follow-up questions. Wanting to really understand what I meant, saying things like "that's so funny, I never thought about that before."

I learned that her father, after a modest upbringing, had enjoyed a lucrative decades-long career as a Manhattan stockbroker. She grew up in a wealthy Long Island neighborhood and went to elite prep schools until the financial crisis took away most of their assets, including their home. Now she lived in a small apartment with her brother and parents in Boca Raton.

I told her about my drug addiction, my failed relationship with Sarah, and recent creative struggles. She described her harrowing recovery from a nearly decade-long eating disorder, sexual assault in high school and alcoholism in college. I discovered with delight that she, like me, had made the conscious decision to trade professional goals for developing the philosophical and spiritual self. Our first date lasted nine hours, and we saw each other three times the first week alone.

Life was moving fast. I had just moved across the country, tripled my IoTeX workload, and two new viral TikToks had led to over 100,000 followers and an influx of sponsor interest. Dozens of agent rejections increased the pressure to re-write my first draft. And I wondered whether it was responsible, or healthy, barely six-weeks after breaking up with Sarah to enter a whirlwind romance that was rapidly sinking deep emotional hooks into me. Deeper even, it already felt, than the high point of my relationship with Sarah. How was it that somehow, before even arriving in Florida, I had found someone who appeared, in a way, to be a mirror of myself. A girl from a similar socio-economic background who had also made it to an elite institution and burned out, who had experienced addiction and mental health crises beyond her years, and was now dedicated to healing herself and, hopefully, one day, those around her.

It occurred to me that perhaps my relationship with Sarah had dis-integrated because of poor compatibility, divergent goals, and not because of personal flaws. I had resented Sarah for what I perceived to be her abrupt transformation from a balanced person to a career-obsessed workaholic neglecting our relationship and everything else in her life. But in fact, I realized, if anyone had changed it had been me.

Re-writing the book remained my biggest priority, as well as my greatest source of dissatisfaction. The truth was slowly making its way into the manuscript–including unflattering drug scenes and more accurate portrayals of the fund's performance. But the more I committed myself to telling the truth the more bewildered I felt. I had peeled off the first layer of the onion and not only discovered an endless complex of additional layers, but found my eyes were blinded by tear-jerking fumes. Many nights I would dream about the money I had stolen from my family, or the relationships I had destroyed, and wake up with a desperate urge to escape from my own mind. I had started down a seemingly endless course of painful self-discovery, and I saw no easy path to arriving at a point where I could finally write a book devoid of self-deception.

"I want to be like Thoreau," I told Emily on our third date, "live on a plot of land and build a cabin and just write. I feel like becoming a hermit might be my true calling."

"That sounds wonderful. I've always dreamed of something similar–like living on a sailboat for a while, or on a remote island and just painting and dancing all the time."

"I think I really need it honestly. There are so many things in my past that I need to confront, and it's so hard to do it when you're so busy all the time. I just want to get away and look at myself clearly."

"You know what I think you need?"

"What's that?"

"An acid trip."

Two days later we met again in Delray, sun block and notebook in hand, the accouterments of the upcoming trip. I had five tabs of LSD with me, the leftovers from my journey to the New Mexico wilderness.

"How much are we taking?" Emily asked, nervously digging her right foot into the sand.

"How does two tabs sound?"

"Sure," she said, voice shaking.

"You know one tab in New Mexico made me quit my job to become a writer. Today we're taking two," I said, smiling.

"After this you're going to quit writing and dedicate your life to contacting aliens." We both laughed, and I slipped my hand into hers and set off walking.

"Do you know any private spots we can go to? I hate being around people when I'm tripping."

"Let's just keep walking for a while," Emily said, "the farther north we walk the fewer people."

We took our shoes off and slowly walked past children playing in the surf and dogs chasing frisbees. After about twenty minutes we were almost alone, save the occasional beach runner, and took our seats in the sand, looking into each other's eyes for silent reassurance before popping our respective doses.

We chatted nervously.

"Feel anything yet?" I asked after half an hour.

"No not yet, maybe a little nausea but I think that's just nerves."

After a few more minutes of anxious conversation we grew silent. The drug was taking hold. I closed my eyes and lay back in the sand—my eyelids turning into a movie screen with ribbons of color and swirling, twisting shapes. I smiled, enjoying the show. But then the experience intensified. My body grew heavy, and within minutes it felt as if leather straps were binding me to a steel plate buried deep below the sand. My body, my entire experience, now completely out of my control. I relaxed, surrendering myself to the psychedelic that pierced through my unconscious and dragged painful truths into the bright hospital lighting of my raging consciousness. For the next three hours, I was subjected to what felt like psychological electro-shock therapy.

You stole your family's money to buy drugs! My mind screamed over and over. I watched the smiling faces of my family members, so innocent and loving toward me despite my betrayal.

Tyler hurt the worst. I had stolen $20,000 from him. And through him I was shown the deep, energetic entanglements that I had with my family, and how my lies had torn the delicate fabric that connected us. Possible to ignore for a time, but whose consequences would make themselves manifest in increasingly terrible ways the longer the lie festered.

I felt a tap on my shoulder, and I opened my eyes. Emily was next to me, *that's right, I'm on a beach in South Florida.*

"Are you okay?" She whispered, eyeing me with concern. "You've been so quiet, and you keep making these moaning sounds."

"Yeah," I rasped, "I'm okay. Just... hard."

She nodded, grabbing my hand and squeezing.

After another hour the LSD had begun to wear off and I staggered to my feet. Making my way to the water and wading in slowly, tipping myself on my back, floating. Allowing the waves, no more than three feet crest-to-trough, to rock me up and down. I felt like a blue whale resting on the ocean's surface, rising and falling in seventy-foot swells. Everything magnified to a glorious and terrifying scale. After a few minutes I swam back to shore, plopping back down next to Emily, heaving, catching my breath.

Finally, as the full moon rose over the beach, Emily and I headed home. I could barely talk, all my energy directed inward, focused on processing the huge emotional weight of what I had just confronted.

"How was the trip?" Emily asked, almost in a whisper, sensing my reticence.

"I need some time to decompress," I said, "I'll tell you about it later."

The next day I called Tyler.

"Hey, how are you doing?"

"I'm good. Thanks for asking."

"Listen, there's no easy way to say this. There's something that's been eating me up for a long time now..." I paused, taking a deep breath before continuing, "I lied to you about the money being hacked. I sold Ethereum when it wasn't worth much to buy drugs, thinking that I could just buy it back when I made more money. But then it went up so quickly. I didn't have the ability to buy back even a fraction of it, and then it was too late."

Silence for a moment.

"Wow. You know it's okay. Honestly it doesn't make much difference to me. I kind of forgot about it. That sounds like a really hard thing to deal with, I'm happy you told me."

"Listen," I said, feeling like a boulder was slowly being lifted off my chest, "I know this doesn't make up for it. But I have some money now and I want to repay you at least for your initial investment, the $20,000 you put in."

"Okay, sure. That sounds fair."

I wired him $20,000 that same day, most of the cash I had on hand. I had the same conversation with Evan, with a similar response, sending him $1,000.

I called Tyler again when I wired the money.

"Just sent it, should be in your account by tomorrow."

"Thanks Dean. By the way, I invested in a buddy of mine's real estate deal and lost over half my money. So in a way, you gave me a much better rate of return."

We both laughed.

Finally, it was time to call my parents. I dialed my mom, imagining she would take the news easier, but she didn't answer. So I called my dad.

"Hey, Dean."

"Hey, Dad. Listen, there's something I have to tell you." I told him the same thing I'd told Tyler.

"Listen," he said, his voice warm, "don't think for a minute that you have to repay us for any of it. I made some mistakes when I was younger, some things I regret. And your mom and I completely forgive you. We're just happy you're getting better."

I felt tears come down my face and I held the phone away from my mouth so he wouldn't hear me cry. I stifled the tears and mustered the clearest voice I could.

"Thanks Dad, that means a lot to me."

It was a transformational moment. Proving to me that the darkest parts of my past did not need to be shut up forever in order for me to remain acceptable to those around me. They could be brought to light and absolved in the fresh air of true connection. My crippling fears had been largely unfounded. It was as if I had shoved old food under the couch and pretended for years that I didn't smell the rot. Once I looked into the darkness and really confronted the mess in there, it was the simplest thing in the world to reach in and clean it up.

CHAPTER THIRTY-NINE – APRIL, 2021

Emily and I became exclusive, I found an agent and was accepted into the non-fiction MFA program at the University of San Francisco and waitlisted at Columbia. IoTeX's token had gone up enough that I could buy a two-and-a-quarter acre plot of land in Upstate New York between Rochester and Buffalo—my Walden Pond. One day, hopefully soon, I would go out there and build myself a little cabin. Life was good.

My agent was a grizzled industry veteran named Jack in his 50s who had spent his early career on Wall Street. He knew my world and he knew the literary world, and he told me he could help me bridge the gap. "Just follow my instructions and *God Money's* going to be a huge hit," Jack said, "I can turn you into the next Michael Lewis."

The next Michael Lewis. That sounded good. Puffery was the key to my heart. I was desperate for someone to believe in me, who could speak my dreams out loud. But grandiosity had gotten me into trouble in the past, and I was wary of it even as I indulged it.

I spent the summer with Emily, road-tripping around the country, stopping in Breckenridge for six weeks to write and hike. Jack was hard on me. He told me about another client of his who had just sold his debut book–also a memoir–to Harper Collins for a $100,000 advance. He felt he could swing a similar deal for me, but the manuscript needed heavy re-writing. I told him to pull no punches. Give it to me straight, I can take it.

"There's too much purple prose, do you know what purple prose is?"

"No."

"It's flowery, vague language that doesn't drive the narrative forward. You can write sharp and clear and fast but most of the time you don't. It's a bad habit you have to kick."

"Got it."

He marked up my manuscript, telling me to cut my favorite passages and excoriating me for sections that strayed into abstraction.

I was wrong. I couldn't take it. Every critique Jack leveled at me, full of sound judgment, burned badly, kickstarting a spiral of fear and self-doubt that often left me too shaken to write for days. Finally, after four months, twice as long as Jack expected, he declared that the proposal, which included a fraction of the full manuscript, was finally good enough to shop around to publishers.

In September, I moved into a small Nob Hill apartment and began my MFA at USF while Emily went back to Yale for her senior year.

When I arrived in San Francisco, it felt like I'd walked through a doorway of infinite possibility. Jack sent off my manuscript to twenty-two publishers. "We'll know in a month if we get any bites," he said, "best case scenario a few editors get into a bidding war."

I arrived for my first MFA class at the USF campus and sat down in a small conference room. My cohort, which would be the same for the next two years, consisted of seven women and me. The program, which cost $8,000 a semester, included two two-hour workshops a week. Sixty-four hours of total class time per semester, I calculated, or $125/hour. Our reading list included a book titled *Appropriate*, which examined cultural appropriation and what writers from certain racial backgrounds should and should not write. For our first class we were asked to bring in an excerpt from a non-fiction work we admired. We heard passages from *Know My Name*, the memoir of Chanel Miller, the victim in the Brock Turner assault, and *In The Dream House*, a memoir written by a lesbian describing her abusive relationship. I read the opening two pages from Hunter S. Thompson's *Hell's Angels*.

Here was a chance to broaden my literary and cultural horizons, to understand the female literary worldview, increasingly dominant in modern publishing, and receive feedback from peers outside my normal target audience. But as the weeks went by I received almost no concrete criticism of my writing, even when it contained, to me, obvious flaws. The professors, and by extension most of the students, had adopted a methodology of affirmation that seemed more interested in making students feel good rather than exposing their blind spots. The institutionalization of "everyone gets a trophy."

In early October, Jack sent me an email telling me that sixteen of the twenty-two editors had passed on the manuscript.

I wrote back, pleading for more info–"Did they say why they passed on it?"

"Too raw," he answered, tersely, "basically you're too close to the events. You need a few more years."

The next day he called me.

"Listen, I have a proposal, what if you write a more technical book that explains crypto and Bitcoin to the average person? And then once you're done with the MFA you can rewrite God Money and we'll give it another shot with the publishers."

I paused, feeling like a weight had just been loaded onto my chest.

"I don't know, man. I'm really not that interested in writing about crypto and blockchain as a technology. The more I write, the more I just want to focus on the issues that really matter to me. Like addiction and greed and coming of age."

"But I'm telling you, if you want to be a professional writer sometimes you have to focus on what the marketplace wants to read, not what you want to write."

In my heart I knew he was right. But I also knew I couldn't do it. There had to be some way to hack the system, to craft a life that allowed me to do what I loved without having to climb mountains of drudgery for a few moments of peace at the top.

"I'm not interested, really."

"Suit yourself."

"There's still hope though isn't there? I mean with the six editors that haven't responded yet."

There was a long pause.

"Yeah, yeah there's still hope. I'll let you know if I hear back."

CHAPTER FORTY - OCTOBER 2021

I flew to Connecticut and picked up Emily for a five-day camping trip in Cape Cod. I spent the flight biting my cuticles and writing out long journal entries trying to reassure myself that I still possessed a coherent narrative for my life. But when I walked out of Hartford airport and spotted Emily standing outside of a Zipcar waving at me a lightness washed over me. I ran and hugged her.

"Thank you so much for picking me up! You really didn't have to."

"Of course I did! You know I couldn't wait to see you."

It was literally shocking to me how much happiness I felt in her presence. I couldn't stop smiling. It was as if all the problems in my life were just flickering shadows and Emily came along with a torchlight and blew them all away.

We spent the night in her apartment and left for the cape in a rental car the next morning. Waking up the first morning with the stuffy heat of the tent coming down on us. The air was sticky, and Emily lay next to me sweaty and smiling in her goofy way. She rolled over and draped her arm around me, then battened me with her thigh, locking me in place and laughing like she had just pulled a great practical joke on me. The RV resort we were camped in was like a little suburban neighborhood, and we were the vagabonds in a tent that everyone avoided looking at when they walked by. It was past nine and the heat was growing oppressive, and I considered jumping out of the tent, but Emily was convincing in her advances, and I succumbed. I reached down and played with her until she started breathing wetness into my ear and her legs started wobbling. I heard the crunch of a shoe on gravel and turned to see a balding man in a blue pullover fleece watching us through the open rainfly. I zipped it shut and shared a laugh with Emily.

I kept playing with her and she gripped my back tighter and tighter until I felt a gush and her breathing stopped for a few seconds before she turned to her side and gasped and shook, grabbing the back of my head and kissing me fiercely. Then we made love. It was always the same ritual. Her turn, my turn.

We woke up around 9:30 each morning, then lay in the tent and made love before emerging around 10:30. Outside the tent, we ate buttery grits mixed with melted mozzarella sticks, our faces still flushed. The air was cool but the sun was warm and the sky cloudless as we sipped our coffee and chatted about life, philosophy, and our plans for the day.

When we finally did get out the tent that first morning we discovered both of our phones were almost dead. We used Emily's last seven percent to map us to a Starbucks where we could charge up. Before leaving the campground, we stopped at check-in.

The elderly lady at the front desk with a graying bob and a scowl greeted me. "You're late checking in."

"Sorry about that, we tried to check in last night but the office was closed."

"You're lucky we even allow tent campers here," she said, handing me my parking placard. I returned to the car a little disheartened and told Emily what happened.

"Evidently they have a thing against attractive young artists."

We both laughed.

After charging up our phones we went to rent bikes at a shop called Idle Times. The rental man had a deep, rich voice and when he spoke it made me feel like it was going to be a good, relaxing day on the Cape. As we were getting ready to ride, Emily kicked the thick steel kickstand clean off her bike with a shock of force that I had never seen before. The bike guy came out and was not surprised, assuring us "it happens all the time" in his soothing way. Still, I didn't look at Emily the same the rest of the day; her leg power had earned her a newfound respect from me. We charged off into the sweaty October afternoon with the rich sun beating down on us. It felt like I was photosynthesizing, gaining energy the hotter it got.

We biked through marshes and pine forests before getting down towards Eastham where we encountered a nice old man with a gravelly smoker's voice that made me lean in close and say "Sorry?" a few times before I finally got his drift (he told us directions to the beach) and we charged off in that direction.

As we biked I reflected on how Emily was one of the best things that ever happened to me. When I was running the fund I had felt at times that my life was already over. That adult responsibilities meant that my life would forever be a cash-flow statement, and not something that was joyful or meaningful in and of itself. Then, after the fund closed, I believed that my failure to achieve financial escape velocity at the age of 25 meant I was doomed to unhappiness. But Emily had given me new hope. She was not solely responsible for my happiness, but her presence reminded me that well-being was always available to me.

The trip ended and we went our separate ways. Back in San Francisco the MFA program didn't seem so bad anymore. Maybe Jack was right. I would graduate in a year and a half and then I would write the book I really wanted.

A couple of weeks after returning to San Francisco I began suffering from migraines. Sometimes spending entire afternoons in bed, popping Tylenol and googling home remedies. One day, after a particularly painful bout, I was eating pizza before class when I cried out in pain. My right hand instinctively shot up and began massaging the spot where I had bitten my lip. I had never bitten my lip while eating, and so was surprised, as I continued to slowly eat the pizza, that it happened a half-dozen more times before the slice was done.

When I arrived in class I discovered that I couldn't blink my right eye, so I spent the three-hour seminar hunched over, holding down my eyelid. No one in class appeared to notice, and I wondered if I was just imagining things. At a break, I went to the bathroom and gave the mirror my best attempt at a smile: the right side of my face was frozen while the left side lifted up in a startling scowl. *I look like a snarling pitbull when I smile*, I thought.

I finished class and returned home, googling my symptoms and found I had Bell's Palsy, the causes of which include stroke. The UCSF Medical Center was just half a mile from my apartment, so I went to the emergency room, hunched over, holding my eye as I walked.

At the intake counter I gave the nurse my best snarl-smile.

"The right side of my face is frozen," I said.

The nurse looked concerned.

"How long has it been like this?"

"I don't know, a few hours. I noticed it when I smiled at a little girl and she started screaming."

"I'll get you right in."

For the next twelve hours I lay on a bed in the hallway, bright lights and the sound of doctors and nurses shuffling by. Periodically someone would come to check on me and say "it's probably just an infection, but we'll keep you for a while to make sure it doesn't get worse." Looking at my phone hurt too much, and I lost track of time. Like *Groundhog Day,* doctors kept coming by and saying the same thing. "Just an infection," the same statement, different doctor, again and again. Sometime around four in the morning I got a CT scan.

"It's not a stroke," a doctor said, examining the results.

"So what is it?"

"I don't know."

I returned to my bed in the hallway and lay in a haze between sleep and wakefulness. The migraines were almost unbearable, and I over-heard an elderly lady, attended by her haggard daughter, moaning loudly a few feet away.

"I can't bear it. I really can't stand it any longer. I don't want to live anymore!" She cried out suddenly.

"Please, doctor," the daughter said, grabbing a physician who was speed-walking by, "give my mother something. She's in agony."

A few minutes later, a nurse hooked her up to an IV. Her moaning stopped, and she began to sing.

"Row, row, row, your boat, gently down the stream. Merrily, merrily, merrily, merrily, life is but a dream!"

"Quiet, Mom. You'll disturb the other patients," her daughter warned.

"Oh, god, but I feel so good!" she cried. "I can't believe it! I feel completely cured."

"Mom, that's because they gave you morphine."

"Oh, but you don't understand. I feel completely better!"

"I know, Mom, I know. But it's just the pain medication."

Finally, around 9 a.m. I was released from the ward, equipped with nothing but an eye-drop prescription to keep my unblinking eye from drying out, and admonishments to return to the emergency room if my facial paralysis worsened.

Over the next few days, the migraines worsened but my facial paralysis stayed the same. I lay in bed, spacing out doses of acetaminophen so I wouldn't go over the daily limit, and stopped going to class. I became an expert at eating with only the right side of my mouth and could drag myself out of bed for forty-five minutes a day to use the stationary bike in the USF gym at low speeds. My spirit rebelled against the lethargy. I sought out stimulating supplements like concentrated caffeine drinks and the over-the-counter drug "kratom" to give me an artificial boost of energy. But using over-the-counter drugs was like fighting the wind with a fan. Each passing day as I lay in bed, alone in my apartment, my despair mounted. I began to feel like my energy would never return, and I fantasized about stronger stimulants.

I regularly visited the UCSF urgent care to discuss my case with the internist. He suspected, just like the bevy of doctors in the emergency room, that I had suffered from an infection of some kind but didn't take any further steps to diagnosis.

"It will probably just get better with time," he told me, "try not to get in your head about it."

Three weeks went by like this. My friend Johnny came to visit for a weekend. He sat by my bed and we talked and occasionally went out for walks. When he left I was secretly glad. It was easier for me if people in my life didn't see me in this state. I called Emily and gave her an update.

When she picked up I listened to the sound of her voice and felt warm. *It's so simple*, I thought, as she updated me about her life, *just hearing her voice makes all the pain bearable.*

"No there's no diagnosis yet," I said, in response to her questions, "maybe it's just my body reacting to being apart from you."

She laughed, "I'm sure that's it."

She was busy, she said, finals were coming up, and she didn't have much time. After we hung up the pain worsened. I checked my portfolio and saw my IoTeX tokens had appreciated nearly $70,000 in the last thirty-six hours. I rolled over and searched with my hand for the cold side of the pillow and smothered my forehead with it. Finally, I felt well enough to get up. I ordered a $17 lox bagel for pickup on Uber Eats and walked through Lower Sunset, which felt like a movie set, and hurriedly took the bag with my food from the Sikh man behind the counter and walked out.

After a few blocks, my head felt heavy and I sat. I watched people drift by, hunched and shuffling, the gait of vague discontent so common in cities. I got up and kept walking, feeling an energy return to me. I decided to continue to the Haight. I handed a rough-looking bearded man wearing a ripped tie-dye shirt a $5 bill, he thanked me. I kept walking to Walgreens and bought some razors and a $4 Starbucks cold brew coffee. I drank it, returned home, and lay in bed for a while.

The next day, while browsing Reddit, I discovered Bell's Palsy was a common symptom of Lyme disease, a tick-spread infection that can make its way to the brain. If untreated, it leads to arthritis and chronic pain.

I went to the urgent care and shared my discovery with the internist. He was initially dismissive but agreed that I should take some blood tests to be sure. After a ten-day wait the results returned positive. I called my mom.

"Hey, Mom," I said, my voice achey.

"Hey, sweetie. How are you feeling?"

"I have some good news. I finally have a diagnosis. It's Lyme disease. I must have gotten it when I was out camping with Emily."

"Lyme disease! Wow, but they can treat it, right?"

"Yeah, just two weeks of antibiotics and I should be good to go. But I feel really low now, even though I know I'm going to get better."

"Yeah, that's very natural. That's a major illness. Just know that you're always welcome to come home. You might be more comfortable here."

"Okay, I'll drive up. I don't want to be in this apartment any more to be honest."

After we hung up, I got out of bed, suddenly feeling like I was cured. *What a remarkable difference a reason for suffering can make to the human soul!* I thought. I pumped my fists up and down and jogged in circles in my room but the migraines hit me again and I collapsed back into bed, grabbing my laptop to email my professors that I was dropping out of the MFA. I knew that the MFA was not the answer to my creative paralysis. Stuck between a dead project that I couldn't quite let go of and the heavy impossibility of starting a new book entirely. I needed a total reset, some kind of fresh inspiration that would not come in a classroom. "Are you sure? Sometimes it's better to just power through," one of my professors wrote back. I didn't respond. *Good riddance*, I thought, *now I can start living again.*

CHAPTER FORTY-ONE – NOVEMBER, 2021

Four days after starting antibiotics my recovery began in earnest. At home now, I spent three hours with my dad in the dirt excising a stump in our front yard. It was like struggling with a kraken. It felt so good to use my body again, to feel strong and useful.

But as the days passed and my physical symptoms lifted I noticed that, except for short-lived spurts of well-being, my happiness didn't grow with my physical vitality. Emily was in the middle of finals and we didn't speak for almost ten days. And so my energy went inward, dedicated to self-diagnosing the causes of suffering. If I examined the facts of my life—imagining myself as someone on the outside observing me and writing down what they saw—I *should* have been happy. I had a loving girlfriend and family, good job opportunities, a large social media following, and extra cash. It was these facts that made me fundamentally skeptical about the process by which society expects me, expects all of us, to achieve happiness. *Maybe my problems are really spiritual, outside the realms of Western medicine, philosophy and science.*

It is surprising that more people don't kill themselves, I wrote in my journal. *Life is generally cut through with unpleasantness. Even in a wealthy developed society, I could have the most pampered lifestyle with nothing but free time and I still would find ways to be thoroughly unhappy. This is my special genius. My life is already unbelievably comfortable, and yet I don't enjoy most of it. I have a sense that my body is not really mine. It's itchy in a sense, constantly telling me it doesn't like to Be. I would do anything to be a happy person. Or at least that's what I tell myself. Maybe I look down on happiness as a sign of idiocy. As indicative of poor mental faculties and lack of philosophical sophistication. In the dark cave of my mind I harbor a certain disdain for other people that I would be ashamed to admit publicly. A kind of looking down upon others and especially myself for indulging in the weakness of wellbeing. These negative thoughts seem to happen against my will, independent of external circumstances. Wealth means little when you do not have ownership over the real estate of your own mind.*

Here I was, exhausting an outrageous quantity of raw will each morning to break my glassy stare from the ceiling and begin my tasks. I had tried many things to get myself back, taking SSRIs, exercising obsessively, or pretending I was in a play, acting as a happy person hoping one day the drama would make its way from the stage and into reality. My suicidal fantasies returned, and I would visualize, often for hours at a time, placing a .44 magnum pistol (or some other, equally massive handgun) to my head and pulling the trigger. I relished the visual of the bullet crushing the side of my skull, rampaging through brain tissue, before exiting the other side and turning my shitty brain into scattered cow pie.

I felt trapped in a maddening stasis by my addiction. Afraid that starting a company or pouring myself back into writing would trigger a relapse. Sobriety had become my main priority, as I learned it had to be. In December, a few times a week, I would drive to the sauna for thirty minutes, emulating the followers of a sect of Zen Buddhism who sit on the end of a spike to stay in the moment. A wall around every second. *One. One. One.* All I had to do was make it to the next one, watching the sweat drip off my forehead and onto the floor. In the sauna, I dropped out of my head and into my body. I could feel and process my emotions without getting stuck in thought loops disconnected from my actual experience. It was in the sauna that I first experienced the intimate connection between emotions and thoughts. Many thoughts, I discovered, appeared to be simply the cognitive discharge of a body sensation, not a statement of fact about my reality delivered from on high. But these insights could only take me so far. I usually left the sauna feeling better, but the old patterns would return within a few hours. And it was in this trapped feeling that I decided I only had one option left. To return to drugs. After nearly three years sober, sitting on my laptop in my parents basement while they prepared dinner, I gave in totally to despair. Here I was, days away from turning twenty-six, living once again at home as if I were still a child. The fund, the MFA, the book, everything that was supposed to bring success had failed, and I was right back where I started. It was an unbearable feeling, and it was in this feeling, just before my Mom called down with her familiar "Dean, dinner's ready!" that I went on the deep web and ordered a fresh shipment of Adderall and cocaine.

CHAPTER FORTY-TWO – DECEMBER 2021

The day after my 26th birthday, on December 13th, the shipment arrived. My parents left for a week to visit my maternal Grandfather who was undergoing cancer treatment.

"We'll be back a few days before Christmas!" My mom said, cheerfully, "have a good time honey and try not to burn the house down."

That morning, Jack emailed to tell me that the final six publishers had rejected God Money. The book, on which I had rested so many hopes, had hit a dead end.

But I didn't mind. I had in my hands the key to my future. After my parent's car disappeared from view on the gravel drive, I pulled out my phone and set a five-minute timer. I sat, package in hand, staring at the timer click towards zero. After five minutes, I could be reasonably sure my parents wouldn't return because they had forgotten something. When the timer went off I ripped open the package, greedily inspecting the contents. An eighth of an ounce of cocaine and thirty pills of Adderall. I started with cocaine. Sitting on a wooden chair in front of a wooden desk in the dark basement of my parents house, heavy rain pattering against the windows. I poured a line onto my phone and crushed it up. The sight of the prepared powder made me hesitate. Dimly I thought of the sobriety

I had fought every day for a thousand days to preserve. But the bright light of the memory of previous highs crowded out the rest, that glorious surge of energy that broke through sluggish patterns and delivered me to the heights of ambition and righteous action. Like a bungee jumper taking that final, definitive step off the edge, I took a deep breath and in a single, determined movement bent over my phone and sucked up the line. The rush, still so familiar to my nervous system, was like a nuclear detonation of confidence and enthusiasm–ushering out in an instant every insecurity, sense of failure and pain. I leaned back and savored the feeling, before lurching forward at the crystallization of a new insight– *God Money* the book had failed. But I could redeem myself by doing something even more impressive: I would make *God Money* the movie.

I spent the next two hours crafting an email to Jack, using the same power of language I had employed four and a half years earlier to launch the fund. "I can easily secure funding to make God Money a movie. My industry connections will be more than happy to fund a project that simultaneously promotes crypto and tells a heartrending story of greed and loss."

For the next two days I didn't sleep. I spoke to over a dozen potential investors–from the IoTeX founders to my former teammates at EtherMosaic. My drug-fueled enthusiasm was working–$500,000 in verbal commitments.

Jack called me, ecstatic.

"I read your email. Film production is my first love!" He practically shouted into the phone. "Here's the process. You and I will work on a proposal called a treatment for films. We use the treatment to get your investors to put up the first couple hundred grand which I can use to hire a professional screenwriter. I know the guy who wrote *Boiler Room* and he'd be perfect. I can probably get him to do it for

$85,000. Then we can use the script to get a director and actors on board. After that you can raise the rest of the $5 million we need to get the movie done."

I was in a frenzy. I called Emily and talked for ten minutes straight about my plans.

"That's so great," she said, after I finally lapsed into silence, "but it does seem like a pretty abrupt change. I thought you wanted to be a writer."

Annoyed, I yelled into the phone, "this is so much bigger than a book! The whole world will see this movie!"

She was quiet for a moment.

"How about I come out and see you, after Christmas?"

"Yes! I would love that, you can help me draft the proposal."

"Yeah, it would be so fun to work on a creative project together."

My enthusiasm picked back up.

"You know what? Let's go for a road trip! Before you have to go back to school we can go around the country for a couple weeks. It'll be great, nothing fuels creativity like being on the move!"

"Really? That sounds so fun! I can't wait."

A week later my body, exhausted from lack of sleep and heart-palpitating drug use, collapsed. The treatment that Jack mentioned, which at first seemed like the simplest thing in the world, the smallest creative effort for a huge reward, now felt insurmountable. When my parents came home I stopped using and rested for two days before restarting the cycle.

On Christmas eve I stayed up all night in my room, popping Adderall and ignoring my parents and brothers' requests to spend time together.

"You feeling okay?" My Mom asked, knocking at the door.

"Yeah, I'm okay Mom. Just working, I'm sorry."

"You sure you don't want to come out and watch a movie with us?"

"No, that's okay, you guys go ahead."

There was pain in my voice, the pain of drug use and frustration by the continued impossibility of writing the treatment. Jack had sent me several examples, but they all had culturally relevant storylines, a protagonist overcoming racism, a broken home or homophobia, that my story seemed to lack. The drugs, which had worked so well for a time in the financial world of numbers and bold claims, failed when faced with the emotional, almost spiritual task of storytelling. The day after Christmas I sent Jack a rambling, four-thousand-word document.

"I'm sorry Dean, but this just isn't even close," he wrote back, "it lacks heart. I added comments but really the entire thing needs to be re-written. Take as much time as you need."

Two days after Christmas, after refreshing my Adderall supply with a shipment from the deep web, I hit the road with Emily. We drove south to Sedona and then east to Texas. We stayed in hotels to avoid the freezing winter temperatures and I would stay up all night, popping Adderall in a miserable effort to write a meaningful treatment.

"Why don't you come to bed?" Emily asked, late one night.

"I can't, I'm working."

She sighed, rolled over and went back to sleep. I knew Emily noticed something was wrong, but I didn't care. The movie was everything. This was my last chance at redemption, at happiness itself.

During the long days in the car I was mostly silent, putting in my airpods and listening to music or comedy tapes, tense from the Adderall and lack of sleep. Emily, bubbly and effusive at first, grew more silent as the trip progressed.

"What's wrong?" she asked one day, "you're not talking to me and you just seem kind of moody all the time."

"It's this fucking treatment, I just can't seem to put it together. Nothing is coming to me."

"It'll come, just give it time."

On Adderall the part of myself that felt the warmth of Emily's presence and her love was layered over in an armor of rigid monomania. An emotional tradeoff that was increasingly meaningless in light of my frustrated creative efforts. Just looking at the treatment made me feel nauseous. Ten days into the trip we camped on the beach in South Padre Island in East Texas. Night had fallen when we arrived so we lit a fire and chatted, watching the shadows from the flames dance on the sand. The wind had died and the only sound besides our voices was the lap of the waves against the shore. Despite using Adderall during the day I felt strangely at peace.

"I'm off to bed," Emily said, "good night, love you."

"Good night, love you too," I said, smiling at her, before returning my gaze to the fire and lapsing into a pleasant reverie. My mind turned over to the treatment and I thought about the deeper purpose behind the film, and *God Money* in general. *To touch people's hearts,* I thought, *that's what it's all about. But how can I use Adderall, which clearly closes my own heart, to write something that touches the hearts of others?*

This idea struck me as incredibly profound and I felt myself becoming deeply moved. I reached into my bag and pulled out the zip-lock with the pills in them. I stared at the little orange discs with a growing disgust before I lurched to my feet and began walking towards the water. When I reached the water's edge, I pulled open the bag, reached in, grabbed a handful of pills, and launched them into the ocean. Then I turned the bag over and emptied the rest into the water.

"This whole thing was dumb," I told Emily the next morning, "I don't know why I thought I could make a stupid movie."

"It wasn't dumb, you were excited about it and important people were getting behind it! You really had, still have to be honest, a shot at making it happen."

"It just isn't what I actually want. I mean my heart isn't in it. It's just a big fucking ego trip to try to make myself feel better about the book not getting picked up."

"No, you're passionate about your story and you just wanted to find a way to get it out there. And just because a few publishers said no doesn't mean it's over. You can re-write it, you can work on another book. These things are hard and they take time."

I looked up at her smiling.

"I really love you, you know."

"I love you too."

I couldn't bring myself to tell Emily about my relapse. It had been a betrayal, using drugs right under her nose, and I worried she might not forgive me. But as we made our way back to my parents' house, my mood improved and I began to feel a profound sense of freedom.

"I think I'm gonna go on a long trip," I told Emily. "You're in school right now, and I feel like there's this huge amount of space that just opened up. Like I'm really done with *God Money* this time. At least for a while, maybe a year, maybe longer. The publishers were right, I am too close to the events. I need to clear my head."

"Where are you gonna go?"

"I think I want to go to Nepal. For a few months at least. And then, maybe, once the spring comes around I'll go to my property in New York."

"That sounds lovely, I'm so excited for you! You know the Buddha was born in Nepal."

"Really? You know I was thinking this might be like a spiritual pilgrimage for me, or something like that. I just wish you could come with me."

"I think it'll be good for you though, to do a solo trip. Especially somewhere kind of rogue like Southeast Asia."

"Maybe once you graduate you can come join me? Wherever I am at that point."

"Yeah, maybe! We'll talk about it when the time comes."

When we stopped for the night I booked a one-way flight to Kathmandu leaving in a week. The longer I stayed at home the more risk there was of a relapse. In Nepal it would be functionally impossible to use the deep web. In the Himalayas, if nothing else, I would find sobriety. And I hoped, with any luck, I might even find some happiness.

CHAPTER FORTY-THREE – EARLY FEBRUARY, 2022

I landed in Kathmandu and headed to a work exchange with a Nepalese family in the hill country. My mind and body were in a fragile state–rubbed raw by the harsh chemical sandblasting of stimulant use. At home, I slept early and long and would get tired after even minor exertion. After clearing customs I boarded a series of buses that ferried me through the dusty urban sprawl, stopping regularly to let a herd of goats or cows cross the street. The bus was crowded, standing room only, and I was constantly steadying myself so as not to hip-check the people jostling at my sides. In 2015, a magnitude 7.8 earthquake had leveled much of the capital, rebuilding had been slow. Many brick and stone buildings, red and yellow and gray and always dusty, stood with gaping holes in their roofs and sides, only partially rebuilt or given up entirely. Wood fires everywhere. Men and women squatting in the street rubbing hands over the flame or stirring a pot. The smog from the fires replaced the sky with a hazy incandescence. We passed people–usually men but some women too–sitting on the side of the street, skeletal and wan. I realized that they were starving. I had never seen a starving person before. A creepy, eerie sensation came over me. Like I wanted to both scream and bury myself deep underground.

But despite all this there was cheer on the bus and in the streets. Music poured from every angle, mostly shrill Hindi pop. The bus driver too had a speaker sitting to his right contributing to the din. Children everywhere–laughing and playing in the streets, and striped and spotted dogs running and slinking and sleeping alongside the livestock.

The journey was only forty miles but it took four hours. After a while we left the city and began to wind up swirling mountain roads. The air got fresher as we climbed and I pressed my face to the window to try to catch a glimpse of the Himalaya but it was too hazy. Finally I got let off in a small town and I asked several people if they knew where "Biru's house" was. Some people did and I was sent up a long winding gravel road, arriving at an even smaller village where I found a three-story concrete house painted hot pink. Biru, a man in his mid-30s who was plump and short but full of energy, came out and greeted me with a shout and a hug and I was introduced to his grandfather, parents, brothers, nephews and nieces. I couldn't tell how many people actually lived in the house, maybe eight or twelve.

They were farmers, Biru told me, in good English. Growing everything they ate. His parents and grandfather spoke no English but the younger people did.

For the next two days I mostly slept.

"No problem," Biru said, "you rest. It's too early to plant still, so there isn't much work." I came down for meal times and to chat. We ate Dhal Bhat–rice and lentils and spinach and spices for breakfast, lunch and dinner.

"Do you always eat Dhal Bhat?" I asked.

"Every day," Biru responded, "we never get tired of it."

They were practicing Hindus, and, in the spirit of my new sur-roundings I read *The Razor's Edge* and *Autobiography of a Yogi* in my room at night.

On the third morning I woke up before seven and doused my body in cold water (there was no water heater in the house) and when I stepped outside I took in my new surroundings for the first time. The farm was terraced, descending rapidly down a dark green mountainside overlooking the smog-covered morass of Kathmandu. But it was not tranquil. A great noise rose up from the streets and houses. And it was in the noise, so surprising in the otherwise bucolic landscape, that I grasped another big difference between Nepal and America. It wasn't the obvious wealth difference, which was immense–Nepal's per-capita GDP sitting at less than 2 percent of the U.S.'s. Instead, it was a physical experience, one I felt deep inside, reflected in the function and energy of the neighborhood. American neighborhoods, especially the suburbs of wealthy coastal cities, are quiet. At times the quiet seems peaceful, but it is also vaguely eerie. Large houses encase separate organisms, reaching out into the world through screens: working, ordering, entertaining, even dating, all inside the crude metaverse of the home. They can be fundamentally lonely things, suburbs. And the greater the separa-tion, the longer the driveway, the wider the lawn, the more desirable. Everyone wants a Versailles, but unlike Versailles, they do not receive a constant stream of official visitors, or many visitors at all. In Nepal, the neighborhoods, built on terraced hills, were alive–shouting children, scraping tools, animals, and the accordion honks of buses and motorbikes that filled the hills with festive blares. The Nepalese neighborhood in the town of Phaskot, where I was staying, was like a flock of songbirds in a tree. It was certainly not a utopia in every sense—instability and brutal poverty constituted the main facts of economic life. But happiness sprang forth from everyone I talked to. The hills of Phaskot bled good karma, it appeared. And the urgency to answer the question, "What will you do with your one wild and precious life?" was diluted by the promise of ten thousand future lives, until the anxiety of the inhabitants was swept away in an endless ocean of existence. I reflected on the many reasons in America, despite access to vast wealth, I had failed to find a stable happiness. But I began to see some possible reasons why.

Over the next few weeks, I pretended to help on the farm (I was mostly useless and there was no real work in early February) and explored the neighborhood. I offered to pay Biru $10 a day–more than three times the average daily wage in Nepal–for my lodging because of how little I was working.

"You're feeding me and I'm hardly lifting a finger."

He protested, but when I produced the crisp bills he accepted.

As the days passed I was increasingly disturbed by my recent relapse and lying to Emily. "I have to tell you something important. I'm pretty ashamed of it but I feel I need to be straight with you," I texted her. When we talked later that day I told her about ordering Adderall on the deep web and using it almost every day on our trip, explaining that that was the reason I had been staying up all night and why I must have seemed so distant and at times even rude.

There was a long silence after I finished speaking.

"I appreciate your honesty."

"Anything else?" I asked, heart beating fast.

"No, not really. I mean it hurts. It would have honestly been totally fine if it had been a one-time thing and you had just told me right away. But the fact that it was over several weeks, I mean you lied to me that whole time. That sucks. It's kind of a betrayal, but I do appreciate your honesty."

"I understand that, I can't express to you how sorry I am. I really wasn't in my right mind, I mean the movie thing was so stupid. It was like this crazy obsession that took hold of me."

She was quiet for a long time again, then: "Yeah it just... it just sucks that you prioritized that to the point that you were using drugs and lying to me."

I gripped the phone tighter as I fought to steady my voice, which, I worried, was starting to sound pleading.

"I know. I mean that's really why I came out here. To try to figure out why I do things that I like. Why I'm so compulsive and do so many things to hurt myself and those I love, there's a lot of healing and work I need to do. I know that. I'm sorry."

She sighed.

"I respect that, and I really am proud of you for going. I mean, it's going to be okay. I can forgive you, I think, I'm just gonna need some time. And I'm just so busy it's hard to process things you know, and this one's gonna take some processing."

"That makes sense. Do you want to take time off from talking?"

"I don't know. No, I don't think so. Let's still talk, I'm not, like, breaking up with you or anything."

"That's good," I said, laughing awkwardly.

"Okay, well I gotta get back studying."

"Okay."

"Yeah, talk to you later."

"Bye."

She hung up. I sat in my room in stunned silence. It had gone reasonably well, we hadn't broken up. But something in her voice, a dark bitterness, hinted that this had not been a harmless mistake patched over by a noble confession. That I had done something irrevocably bad, and that, at least for now, I was powerless to make it right.

CHAPTER FORTY-FOUR – LATE FEBRUARY, 2022

After three and half weeks with Biru's family I moved on to Pokhara, the second largest city in Nepal and the basecamp for the Himalayas. I was set on hiking the Annapurna circuit, a popular three-week trek around the Annapurna massif culminating in a crossing of Thorong La pass at 17,769 feet. I wanted solitude, and with heavy snow still falling above ten thousand feet along with the added deterrent of COVID, I expected to find it.

I texted Emily from the bus to Pokhara–"Leaving in a couple days for the mountains, might not be able to talk much for a couple weeks–cell service will be spotty."

She didn't respond.

As soon as I arrived in Pokhara I went to a trekking company to hire a guide. His name was Krsna, and we met up the next day to board a bus to the trailhead.

His appearance suggested he was late middle-aged, quite frail, equipped with ratty tennis shoes and a backpack no larger than a school child's. His small pack made me self-conscious about my seventy-liters filled with North Face gear and my goose-down sleeping bag.

On the third night, after about twelve miles of trekking we stopped at a small hotel in a village around 6,000 feet. The room was roughly five by ten with exposed plywood walls and a single-size mattress. Luxurious compared to tent camping. After dropping my pack I went outside and discovered I had a neighbor. Apparently a Nepali man with a long, greying beard, smoking a cigarette and muttering softly to himself. I studied him for a moment and, probably sensing he was being watched, he turned and met my gaze. His eyes stunned me. They were bright blue, and burned with a ferocious intelligence that cut right to my core. He said nothing, but his smile, which lit up his face when he saw my awed expression, was so warm and inviting that I instinctively took a step towards him.

"I'm Dean," I said, holding out my hand. He let my hand hang, bowing and saying softly in good English "my name is Sumar."

"Are you here on a trek?" I asked, dropping my hand.

He laughed. An unusual laugh that started deep in his belly, rolling up his torso and shaking his whole body in childlike delight.

"Me? No. I am a Sadhu. I am searching for truth."

"For truth? What do you mean by that?"

He shook his head, his expression growing suddenly grim.

"It's too much to explain right now. Let's talk after dinner."

That night at eight, after finishing my Dal Bhat, I wandered through the tiny village. Two children played with a fraying soccer ball under a single streetlamp. Because of the hills, there was no light pollution, and only a few sprinkles of light betrayed a couple of tiny villages twinkling on the horizon. I couldn't keep my mind off Sumar, his eyes and his obscure way of talking. When I returned, I spotted him standing in front of the kitchen–he waved me over.

"Still want to talk?" He asked.

"Of course."

"Come to my room, we can talk better there."

We sat on his bed, and he offered me a joint. I took it.

"You will understand me better if you smoke this," he said, laughing heartily.

"Do you smoke every day?"

"Every day. My body wakes me up around four, and I sit upright as if lightning had struck me. Then I sit in meditation for the next eighteen hours, with only short breaks to stretch or go to the bathroom."

"That's quite a serious schedule."

"That's why I smoke all day long," he said, laughing again.

By US standards, I reflected, he was a stoner wasting away in a cloud of weed smoke. But here in Nepal, he was a Sadhu, a holy man. Socially accepted and even revered. I asked how he supported his lifestyle.

"When I was working, I managed to save about 1.2 million rupees, which I think is around $15,000. I live off the interest, about $500 a year. I eat only one meal a day and buy my weed in bulk. The dealers give me a big discount, about seventy-five percent off the normal price. They call it the 'Sadhu discount.'"

I laughed, explaining to Sumar how absurd it would be in the US for weed dealers to offer steep discounts to people who claimed to be holy men.

"Yes, I understand in the US you don't have this idea of a Sadhu."

"No. We have TikTok stars but no Sadhus," I said, smiling, "so tell me, why do you meditate so much?"

"One day, when I was still working in the city, I was meditating when my reality broke apart. I discovered a new reality, a more real one, where my experience was only bliss. I met God, if you understand me. Now, when I meditate, I spend all day with God. If I did not have to sleep I wouldn't, because it takes me away from Him."

Having just read the *Bhagavad Gita*, I told him I knew, intellectually at least, what he was referring to. The Hindu notion of "maya" or illusion refers to the false physical reality we mistakenly accept as true. Brahma, or god, is the metaphysical substrata, a kind of soul-innervating energy that pervades all beings but is invisible to them as long as they are wholly consumed by their bodies' senses and desires. It was an idea that had astounded and seduced me. It was so relieving to discover that this world where I was a depressed drug addict might only be an illusion.

"Ah so you understand me perfectly then," Sumar said, when I finished my diatribe.

"Not exactly. I mean I can explain it fine, but do I really understand? I doubt it."

He nodded, "yes, sometimes I feel this way too. That's why I call myself a seeker."

"So you don't think you've found exactly what you're looking for then?"

His expression grew grave.

"No. Even though I feel I am with Him, I feel also that there is a place beyond that one. Where I become Him, where I am Him. That is the truth I want to find."

"What will you do if you find that place, where you become God?"

He looked at me seriously.

"Do you know what a Bodhisattva is?"

"No."

"A Bodhisattva is an enlightened being, one who has become Him," he pointed up to the sky at the word 'Him,' "who comes back to the realm of illusion to bring others into truth. I suppose I would become like that. One of those great beings."

"And what if you never reach ultimate truth?" I asked.

He shrugged, then, looking at me with a sincerity that seemed to me to be absolute, he said "in that case it was not meant for me in this life." I noticed in his eyes a gleam of serenity at his words, as if to say *it doesn't matter to me one bit if I really achieve my goal, what matters is that I am on the right path.*

I could have talked to Sumar all night, but Krnsa shouted something in Nepali from the next room, and Sumar told me he was yelling at us to go to sleep. I nodded, thanked Sumar for his time and went off to bed.

A week into the trek we arrived in Manang at 10,500 feet, the final supply outpost before Thorong La pass. We spent two nights there to acclimate and on the second night Emily finally responded to me.

"Hope you enjoy the hike!"

It was a terse reply, and I read all kinds of terrible conclusions into it. She must have found a guy at Yale, probably a six-five rower or lacrosse player from a rich family. A nice, healthy young man perfumed with success, much more fun at a party, and most importantly not a drug addict.

But after we left Manang and hiked towards the summit, my worries about Emily receded into the background. The dropping temperatures and the hip-deep snow had snapped my awareness back into the body. I focused only on the next step. Two days later we arrived at the final base camp at 15,000 feet. As night fell the sky cleared and temperatures plummeted to below -20 celsius, or around -5 fahrenheit. I piled blankets on top of my sleeping bag to try to stay warm in my unheated room. Finally, after midnight, I fell into a fitful sleep. At 4:30, we broke camp and started up the mountain. A recent blizzard had covered up the path leading up to the pass.

But as dawn broke and we reached the top of the pass I was overwhelmed with bliss. That night, I wrote about the experience in my journal: *As we hiked over the Thorong La pass I felt full of sweetness and accomplishment mixed with the nostalgia for the end of this life-fulfilling journey. I will never forget this day, already ten years lived before the afternoon, I could have cried if I had had the energy. My heart was full of love. Forgive me for not wanting to let go of something already gone. I wanted it to stay yet I knew I would never feel this way again, not exactly anyway, in some other form perhaps, if I'm lucky. Each hiker's smile was so genuine, so pure, so full of love. It was not put on, but infused with an authenticity so rare.*

Lyme disease has been incredibly humbling for me. I did not even feel the tick bite into me, and its effects lay me in bed for an entire month. It gave me a newfound appreciation for the fragility of virility. The capacity and energy to MOVE is fickle. It made me realize the profundity of the usually trite statement that we have so little control over our own existence. The only free will we have perhaps, if one can call it free will, is to move closer to God. Embracing, on a deeply experiential level, the fragility of existence. We are like a daisy whose pedals can be blown off with a single gust of wind. But every winter has its spring, and it is a sad flower that hangs tight to its pedals after its color is gone. Let them fly away with the wind, and in a short time the buds of new growth will form and you will stand the brighter for it. The crossing of Thorong La was a validation that my winter was over, spring had come.

I texted my mom a photo of me at the top of Thorong La and she responded:

"It makes me so happy to see you so happy. It's been a long time since I've seen you smile like that :)"

CHAPTER FORTY-FIVE -
MARCH, 2022

I said goodbye to Krnsa and stayed alone in Muktinath for several days to try my hand at meditation. I booked a room in a hotel, which was free as long as you bought a daily meal from their kitchen–and spent my days sitting cross-legged doing my utmost to let the outside silence overtake the noise in my head. Periodically I would walk outside and look towards Thorong La, trying to hold on to the fading high of the crossing.

My text describing my conquest of the pass had elicited no response from Emily for two days and in the long hours of solitude the peace I had hoped to cultivate gave way to ruminating frustration that at times bubbled over into rage. In a rush of resentment I sent her an aggrieved text.

"It's crazy to me that you can't even take thirty seconds every couple days to write me a text... Do you even care about me anymore?"

A day later I received an hour and a half voice note. At first her words were inscrutable and then, as I listened, heartbreaking.

She began by detailing a series of sexual traumas and betrayals from boys in middle school through her time in college. Before meeting me, she continued, she had become fundamentally skeptical about forming a deep bond with any man. With me, she said, she had regained hope as her trust grew, but lying about my Adderall use had reopened old wounds.

My mind was reeling with a mix of sympathy and indignation and I mentally prepared a series of logical arguments for why she should stay with me. *If I could only speak to her directly I could get her to see my point of view*, I told myself, over and over. Finally I got her on FaceTime.

"Drug use isn't sexual assault." I began, "I never violated you physically; why are you comparing the two?"

"It's an issue of trust," she said, "it's still a violation."

"But it was hurtful to myself more than anything. It was about me; it had nothing to do with you."

"How can you say it had nothing to do with me? Isn't that the whole problem, that you weren't thinking of me?"

"But I was thinking of you. That's why it was so painful for me, and why I told you about it as soon as I really faced up to what I had done. You even said it would be okay, but now you're acting like you want to break up."

She was silent for a moment.

"I know, and I'm really sorry about that. I have this tendency to avoid hard confrontations. To just pretend that everything is okay to avoid hurting people. I wasn't really sure how I felt in the moment to be honest, and I think I wanted it to be okay when it really wasn't."

I fell silent. Looking at her face through my phone, I felt a void grow between us, as if I was talking to a stranger.

"I'm going to need time to heal," she continued, "I think we should take a week break from talking and then we can figure out where we stand."

After we hung up, I was in a state of fear and bewilderment, and, throwing meditation to the wind, I decided to return to Kathmandu to distract myself.

Within a day of returning to the capital I was wandering around the tourist district of Thamel, feeling sorry for myself, when a Nepali man, who looked to be in his mid-20s, sidled up next to me and began speaking rapidly in English.

"Hello sir, it's a pleasure to meet you, my name is Sonu and I work for a painting school. Would you like to come with me and meet the children?"

Probably a racket, I thought, not breaking stride. I was in a bad mood, and wanted to be left alone.

"No thank you," I said, not looking down.

With lurid scenes of real depravity and poverty, visiting Westerners with any tenderness in their heart are ready to open their wallets in response to the immense material suffering around them. Even a relatively small amount of money, a few hundred dollars, can be life-changing in a country where the per-capita GDP is only little more than a thousand dollars a year. But scam artists are known for convincing tourists to wire money to "orphanages," only to have the money directed to their personal accounts.

"But sir," Sonu persisted, "these are not normal paintings. They are spiritual, depicting great Bodhisattvas and Hindu mystics."

At his words the memory of Sumar returned to me and I stopped short, looking down at the stranger. He was much shorter than me, but was well-built with a bright face and a body that was palpitating with vitality. His eyes were pleading and warm, and I saw in them an earnestness that I hadn't expected. I had nothing better to do anyway, I decided, agreeing to follow him.

When we arrived at the painting school the last of my defenses melted away. Children crowded around me, proudly showing off their work, colorful acrylic depictions of Buddhas and Hindu gods with hell realms and pure lands intermixed around them. I was impressed by the fine craftsmanship that went into the better works and spent around 30,000 rupees, or around $250, on a painting by a "master student" and shipped it off to Emily. *If nothing else this will show her I still care about her*, I thought, feeling a mixture of ruefulness and real tenderness.

As we walked out, Sonu thanked me profusely.

"Please, let me show you my home in the slums," he said, evidently not wanting to let me go, "this is the real Kathmandu that most tourists never see. On our way we will walk through the oldest street market in Nepal, most tourists never go there also, but I will show you!"

I let him lead me on the "five-minute walk," which turned out to be almost an hour. Sonu had a habit of vastly underestimating the time it took to reach destinations. This was all the more exasperating because he walked so quickly that I had to periodically break out into a light jog to keep up. In the street market, I bought a bag of ashwagandha powder while Sonu blasted me with a speech about the sights in Kathmandu, which was so rapid and efficient that it was apparent he had given it hundreds of times before.

Finally we arrived in the slums. They were, in a word, compact. Consisting of long, winding blocks of two-room cells completely infested with flies. Wafered aluminum sheets served as the only meager insulation from the harsh Kathmandu winters. Reaching Sonu's home required navigating a labyrinth of gates and alleyways: "There is a rich woman who owns our neighborhood," he told me as we walked, "we are six months late on rent, but she has not removed us. No one is paying rent anymore because COVID killed the tourist trade. Now we can't think about finding money for rent, we only think about our dinner." We turned a sharp corner and Sonu cried with delight as he picked up a young boy who had run to him. He must have been no more than two years old and wore no pants. Sonu swung him around in his arms and tickled his penis, which I thought was odd.

"This is my nephew," he declared. Sonu's neighborhood was like a human jungle. There were no animals, because there was no space for animals. But there was music and dancing, adults and children running around by the dozen. There were infants and toddlers everywhere, running and crawling in the dirt, most were completely naked.

As I looked around, I noticed one of the older men staring at me. "Look at this privileged Westerner coming into our slums," I assumed he must be thinking. But then the man began to cry.

"Why is he crying?" I asked Sonu. He went up to the man and spoke to him for a moment before returning to me–"he says you remind him of himself when he was a young man. He is crying because of the sweet memories of his youth."

A group of guys around my age crowded around me, "my friends!" Sonu announced joyfully. I complimented one of their t-shirts, a multi-layered cotton patchwork, and he ripped it off and handed it to me. I shook my head, "I can't take your shirt." Sonu looked at me horrified, "you must take it! And give him yours in return."

I nodded, took off my shirt with the Liquid Freedom logo, and handed it to him. I thought of the strange twists of fate that had led a young man living in the slums of Kathmandu to come into possession of a T-shirt featuring the logo of an obscure cryptocurrency startup.

A woman prepared our dinner over a wood fire.

"What is she making?" I asked Sonu.

"Dhal Bhat."

"Of course, why did I even ask?" I responded, laughing.

When it was ready, the woman served me in a wooden bowl and Sonu ushered me into the backroom of the house.

"For your dinner," he said, in a whisper, producing three small pieces of chicken from an iron pot. He glanced over my shoulder to make sure no one was watching as he dropped them in. "We reserve meat only for very special occasions."

I began to protest but I saw in his eyes that it would humiliate him to refuse. The meal was the best I had in Nepal. The spices of the Dhal were extraordinary and I thanked him effusively.

"I should probably be getting back to my hostel," I said, as I finished my meal.

Sonu shook his head, "no no you are my guest. You will sleep here with me."

He ran into the back room before I could protest and returned with a yoga mat, which he rolled onto the living room's dirt floor.

"This is the men's room; we will sleep next to each other." As we prepared for sleep at least a dozen other men packed into the space, shoulder to shoulder, with no more than six inches between us. Sonu was beside himself with excitement.

"An American my friends!" He shouted to the group, "sleeping with us tonight, think of it!" He bellowed with laughter and many of the others laughed also. I smiled, feeling embarrassed but happy.

A couple hours after we all fell asleep someone farted so loudly I woke up. A general conversation and fits of laughter broke out that lasted for almost twenty minutes before a consensus decision, inscrutably achieved, sent us all back to sleep. This process was repeated every couple of hours, a fart or a shout would wake us all up and conversation would ensue and then break apart again and we all fell quiet.

I woke up to Sonu shaking me.

"What time is it?"

"About five am. We rise early in the slums."

I blinked my eyes open, he looked fresh as if he had been up for hours.

"Please, there is no time to waste, we have a big day ahead of us." For the next nine hours I let Sonu lead me on a whirlwind tour of Kathmandu. He noticed my interest in the "babas," another word for "Sadhu," who lived on the streets.

"You must meet the Aghori Babas," he declared.

"What are those?"

"They live on the remains of the dead."

He took me to a cemetery where a few men, dressed only in loin-cloths despite the cold March weather, sat in a semicircle smoking out of a large pipe.

"You see their faces?" Sonu asked, "they smear themselves with the cremated remains of the dead. Many of them are attacked by the families of the dead, because they eat their bodies." I studied the men with a mixture of awe and disgust. Then one of them turned and smiled at me, he had eyes like a demon.

"Let's get out of here," I said.

That evening I said goodbye to Sonu. Gifting him my Apple Watch and all the cash I had on hand, close to 20,000 rupees, or around $170, to help him with expenses.

"May god bless you," he said.

I returned to my Hostel in Thamel with a full heart and spent the rest of the week wandering the streets and writing long journal entries. Finally the time came for Emily and I to speak again.

An icy shiver ran through me as I pressed the call button and waited for her to answer. But as she picked up, a calmness spread over me, and I listened with equanimity to her soft voice, which I also sensed was full of resolve.

"Hey, how are you?"

"I'm good." My mind was full of stories I wanted to tell her. About my adventures with Sonu and the pass but I knew now wasn't the time. I bit my tongue and focused. "So, how are you feeling after this week? Have you made up your mind about... us?"

"Listen, I care about you so much," she began, "I just want to start with that. But, to be honest, school is so hard. It's taking everything I have to finish my degree, and I just don't think I have the emotional space to continue a relationship. So I think at the very least we should take a break until I graduate. And then, maybe once that's over, we can see what happens. But for now I just can't do this Dean."

To my surprise, a warmth spread from my belly up into my chest. I realized it was pride. Pride in Emily for taking a stand and saying what she really felt, even if it was hard. And I also heard in her voice a conflicted conscience. She was, understandably, emotionally overwhelmed. But, I hoped, with time and space she would come to see that what we had was too good, too powerful, to give up forever.

"I understand. And honestly, I'm proud of you. Proud of you for saying what you really feel, and taking space when you need it. I'm so sorry, again, for what I did, and I also care about you so much. But to be honest, it's going to be too hard to resist the temptation to text you. Let's block each other's numbers. And then, on graduation day, unblock me."

"Okay, goodbye, Dean."

"I'll call you right when they hand you the diploma," I said, laughing.

We hung up and I sat in silence. I felt, for once, clarity. And as I continued to sit a blazing energy formed in my heart in response to that clarity. My property, my Walden Pond, was my next destination. I would work with my hands, connect deeply with the land and confront, in Thoreau's words, the essential facts of life.

I booked a flight home, ending my trip. Awash with activation energy from the breakup, there was, it seemed, no time to waste. I had gotten what I came for. In Nepal I had dried out—my sobriety felt stable once again. Sumar had shown me the bliss one can find in solitude. And the hike had revealed the clearness of mind and heart that I could find in the outdoors.

In my mind's eye I imagined the property as a spiritual oasis, a playground of self-development, free from the strictures of urban society and insulated from the psychologically corrosive forces of modern hustle culture. There I would find peace. Constructing a life that cost little, thereby removing the tremendous pressure to make money. With financial pressures thus reduced, I could explore my inner world undisturbed. But I sensed, dimly, that I also wanted an escape. A challenge so far outside my comfort zone that it would distract me from the emotional pain of losing Emily and the creative pain of my unsold book.

With these mixed and, at times, contradictory emotions swirling around in my all-too-human heart, I boarded the flight home.

CHAPTER FORTY-SIX – APRIL 2022

Back home at my parents' house. My base of stability and support to which, at twenty-six, my life still seemed irrevocably anchored. But soon I would have a new base, built with my own hands according to my whims. Once again, I packed my life into the Sienna and readied myself for the long drive. Reinventing myself for what seemed like the fifth time in as many years.

"This is your second midlife crisis and you're only twenty-six," my mom joked as I loaded up the car.

"Only second?" I answered, smiling.

But as I was about to leave she grew more serious. Standing by the door, final bag in hand, she pulled me aside for a parting speech.

"Dean, you know I just have to say, you have such a rare expertise in the crypto industry and I can't help but feel that you are throwing away your best chance of financial freedom at a young age. Not everybody in their mid-20s has the skills you have, and the ability to earn a six-figure salary in a growing industry. I just want you to consider what you're giving up. With compound interest and everything, it's really a fortune in the long run that you are sacrificing."

I set down my bag and l looked at her with sadness, my eyes welling with tears as she spoke.

"You don't understand," I said, shaking my head, "it doesn't feel like I have a choice. Practically everyone I went to school with is like that. Working a good job, stacking savings, some might already be millionaires, who knows. Five years ago I was the best of them, I had a fund, I was going to be rich before I turned twenty-five. But here I am. I'm..." my voice began to break, "I'm an addict, Mom. I'm a drug addict. And it feels like if I worked that kind of job, I would relapse."

She looked down.

"Yes I... I don't think I realized. I'm sorry. You're doing your best, and what's right for you, I understand that."

We hugged and a moment later I was behind the wheel, feeling the crunch of the gravel beneath me as I pulled out of the driveway, sensing a strange nostalgia for a moment that had not yet passed. A bittersweet intuition that this was one of those defining moments in the arc of my life. The last glimpse, perhaps, of adolescence.

It took me nine days to reach the property. Sleeping in Walmart parking lots or camping in National Forests to save money. I gutted the backseat of the Sienna, replacing the seats with a twin bed and a cooking station and paying for gas and food with TikTok sponsorships and the occasional, ghost-written article on crypto.

Three days into the drive I stopped for the night at the Walmart in Missoula. My mom's words rattled around my brain, and, as I covered the windows with smelly T-shirts to block out the bright industrial lights illuminating the parking lot, a depressing thought struck me: *I'm a complete fucking loser.* I recalled my now shattered self-image of someone on an escalator heading inexorably into the

American upper class. Redirected by addiction and depression, I had been forced to go inward, to embark on a spiritual path to investigate the root causes of my self-destructive compulsions and avoid slipping back into the hell of active addiction. But at what cost? I was on track to end up far worse financially than my parents. Maybe addiction had been worth it if it meant I could still hold on to the chimera of success. Now I felt like a loser, a detached amoeba, bereft of purpose, having thrown away my propitious education and upbringing. Staring not even mediocrity in the face, but outright destitution. *But still, I'm only twenty-six, I have my whole life ahead of me.* This was a thought, mostly ineffective, I often employed to fend off the gnawing anxiety of a wasted life.

I sat upright, leaning my back against the backside of the driver's seat, ruminating. After an hour my dark thoughts seemed to subside, and a new thought emerged that restored some hope. Even though I felt like a loser, I was sober. Bravely facing all the uncomfortable emotions that I had previously kept away with a chemical HAZMAT. And I took some extra solace in the idea that these feelings of insecurity and my profound sense of personal deficiency were not meaningless. They were teaching me compassion. After four years of on-and-off sobriety I had come to understand myself better, and through that understanding had become a better friend to myself. Not a perfect friend, but at least a present one. And that was perhaps the greatest accomplishment of my life so far.

CHAPTER FORTY-SEVEN - MAY 2022

When I first drove up to the property, my stomach dropped. *This can't be it*, I thought. It was completely overgrown, and the promised driveway was nowhere to be seen. It was a wasteland—dead Ash trees everywhere, killed by blight, freeing the sunlight to supercharge the wild underbrush that made everything but the property's periphery inaccessible. A jungle of blackberries and raspberries and poison ivy which climbed the dead trees and hung over the property, dropping seeds, mocking in their superiority. But I was bubbling with energy and my initial disappointment turned to resolve. I took the few old tools my dad had gifted me—a pair of clippers and a rusty shovel and rake, and began attacking the rectangular strip of brush that appeared to constitute the old driveway.

It was early May when I arrived, and recently melted snow turned the freshly cleared ground to mud. The first day I made enough space to park my van. After ten days, I had opened up the driveway two hundred feet back to a clearing where I decided I would build my cabin. I moved my base to the clearing—setting up a tent and canopy, surveying the property with delight. Boundless life came forth in the rising crescendo of spring. I had worried the property would seem lifeless because so many of the larger trees were dead. But their open canopies and deteriorating wood were a haven for woodpeckers and songbirds, who flocked to the property in droves, announcing dawn with a manifold symphony. I recalled how I used to wince at the sounds of the birds. Their songs signaling the start of a painful withdrawal after a long night of binging. Now it was pure music.

Every day I discovered some new charm. A maple sapling or a flowering dogwood. The grass seemed to grow an inch a day, it was insatiable, the life that had so recently been starved of sunlight in the deep snow. One day I stumbled upon three small ponds harboring hundreds of tadpoles. Then the ponds dried up at the exact moment they turned into frogs, hopping all over the property and bringing a hundred smiles to my face. Before long I realized I was falling in love with the property. It was like having a child, everything it did delighted me. Some new sprout would catch my eye, and I would stop for several minutes to examine it. It felt like the whole universe was packed into these 2.2 acres, and each day I discovered a new planet. Then the fireflies came. They were perhaps my greatest delight. As night fell over the property thousands of blinking green and yellow bugs bounced around the meadow, the stars of the Milky Way brought down to earth.

Some people go their whole lives without seeing the blue sky, I wrote in my journal one night. *They never see it. Not even once. I lived over two decades without really seeing it. Our eyes glaze over. What's wrong? Nothing really. Just busy. Busy with the day. Distracted by life. Caught up in anxious thoughts, fog for the senses. Never forget. Never forget that beauty awaits you at every single moment. Yes even on an overcast night. The moon peeks through. It's there waiting.*

The property was a mile from the Erie Canal, and so in the afternoons I would take walks along the water, listening to lectures by the Buddhist master Thich Nhat Hanh. He taught a lesson of simple happiness: "Every mindful breath is a moment of enlightenment. Every step taken with attention is an enlightened step." In my solitude, his teachings began to penetrate into my subconscious and down into my nervous system. A source of calm, I would return to his words when my mind became overwhelmed by the great task ahead of me. I didn't have a clue how to build a cabin. I had less than $10,000 left, which had to cover tools and materials as well as food. There was also the problem of electricity. I used some of my precious funds for a generator and solar panels, relying on the outlets in the local library to charge up in the meantime.

As the days turned into weeks the work, so liberating and expansive at first, began to feel, at times, like drudgery. The prospect of months and years of the same made me afraid. The fast-growing grass, initially awe-inspiring, became a burden. Another task to complete to keep the property habitable. And then loneliness. At night my thoughts turned to Emily. It was always the same routine: as darkness fell I sat down in the grassy meadow under the stars to meditate. But my mind would be a fury of activity and I would rise after only a few minutes, opening YouTube to a talk by Tich Nhat Hanh, telling myself I needed more teaching before I could begin the practice. I would think of Emily. *If only she were here, I wouldn't feel so distracted.* In these dark and lonely nights, I had a feeling, or at least a hope, that she felt the same way. It was now late May; I checked online to confirm the last finals were over–graduation now just days away. I unblocked her number and sent a text. It didn't go through. *I'm still blocked*, I thought, then: *what if she never unblocks me?*

I paced around the property, considering what to do. She may have decided to move on completely, another guy perhaps. But I had changed. I felt calmer, more grounded, totally committed to my spiritual development. If only I could see her, show her who I was becoming. I opened Google Maps and found that New Haven was only a six hour drive away. I could do that in an afternoon.

Tomorrow afternoon, to be exact. I had her address, I would show up and present myself, accepting totally her reaction, good or ill.

The next day I set off eastbound on I-90. With each passing exit the ball of nerves in my stomach grew tighter and by the time I arrived in New Haven I felt like screaming. I pulled over once I got off the highway, closing my eyes and following my breath. I recovered somewhat and continued the drive to her neighborhood. I parked my car askew, and picked a bundle of Lilac's from someone's yard, feeling proud of myself for being so romantic, wandering up and down Edwards Street hoping that I would run into her. To meet her on the street would save me the embarrassment of ringing her doorbell and having her roommate answer. No sign of her. I tried to work up the nerve to ring her doorbell, I would do that soon, I decided. Then, a thought: *She might be at East Rock*, a large park on the edge of campus that she had talked about often. "I go there almost every evening," she had said. *At East Rock, I thought*, not at home. *Ring, ask, and go to East Rock*. I walked up to her door, Lilacs in hand, heart pounding, and rang once, twice. Nervous. *Maybe she's moved out already*. Finally I rang a third time. Nothing. Not even a roommate. I dropped the Lilacs on her front porch and drove to the park.

I'm literally a stalker, I thought, as I drove. Nobody seemed to pay me much notice. Stalking did not appear to register on their radar of possible motives for driving a motor vehicle. I entered East Rock and sent her an email, "Hey, I'm in New Haven, are you around?" I checked it every two minutes. No response. Damn, East Rock was gorgeous. It was raining. It was pouring, and I was soaked. *Emily, here I come*. Night was falling and the park was huge—over 400 acres—she could be anywhere. I climbed to a war monument that sits at the highest point in East Rock. I was officially a stalker. No other way to put it. Driving six hours without telling her I was coming and then wandering around her neighborhood. When I got to the top there was no Emily, just rain. I drove back to her street, parking a few doors down, DMing her brother, John, on Instagram and a couple of her Yale friends. No cigar. Finally I gave up, checking into a hotel nearby.

Then, around one in the morning, I got a response from Emily.

"Oh my gosh, I had no idea you were coming! John just texted me. I was out at East Rock on mushrooms and I just got home. I'm free tomorrow. Let's meet up!"

The next afternoon, I sat at the Yale green waiting to meet Emily. The sound of students laughing mixed with the spring sun and soft breeze and I felt happy. I reminisced about the week leading up to my own graduation; full of bright hopes and the satisfaction of accomplishment. Then I saw Emily appear out of the crowd, walking towards me. I wanted to leap up and ask her to get back together with me but I checked myself–I had to get a sense of how she was feeling before pushing my agenda onto her.

"It's so great to see you!" I said, standing up to hug her.

"Great to see you too," she said.

She was friendly, but I sensed her cautiousness, sizing me up. I played it cool, casually asking her about her life. She told me about the stresses of school, how completely the effort to finish her coursework had consumed her, and how difficult it had been to stay grounded through it all. I listened, trying to read through the lines. As far as I could tell she had spent the last four months entirely dedicated to finishing school. No time for other guys, thank god. I told her about the property. About the birds and the frogs, the driveway I had cleared and the cabin I would build.

"It sounds so beautiful!" she said. "I relate to what you're saying so much. I feel like East Rock has been for me what your property has been for you. I can't tell you how busy I have been with school. I haven't had a chance to catch my breath. But I went to East Rock almost every night when I wasn't cramming. It was like the only place I could be myself, where I wasn't lost in old ideas of myself, or ideas that I had to be this successful, popular Yalee."

The property can be your East Rock, I thought, but out loud I asked if she wanted to walk to East Rock.

"I would love that," she said.

As we walked, I told her about my commitment to spirituality, and how I was listening to Thich Nhat Hanh almost every day. She shared insights from her meditation practice and the deep relationship she had developed with the forest. As we talked, I sensed a glibness in our speech that papered over the deeper feelings we seemed to share. When we arrived in East Rock our conversation trailed off. We had run out of friendly pretense, the time had come to face the elephant.

"Do you want to sit down?" I asked, my voice shaking slightly as I pointed to a large rock next to the river.

"Listen," I began, as we took our seats, "I'm sorry for not being the best partner to you. I have a lot of healing left to do from my addiction, and I think being at the property is exactly where I need to be to do that healing."

"It's not all your fault. I have been so stressed this year," she said. "And to be honest, I was never fully convinced the breakup was the best thing. My friend Jacob came to visit right after we broke up. He told me that when he broke up with his girlfriend, he was one hundred percent sure it was the right decision. When he told me that, I realized that I wasn't sure. I have never been sure. I literally just finished finals two days ago, and so I haven't had the time to really think about it. But when I heard you were here yesterday, I had last night to really sit with the possibility of us getting back together."

"And?"

"And it felt right."

I put my arm around her, and she leaned into me. We continued talking before rising to head up the mountain. We arrived at the monument as the sun was setting, Emily turned to me and kissed me.

"I want to come stay with you at the property."

"I would like that."

"I'm going to go home and decompress at my parents' house for a month or so. But then I'll come stay with you in early July."

"Okay. Whatever you want," I said, smiling like an idiot at the orange sky.

CHAPTER FORTY-EIGHT
– JUNE 2022

I had a few weeks before Emily would arrive, time I spent poisoning poison ivy, cutting dead trees, planting new trees, and planning the cabin's construction. I called the local code officer, Karen, who offered to come out and walk the property. She pulled up in an early 2000s Dodge Caravan and stepped out with a bristle in her step and a scowl on her face. She was probably in her early 50s and wore a flannel shirt with cargo pants. Her brown hair was pulled back in a tight ponytail, and her eyebrows appeared permanently knitted together based on the thick crease dividing them.

"Wow this is a piece of shit," she said, scanning the property from the road, "how much did you pay for it?"

"$15,000."

She shrugged, "well anyway, that's a good deal. Your little slice of paradise." She chuckled, "so what do you want to do with it?"

"I want to build a cabin, or a tiny home."

She looked at me warily, "don't tell me you're another one of these hippies. We've had a lot of young people coming out here wanting to live off-grid and shit in the woods. You can't live in a cabin in Orleans County, you just can't."

"Why not?"

"First of all, the minimum house size is 900 square feet."

"Are there any exceptions?"

"No exceptions."

"Okay, are there any other requirements?"

"Septic, of course. Which I'm guessing is going to run you around twenty thousand, fifteen if you're lucky. And then you'll probably want to run electric which will cost you another few thousand."

"Thank you," I said.

I watched her drive away, shaking her head. She hadn't bothered to walk the property.

The sun was beating down and I suddenly felt very hot. I swatted at a fly buzzing around me, then walked up the driveway and sat down on a stump, dropping my chin into my hands. It was very quiet now, the fly had left. I took a deep breath and exhaled a sniffle-cry that sounded like a dog whimpering. I looked up and then around, feeling embarrassed although I was alone. I laughed and then took out my phone, swiping on TikTok for a while, trying to ignore the anger that was slowly building in my chest. *This is my property*, I thought, *people have built homes without code officers for millennia and got on fine.* I traded TikTok for Google and searched for the local building laws. Reading through documents that looked like they had been typewritten and then scanned, I learned that you could build a shed without a permit as long as it was under 200 square feet. That was it.

I would build a shed and call it a cabin. Problem solved. I stuck my middle finger in the air at an imaginary Karen.

In the short time I had lived near Holley, a town of about 1,500 that was only a three-minute drive away, it dawned on me that the property was not in the middle of the wilderness, as I had imagined. It was surrounded by a proud community of long-time residents who, while outwardly friendly, at times disclosed a fiercely territorial and even outright antagonistic attitude towards outsiders.

One morning a few days before meeting with Karen, I was clearing brush, sweating shirtless in the hot sun, when I heard a woman shouting up the driveway.

"Is anyone there? Hello, is anyone here?"

I turned and saw a woman, probably in her late 30s, walking up the driveway frantically waving her arms at me. I dropped my clippers and sped-walked towards her.

"What's going on?"

She was heaving, on the verge of a panic attack, "are... are you Dean?"

"Uh, yes I am."

"I'm Gina," her voice shook, "I live in the house behind you, I just had my mailbox smashed!"

"What do you mean, who smashed your mailbox?"

"I'm positive it was Keith."

"Who's Keith?"

"He lives a few doors down, he's the one with the confederate flag on his porch. I reported him to animal control yesterday because he was keeping a pet deer. Which as you know is animal abuse, and I think this was his way of retaliating."

I didn't understand why keeping a pet deer was animal abuse, but I tried to put on a sympathetic face for Gina.

"Did you see him smash your mailbox?"

"No I didn't, but I just called the sheriff and want to make sure I'm not in danger."

"Okay well feel free to stay here until the sheriff comes, I'm sorry that happened to you." I put my hand on her shoulder and asked her to sit down. She nodded, thanking me. We chatted for a few minutes while we waited for the sheriff.

"If I had to do it over again," Gina said, shaking her head, "I wouldn't have moved here. My advice is to pack up and get out of here while you can."

At the time I dismissed Gina's words as the paranoid expression of her panicked state, but after meeting with Karen I feared that perhaps she was right.

The night after Karen came, after sitting down to a meditation, I felt a calm descend over me. I took out my journal: *It seems like one of the biggest obstacles to deep relaxation is the terrible fear that I will miss something important that my brain comes up with. The conversation with Karen today kicked up a lot of mental dust and I can't help but feel some insight, some Big Idea will strike me that will make it all okay. And then there is that terrible feeling akin to a desperate need to exit. To escape. This hits me every now and then, and it's one of my greatest triggers. The feeling that I simply cannot go on feeling how I'm feeling. That I must take a drug to totally overwhelm the negative. But today I can stand proud because I didn't give in: I have proof now that happiness is possible in sobriety. The past couple of days I experienced a wonderful sense of peace and clarity. I am beginning to touch true peace living in the woods. Not always, but I am approaching it, I can feel it. A year or so in the woods will bring me much closer to peace of mind. I'm realizing now the absolute fruits of spiritual practice. It seems to me that the whole game is to get high. It's always been your game and it's always been everyone's game. To get as high as possible as often as possible. And the spiritual game confronts that directly. It aims to get you as high looking at a daisy as snorting cocaine.*

As I sat in the dark listening to the crickets and watching the fireflies, I felt an intense craving for community, for structure. I googled local meditation centers and found the Rochester Zen Center was offering an intro to meditation workshop. A few days later I joined about forty other people as we crowded into the "zendo," the meditation hall. We were told to bow to a big altar of the Buddha at the back of the room as we walked in, which I did half-heartedly. *This better not be a cult,* I thought, feeling resistance to the Zen forms.

We sat on cushions facing the wall and were given instructions by a late-middle-aged woman named Donna with short white hair and blue robes.

"At the Rochester Zen Center, we practice Zazen," she began, "a form of meditation that has been practiced since the time of the Buddha 2500 years ago." We were supposed to sit perfectly upright and yet stay totally relaxed. Then: "just feel your whole body breathing." Three bells rang out to start the first thirty-five-minute meditation. A fragile silence descended over the room, each posture shift or loud breath intensely audible. A few minutes in I felt hands on my back, pulling me straighter. I grimaced, trying my best to maintain perfect posture while following my breath. Twenty minutes in, my legs began to burn and I shifted continuously in my seat, a loud rustling each time that made me blush with embarrassment. Finally the bell rang out and I let out a long breath before standing up, intensely relieved. We sat two more 35 minute rounds before lunch, and then, after eating, the "Roshi," or head teacher, gave a talk and answered questions.

"You clean up your house. Why don't you clean up your mind?" He said. "The practice of Zazen is not about getting high," he continued, "it's about freeing us from attachment." I didn't know exactly what he meant but it sounded profound.

The Rochester Zen Center, I learned, was founded in 1966 and was the first center on the East Coast to practice Japanese Zen. Philip Kapleau, the founder, (referred to in Zen circles as "Roshi Kapleau") was a court reporter at Nuremberg[5] before going on to study Zen in Japan in the 1950s under Haku'un "White Cloud" Yasutani, a legendary figure who taught Kapleau a blend of two popular sects of Zen–known as Soto and Rinzai–which he brought to the U.S. with the founding of the Rochester Zen Center.

In the afternoon we sat three more rounds. My legs and back were on fire and I shifted constantly to keep the torment at bay. I forgot all about my breath. But when the bell rang signaling the end of the last period, I felt lighter. When I got back to the property that night I prepared a dinner of pasta and steak, biting into the meat I experienced an explosion of flavor and sensual pleasure that surprised me. My vision seemed clearer and the air was almost sensual against my skin.

I read *The Three Pillars of Zen* by Roshi Kapleau. He described the koan system at the center of Zen teaching, where you grip an unresolvable paradox in your mind for days or years until your rational mind collapses into open awakening. A so-called "fundamental

---

5   The Nuremberg trials, 1945-1946, was an allied-led effort to bring to justice many of the most notorious criminals in Nazi Germany.

koan" like—"What was your face before your mother gave birth to you?" Could be appropriately answered with: "The wind in the trees, the birds singing in the forest." The answer was not what you said, but how you said it–physically manifesting insight into your true nature rather than expressing it through abstract concepts constructed by the rational mind. An answer which points to what is alive in you right now, which can change over the course of your life as you develop and deepen your understanding.

The explicit goal of Zen Buddhism, I learned, was to make any distinction between you and anything outside of you disappear. The realization of this insight was called "Kensho," a blissful and profoundly transformational experience of awakening that is the explicit goal of many Zen practitioners. Kapleau's book–which included a biographical portion describing the Kenshos of ten Western practitioners–lit a fire under me, and rarely did an hour go by when I did not think about achieving Kensho.

I signed up for a two-day meditation retreat with the Zen Center in early September, hoping, believing, that I would experience this mysterious and tantalizing awakening.

Chapter Forty-Eight - July, 2022

In early July, Emily arrived. Picking her up from the Buffalo airport I imagined all my happiness on the property would be multiplied tenfold by her presence.

"So I have to warn you," I said, glancing over at her from the driver's seat, "the accommodations are not exactly palatial."

She laughed, "I'd expect nothing less."

"But don't worry, by winter time we're gonna have a beautiful cabin built. With insulation and wood heat, it's going to be better than the Ritz."

She smiled: "I can't wait."

We stopped at Niagara Falls before heading to the property. The sun was setting and as we stood over the viewing platform feeling the mist in our faces I had a thought that I would never be sad again.

When we arrived at the property that night I introduced her to our home for the next few months: a two-person REI tent with a twin air mattress that needed to be refilled every few nights. She didn't bat an eye, "this is perfect," she said, I felt my heart grow warm.

"I'm so happy you're here," I said, grabbing her hips and pulling her in for a kiss.

"Me too," she said, breathing deeply and smiling.

A few days later a truck trundled up our long driveway and deposited a cubic, plastic-wrapped pile of wood. It was the shed kit I had ordered from Lowe's for $4,700, which included pre-cut lumber and instructions on how to build a 16x12 shed.

The next morning I was startled awake by hard rain seeping into the tent. The rain pounded through the morning, so we broke camp and went into town. We hit the gym and stopped by the library until the storm passed.

We returned to the property later that day. I planted a blue spruce tree and christened it with kava tea.

"May you be rooted," we said.

The sun came out. We pulled everything out of the tent and stacked it up by the fire. I had a terrible time starting it because the wood was all wet. I decided I would postpone the cabin build for a few days and put together a wood shed.

We developed a routine—every day I would chainsaw dead ash trees into blocks and hack them into firewood with a splitting maul. Then, after work, I would build a bonfire and we would sit around for hours reading and talking and meditating. At sunset we would go out onto the road and watch the orange and reds spread across the horizon over the farmland. The night of the rain we burned veggies in a red dutch oven and ate pesto-slathered superfood pasta from Wegmans. I meditated and felt my breath was the most pleasant thing in the world.

For fun, I built a "hippie hot tub" using a $129 six by two galvanized steel feeding tank from Tractor Supply stacked on cinder blocks. I filled it with water from the well and built a fire under it, after thirty minutes steam would peel off the top and we would trade off relaxing in the warm water and then running to the fire to dry off when we had enough.

But as the days turned to weeks I began to resent Emily. I watched her sit in a chair and read or meditate or journal while I labored with the lumber, hauling it up to the build site and digging holes for the raised foundation.

"Why don't you help out a bit?" I snapped, looking at her vengefully.

"Dean, I just want some time to relax. I will work, but I just finished a really stressful school year, so I need to rest."

"But you've rested enough! You've been here five weeks and you've done next to nothing!"

"Don't you understand, building a cabin is your dream, not mine!"

She got up and stormed off, disappearing down the driveway, leaving me shaking with anger. I lit up a cigar to relax my nerves, and when she came back an hour later I apologized.

"Look, I'm sorry," I said, "my emotions are just so raw out here. Everything feels amplified and there's nothing to distract me. I know the cabin is my dream, and you should be able to relax."

She accepted my apology and we were okay for a while. That night we went to the gas station and bought some scratchers. We lost on all of them. I caught a look of myself in the bathroom mirror and saw my clothes were dirty and my beard was growing long. When I walked out a woman stopped me to ask if I worked in landscaping, "I got a lot of work I need done on my property," she said, "in case you're looking for jobs." I laughed and told her I had my work cut out for me on my own property, but I appreciated the offer.

By mid-August I finished the foundation of the cabin and began to work on the frame. Emily and I visited the Zen Center for Sunday service and we talked to the teachers about living in the woods and building the cabin.

"You should use the construction process as your spiritual practice," the Roshi suggested, "when you carry a board, just carry the board, don't think about anything else."

When I carried a board, I watched my mind fly in a thousand different directions. Sometimes I would even drop it in forgetfulness and rush off to take care of something else. When I focused on only the board, I succeeded. Still, I lost myself in anxiety many times. I threw nails, scattering them. I kicked the floor frame. I screamed and dropped to my knees with my head in my hands. *Jesus*, I thought, *I'm so fucking far away from Kensho, I can't even nail a board without losing it.*

According to Zen teaching, everything is intrinsically perfect. Our conceptions and delusions impose a false idea of imperfection. We are perfect even in our apparent flaws. You would never critique a tree for being fat. But it's one thing to understand this intellectually. Zen takes seriously the distinction between theoretical understanding and understanding something in your bowels. This point, perhaps more than any other, is what attracted me to Zen. It was the apparent antidote, the medicine, to the over-intellectualization of my mind at the expense of intuition. My whole life I had believed that with enough knowledge, enough information, life would make sense. But where had that led me? To addiction and pain. Zen offered a new path: One that undercut the muddled beliefs of my troubled past and offered a direct route to experiential understanding of life's most profound truths. With the image of Kensho still burning bright in my fantasies, Zen was, if nothing else, worth a shot.

We had no bathroom, so we would dig holes and "fertilize the soil." One day I didn't clean myself properly and suffered three straight days of indigestion. There was a heat wave and I lay all day and night sweating and groaning. I dug a hole outside the tent door and I would periodically unzip and stick my head out and puke into the hole. After I got over the sickness Emily helped me hold the panel boards in place as I nailed them in. Once the walls were up we strung LEDs and placed a small speaker in the middle of the floor and threw our bodies around to music for several hours before collapsing into sleep.

In early September I hugged Emily goodbye and drove to the Zen Center to start the two-day retreat. When I arrived I was handed a brown robe and was given the schedule–wake up was at 4:30 and we were to stay silent all day. We would sit in formal Zazen in the meditation hall for about ten hours–broken up into four blocks throughout the day. We meditated for an hour and a half the first night and then chanted. Old stuff about my failed movie and book came up and I sat most of the rounds burning with shame.

The next morning I woke to the sound of a shrill bell outside my door. I looked at the clock–4:27. I cursed the bell ringer for cheating me out of three minutes of sleep, before forcing myself upright and grabbing my robe. In the bathroom I splashed some cold water on my face, slapping my cheeks hard one at a time with each hand, and then stepped out into the hall to join a procession of about fifty other berobbed guests filing outside for fifteen minutes of walking meditation. The cool air felt good, and by the end of the period I was alert. A sharp bell rang out and we all broke off as one and filed into the meditation hall, bowing to the Buddha altar before taking our pre-assigned seats and beginning the first Zazen period. Back indoors my eyes felt droopy but the pain in my legs and back kept me awake.

We sat three thirty-five-minute rounds, with seven-minute walking breaks in between. By the third round the pain was so great that I became convinced I was doing permanent damage to my knee–but the thought of Kensho kept me sitting. Finally, after what felt like hours, the bell rang out. It was like a choir of angels, the sound of the bell, and as I uncurled my legs I felt the feeling flood back into them, and, to my surprise, as I stepped out onto the Zendo floor and joined the procession to breakfast, the pain disappeared entirely.

By good luck I was one of the first in line for breakfast. The meditation had felt like being locked in a tug-of-war with a bulldozer, and I was ravenous. In silence we ate shoulder-to-shoulder–sugary yogurt with bran meal and dates. The sweetness of the dates nearly killed me and I closed my eyes as I chewed, lost in ecstasy. The only sounds were the scrape of wooden spoons against wooden bowls and the clinical-sounding mastication of dozens of people eating at once. I thought of cows lined up at a trough and I suppressed a laugh.

After breakfast and a short work period where I helped wash dishes we returned to the meditation hall for three more rounds. I got annoyed with the woman next to me who breathed like a whale. *Shut the fuck up*, I thought, with real anger, trying to refocus on my breath. I had switched from sitting cross-legged to kneeling and the pain lessened. We broke for lunch and a short calisthenics period before returning for three more afternoon rounds. This time, even though I was kneeling, the pain returned. During the second round I resolved never to meditate again. *My life wasn't so bad before this*, I thought, *why did I subject myself to this torture?* Then I heard a voice ring out in the Zendo, it was Donna, the same woman who had led the orientation in June.

"We will now begin teacher interviews. If you would like to see the teacher, please stand up now and get in line."

Anything to not sit here anymore, I thought, rising up and joining the line.

I waited my turn behind a half-a-dozen other students to meet with Eryl, an eighty-five-year-old woman who had been practicing at Rochester since the center was founded. Finally, my turn came and I entered a private room and shut the door behind me. She was sitting cross-legged, staring at the floor, and I sat down on the cushion across from her.

"Hey, how are you?" I asked, looking up at her apprehensively.

She smiled, meeting my gaze, "I'm well, how are you?"

I sighed.

"To be honest, I'm in a lot of pain. I came here hoping to get Kensho, but it's just been so hard. I feel like I'm not getting anywhere, my knees and back are killing me."

She smiled warmly.

"This Kensho is just an idea," she said, waving a hand dismissively, "my advice is just to forget about it. And as for the pain, why don't you just sit in a chair?"

"Sit in a chair? Isn't that just giving up?"

"Not at all!" she said, visibly startled, "Zazen should be a beautiful practice of self-exploration, not a masochistic quest to prove to ourselves we can handle pain. Now tell me, what's your practice?"

"I'm just following my breath, although I wonder if that's a good practice, I know in the *Three Pillars of Zen* most of the practitioners Roshi Kapleau talks about study Koans."

She smiled, "Do you know the Buddha was following his breath when he achieved his great awakening?"

I looked at her, surprised, "really? Well if it's good enough for the Buddha, it's good enough for me."

She laughed, "wonderful. Now please remember you are not here to suffer unnecessarily, try to enjoy your practice." And with that she rang a hand bell signalling our interview was over. I stood up and returned to the Zendo, feeling intensely relieved.

I did the final round sitting in a chair. I felt much better. The pain had receded, though now I was fighting fatigue. I gave it everything I had. My thoughts wandered, but I soldiered on. By the end of the round the air started to clear. I felt like I was waking up from a dream.

After dinner we sat four more rounds. I began to experience major hallucinations. A woman appeared on the wall and floated in front of me. I was glad to have something to distract me. Then she disappeared and I had to go back to the breath. By the third round

I noticed, with surprise, that my breath was just breathing itself. I didn't actually have to do anything, it just went in and out on its own. When the last bell rang I stood up and wandered off to bed. Ten hours of meditation, blurry-eyed but clear-headed. When my head hit the pillow I descended into one of the most peaceful sleeps of my life.

The next day was a half-day and when the bell rang out signalling the end of the late-morning meditation block, we all filed out of the Zendo and everyone erupted into conversation. I was startled, two days of silence and suddenly we were all just going to start talking? I slipped out a back entrance and drove home without saying a word to anyone. When I was back at the property Emily was gone—she had just gotten a job at a bakery and must have been at work. I stared blankly at the pile of materials in front of the cabin. Then, without thinking, I pulled out my meditation cushion and sat down. During the retreat I had spent hours imagining how great it would be not to have to meditate. Now that I was home, I could think of nothing else I would rather do. That night, when Emily got home, we decided to sign up together for a week-long retreat at the end of October. I was vaguely aware that something very mysterious was happening to me, but whatever it was, it seemed like the most important thing in the world.

CHAPTER FORTY-NINE – FALL, 2022

The source of all suffering is trying to make permanent what is impermanent. This is the essence of Buddhist teaching. I can't say I've taken to manual labor tasks superbly well. Perhaps it's my own mind chafing against the forced slowness of manual work. Everything takes time. Patience. As a cocaine addict you want new consciousness NOW, instantly, you do not want to wait even a moment to let your body calm down... but the changing of the seasons is slow and so is the calming of the breath in meditation. It always takes time. Pouring down rain. Sitting here cold and fairly miserable with drops coming out of the siding and ceiling. Rough few days. Very little motivation. Lots of stress around slow progress on the cabin and deteriorating financial situation. Savings are very limited, crypto and stocks are plummeting. Flies are bad in the cabin and I realized I didn't build it very well. It's a bit lopsided and the roof is recessed. Oh well, we'll see how it does this winter.

It was early October when I wrote that in my journal, and it was beginning to dawn on me that building a well-insulated and water-tight cabin was not as easy as I had imagined. In the late summer months I had not noticed the small gaps in the roof and siding, but as the rain and cool weather descended over the property every small error was magnified into misery. Thankfully, my Dad, a skilled carpenter, was coming out for five days to help me finish the roof.

When he pulled up to the property in his rental car and stepped out onto the gravel drive, I hugged him, "so great to have you out here, Dad."

"Good to be here, Dean! Thanks for having me." He was in a good mood, and I couldn't wait to introduce him to my natural playground, and all the work I had done on the cabin. But as he walked around the property he became increasingly agitated.

"This place is a mess. Come on Dean, it's so important to keep things organized!" I blushed, conscious of the two days I had spent cleaning up and that this was the best the property had looked in months. He picked up wood scraps that were haphazardly piled in front of the cabin and began stacking them up neatly underneath the foundation.

"If someone comes and sees how you're living they're gonna think this is a drug den. Looks matter, especially if you aren't following code."

"I know," I said, softly, feeling ashamed, "I'm sorry."

He surveyed the cabin, "well it looks okay from the front, let me see what's doing on top."

He grabbed a ladder and clambered up, peering at the roof I watched his face go from curious to grave.

"Dean, this is really bad."

"What do you mean?"

"The whole roof is off, you built it slanted, it's never gonna work. We're gonna have to tear off the paneling and redo the damn thing."

I looked at the ground, crestfallen.

"Do you think we can do it before you leave?"

"We can, but there's no time to waste, we gotta get going today."

"Okay, I'll follow your lead."

My dad, in an instant, transformed into the single-minded manic work mode that I remembered so well from when I was a kid. Cursing and muttering as he tore the plywood paneling off the roof frame, periodically yelling out instructions, "hold the ladder! Hand me that other drill bit! Stack the wood over there!" I rushed around, trying to be helpful but feeling powerless as he completely took over the project I had given my whole soul to for the last three months. But despite it all I was grateful. I knew the cabin needed surgery, and my Dad was offering free labor which I felt prepared to pay for by accepting some mild verbal abuse.

Emily, probably for the best, was to be gone for much of the week working long shifts at the bakery. When she got home from work the first night after my Dad arrived I greeted her, depressed.

"Things aren't looking so good," I told her, my voice low, "my Dad says the whole roof is fucked so we're gonna have to redo it."

"But at least he's here! He can fix it right?"

"Yeah, he can fix it. But I can already tell this week is gonna suck."

"You'll get through it," she said, rubbing my back.

The next day we got started early–the same routine. Dad rushed around, muttering and cursing, complaining about the poor build job– "you really should have hired someone, or gotten some help. It was idiotic to try to do this on your own." I tried to keep a good attitude, reminding myself that he was being helpful, but my stress was building. Periodically, while Dad worked away on the roof, I would steal off to a secluded area and take long drags off a cigar to calm my frayed nerves. *He only sees the bad in it,* I seethed to myself, *he hasn't complimented me once on the fact that I actually built a cabin by myself, even if it is flawed.*

That evening, soothed into a rare calmness by a day of physical work, he reflected. "You know to be fair, I never attempted to build anything this complicated myself." It was the closest he would come to a compliment.

By the afternoon of the third day, thanks to Dad's furious efforts, we had removed the old roof and made significant headway into installing the replacement. The new paneling installed, we got to work on laying the shingles. Up on the roof, Dad gave a long explanation on the proper technique for placing shingles.

"I got it, Dad, I got it," I said, growing exasperated, "I have actually learned something the last few months. Don't forget I built a cabin, even if it is screwed up."

"I know, I know," he said, waving his hand in a way that I perceived as dismissive.

I popped in some headphones and played some music, trying to calm myself down as I worked the staple gun, locking the shingles in place. Everything was fine for a while but before long I heard him shouting, "what, what?" I asked, annoyed, pulling the headphones out.

"Take those goddamn things out of your ear when I'm talking to you!" He bellowed, "I'm trying to tell you you're not doing the shingles correctly."

That phrase, "take those goddamn things out of your ear," was the match that lit the fuse inside of me, and in an instant I exploded.

Three days of cumulative tension, of feeling talked down to and disrespected, burst forth and I leapt off the roof and began to scream, "how fucking dare you! I invite you out to my property and all you do is talk down to me!" I looked into his eyes and saw anger, which only incited me further, "get the fuck out of here!" I screamed, "get the fuck out of here and don't come back! Come on, grab your things and go!"

I watched as he grabbed his bag and went to his car, slamming the door and driving off. My chest was heaving, the rage boiling my insides, and I paced around the property until it calmed to a simmer. I picked up the phone and called Mom.

"Hey honey..."

"Fuck Dad!" I screamed, interrupting her, feeling the hot branding iron of anger pressing freshly against my insides, "he comes out to my property and all he does is talk down to me and criticize me. I can't take it, I can't take it! Tell him not to come back, tell him I want him gone!"

"Oh Dean, I'm sorry, I'm so sorry that happened."

I began to calm down a little.

"It's just. I know he was trying to be helpful, but I just couldn't take it, I couldn't keep accepting his abuse as payment for his help, I snapped. I'm done with him. I'm really done."

"I know Dean, I know, trust me I understand what you're saying. Please, I'll talk to him, just try to calm down."

"Okay, I will, just promise me you'll talk to him for me, and that he won't be coming back."

"I will, I will. He already called me and told me that things got really heated. But I didn't understand how bad it was."

When we hung up I sat down. The anger was so intense it took me hours to calm down. I drank some kava and smoked two cigars and paced and paced. Finally Emily got home and I told her what happened.

She held my hand and told me it was okay.

"You know, I'm not surprised that it happened," she said, "I could tell how stressed your Dad was making you. It wasn't right, the way he was talking to you."

"Thanks," I said, feeling calmer, "it's gonna take a long time, months maybe, before I'm ready to speak to him again."

"And you're totally in your right, you don't owe him a relationship if he's gonna treat you like that."

The next day I surveyed the work. Significant progress had been made, but there were still several weeks of hard work left before the cabin would be ready. I finished the shingling and then cut out a hole in the roof and installed the steel flashing and chimney for the cast-iron stove. The weather was cooling rapidly and many mornings we would wake up to a layer of frost blanketing the property. Finally, just days before we were scheduled to leave for our retreat, I put the finishing touches on the stove installation.

We lit a fire and snuggled up inside the cabin as night descended. Within an hour the cabin was warm and I laughed with delight at our success.

"See!" I said, turning to Emily, "what did I tell you? Better than the Ritz."

We laughed and made love and fell asleep warm and happy.

The next day we woke up late, I made coffee and we milled around sipping and reveling in our new living space when I heard a shout behind me.

"Dean, what the hell is going on here?"

I turned and saw Karen, her face contorted in a snarl, speed-walking up the property. My heart began to beat rapidly.

"Hey, hey Karen, what are you doing here?" I said, suddenly feeling like I might pass out. I looked at the driveway and saw she had pulled up in a new white Dodge Durango.

"What the fuck is all this?" She screamed, gesturing around the property. "It's a shithole, an absolute shithole, and don't tell me you're living in THIS?" she said, pointing a shaking finger at the cabin. She stepped up to it and tore the door open.

"A stove?? Are you kidding me? Get that removed NOW! That is a fire hazard like you wouldn't believe. And nothing, and I mean nothing you're doing here is legal. You are in some serious trouble!"

I gaped at her, stunned, "I, I, I'm sorry."

"And where are you using the bathroom? It smells like piss. You're just shitting and pissing all over the place aren't you?"

"We go into town when we have to go to the bathroom," I said, lamely.

"My ass." She stormed back to her car and came back a moment later with a pink slip of paper.

"This is for you. If this cabin isn't torn down by November 15th, the police will get involved. Do you understand me?"

"Yes, yes, thank you," I said, feeling like I was in the middle of a terrible nightmare.

Then she was in her car, backing out of the driveway in her brand new Dodge Durango, shaking her head and glaring at me like I was Satan himself.

I looked down at the paper, "notice of illegal structure, to be removed in its entirety within fourteen days of receipt. After which time, a $300 fine will be applied for each successive day the structure remains in violation."

My body felt like it had just been hit multiple times with a sledge-hammer and I turned to Emily, "what just happened?" For the next few hours we tried to make sense of our predicament. There were so many questions. How did Karen find out about the cabin? And where would we live? It was already nearly November, the sub-freezing temperatures and lake-effect snows could hit at any moment, camping would soon become dangerous. There was anger and fear and resentment. What right did Karen have to come on the property anyway, unannounced and uninvited, wasn't that trespassing? But through it all there was an awareness that she was fundamentally right and we were fundamentally wrong. We had violated the code, taunting the beast itself, and now had to face the consequences.

CHAPTER FIFTY - LATE FALL, 2022

Just forty-eight hours after Karen stormed on the property, shattering our fragile sense of security and happiness, Emily and I arrived at the retreat center together to begin our first seven-day meditation retreat, known in Zen as "sesshin." On the drive over we forgot all about Karen and the cabin, beside ourselves with nervous anticipation.

"I'm so excited," Emily said, "I've been wanting to do a week-long retreat for years."

"Roshi Kapleau said some people have Kensho on their very first sesshin."

"That's crazy. You and I might literally not be the same people seven days from now."

At seven the gong sounded–the start of sesshin. For the next seven days, we were not to talk, not to make eye contact, and, most importantly, to focus our minds on our practice at all times. The first night we followed the now familiar routine–three thirty-five minute sitting meditation rounds broken up by two seven-minute walking periods. The Zendo, a glass-paneled room with skylights immersed in the middle of a one-hundred-twenty-acre compound outside

Batavia, NY, descended into absolute silence. The lightest breeze or bird chirp flooded the room with sound, and if someone so much as wiggled a big toe the noise was like an air horn piercing the vacuum-sealed silence. Conscious of the sound of the forced air exiting my noise, I hung my mouth open and panted silently through my teeth. The air vibrated with an intensity that far exceeded the relatively casual atmosphere of the two-day retreat. I was surrounded now by sixty human statues, many of whom decades deep into practice lives, veterans of dozens or even hundreds of sesshins. And here I was, the squirrel-minded newcomer threatening to break their tranquility with restless fidgeting.

Scared into an anxious stillness–I tried to bring my attention down into my bellybutton–known as the "hara" in Zen. But the image of Karen kept capturing my awareness–imagining her as a Nazi SS officer righteously executing the Third Riech's heinous decrees.

Finally the third round ended and we all filed off to bed. Still roused into anxiety from the meditation, I didn't fall asleep until 11:30 and woke at 3:45 with terror in my heart–*what if I can't do it, what if I have to leave sesshin early and Emily thinks I'm a giant pussy and leaves me?* But as we sat down for the morning rounds something settled inside of me and my mood lifted. But I had only traded anxiety for physical pain. My knees began to hurt like they were being slowly cut with a serrated blade and I had to use every ounce of restraint to keep myself from shifting in my seat.

The last round of the morning I went to see Roshi in the interview room–her name was Amala-Sensei–a visiting teacher from New Zealand who was in her late 70s and whose thick glasses and white, military-grade haircut reminded me of a drill sergeant. But when I walked in the room, palms sweaty at the prospect of presenting myself to this almost mystical figure of spiritual achievement, she looked up at me with a smile that was so warm my nerves broke into a pleasant ease that manifested in a belly laugh that seemed to surprise both of us.

"In a good mood, I see," she said, as I sat down.

"I guess so. I felt so nervous coming in here, but now I feel okay. Even though I'm already in a lot of pain."

"Is this your first retreat?"

"Yes, can you tell?" I laughed again.

She smiled, ignoring the question.

"What is your practice?"

"Following the breath, although mostly I'm just focusing on my hurting knees."

"I often say that the taste of Zen is pain in the knees. And it's true, pain in many ways is our friend, our teacher. The mind has a way of piling on terrible suffering to what is just a normal sensation. Try to investigate what's happening in your body when you feel pain, rather than simply wishing it will go away. The more resistance you have to it, the more the pain mounts."

I tried to apply Amala's advice–but the pain only grew with each sitting period. In the afternoon I switched to a chair, transferring the pain in my knees to my back and shoulders. On breaks I sometimes found myself walking near Emily but made a special effort to avoid her eyes–I wanted more than anything to ask how she was doing but I knew I couldn't–this was a journey we would each have to take alone.

That evening, sitting in the chair, I felt a wave of anger towards my Dad and Karen that was so intense I bit my lip to keep from scream-ing. I sat this way for nearly an hour, outwardly still but inside shaking. Then the anger melted away and a great calm descended over me that would last for nearly two days.

The pain remained, at times more or less, but there was some distance around it and I was surprised to find that some meditation rounds seemed to end as soon as they began. I became fascinated with the subjective experience of time–how some of the thirty-five-minute periods felt like hours and others no more than a few, fleeting moments. Well-being, it seemed, was inversely correlated with the movement of time. The better I felt, the quicker the hours melted away, the universe's cruel tax on happiness.

But on the morning of the fourth day the calm, which I had hoped would last forever, disappeared and pain roared back worse than before. I found myself shifting in my seat to try to get some relief– "please stay still," the monitor called out. I realized they were talking to me. I burned with embarrassment and suddenly became gripped by a horrifying thought that I would have to leave. That I couldn't handle it after all. For the next two rounds I was beside myself–the pain was so intense it was like sitting in a fire–every part of my legs and back burned with such ferocity that I began to wonder if I was dying. Perhaps my life had been a terrible mistake, I would have killed myself long before if I had known the depths of suffering my body would cause me. I no longer thought about leaving or stay-ing–I thought of nothing but the pain–and the endless rounds that seemed to go on for lifetimes.

Finally we broke for lunch. I could barely walk, even though I had been sitting in a chair my back felt broken. That afternoon, despite popping two ibuprofen, the pain flared up again the moment I sat down. Tears rolled from my eyes; *I have to talk to Amala, the next chance I get I will run to the interview room. I will tell her I'm leaving, that I can't take this anymore.* But almost the exact instant I made the decision to leave, the pain dropped away like a falling glacial ledge.

In an instant I was seized by a profound conviction that no matter what happened in my life it would be okay. I repeated this thought– "no matter what happens in my life, I will be okay," like a mantra a thousand times in my head for the rest of the round, and the tears of pain turned to tears of relief. It was no Kensho, that I knew without a doubt, but something had shifted. There was a spaciousness inside of me that I knew I would work to maintain for the rest of my life.

CHAPTER FIFTY-ONE – WINTER, 2022

"If a man sees Truth in the morning, he may die in the evening without regret."

– Confucius.

When Emily and I returned to the property, glowing with the sweet feeling of accomplishment and inner ease, we were confronted with a dour scene. A cold drizzle was falling out of a gray sky, temperatures in the mid-40s, and the walking trails we had cleared turned to mud. The cabin was also gloomy. Itself gray and surrounded by mud and the door banging harshly against the front siding in the wind, the consequence of the latch I had neglected to install.

I looked at Emily and began to laugh. She smiled and then joined in.

"Wow this place is a piece of shit!" I cried out, joyfully.

I stepped into the cabin, taking stock of the dirty memory foam mattress pad on the floor, the mud-streaked oak flooring I had installed in the back half of the room, and the stacks of unorganized tools and clothing placed at seemingly random intervals. It was cold and damp and thoroughly uninviting but at the same time it felt like home.

"So what are we gonna do?" Emily asked, her voice soft and warm, free from all the anxiety the question would normally have implied.

"We're gonna destroy it."

"How long will it take?"

"Two or three days is my guess. The roof is the hardest part. But we have the law of entropy on our side, things are always looking for ways to come apart, we're just going to help it along."

We got to work, Emily and I. She handed me tools and me up on the roof, tearing off shingles, plywood paneling, and finally the rafters themselves. As I worked, I imagined Karen's face, no doubt smiling with satisfaction at the knowledge of her power. But then there was also my Dad.

"These materials are cheap," he had said, "I give it three or four years max before this thing starts falling apart."

Later he said: "Well maybe if we build the roof right it'll last ten years."

At the time I thought angrily that he had no idea what he was talking about. He couldn't even get his own estimates straight. But now it didn't matter. The cabin, it turned out, would not last a month. Gone before it was ever finished.

After two days the roof was off. We undid the screws connecting the siding and, Emily filming and laughing, I body slammed the walls down, cracking and splitting as they fell. The spectacular unwinding of months of work and years of dreams.

In four days it was done—nothing but a pile of materials. I went to Harbor Freight, bought a large tarp, and spread it over the top of the wood pile, anchoring it down with cinder blocks. Perhaps, one day, I would return and try again. But by next summer, the underbrush would reclaim the ground so that, at first glance, it would look as if I had never been there. In a hundred years the last trace of the materials would be decomposed or blown away. The nails buried under soil and even the synthetic tarp shredded and scattered and gone forever.

I collected as much of the trash and scrap material as I could, loaded it into the back of the Sienna and brought it to a dump. Emily and I ran five loads, one after the other, and with each load I felt lighter. Then, ten days later, just as we finished our work, a lake-effect snowstorm blew in and dumped two feet of snow. We made our way to an inn in Batavia to wait out the storm and plan our next move.

I called my parents and told them what had happened.

"So it's all over anyway," I told my Dad, "the cabin is down, it's done."

"I'm really sorry about how I behaved," he said, "I should have treated you better. Are you coming home for Thanksgiving?"

"Maybe. I might go to South Florida and stay with Emily's family. But then we'll come to your house for Christmas. So we'll be home soon either way."

"Okay, we'll see you then."

"See you then, Dad."

Emily and I meditated in the inn, setting up our cushions on the bed and staring at the inoffensive print of some generic landscape painting on the wall. After a couple rounds I lay back in bed and closed my eyes.

I have to say, everything feels as if I am a child again. The light of life has been turned on once more. All things are shining. I feel my body, my senses. The number one thing is to stop telling stories and get into the body, get into the senses. This is where life is really lived. At all moments a wonderful presence is possible. This is what all great teachers teach. To stop identifying with thoughts and start identifying with the truth of what you're experiencing. What is anxiety really? It is a little tension in the shoulders and neck, a roil in the stomach, everything else is a story going on inside your head! On/off on/off. Continuously everlasting. This is life. I look inside myself and I feel a tingle of a million cells all shimmering with the touch of the bed, the spots of coolness and warmth. I feel the air exiting and entering my nostrils, the roar of the fan in the air conditioner and the soft distant sounds of the car tires on the road. This is life, not the fantasy of the past or the future. NOW. This is Truth! I feel the thump of my heartbeat when I close my eyes. I feel the underside of my feet gripping the earth as I walk, I notice my feelings start to shift negative and I realize I have the power to transform it into joy. I see the dots flashing behind my eyelids and I hear the whistle of the cosmos in the silent room. When the mind is quiet, freed from the exhausting exercise of rumination, it drops into the body and sleeps as the body does at night. It heals itself and is refreshed. The mind is always at work, even in sleep it roars to life with dreams. Waking it never stops as it produces thought after thought and locks into wrestling rumination that saps us. I bite into food and my mouth explodes with flavor, the textures and subtle on/off, and salt and sweet roll around my tongue and I close my eyes and disappear in the ecstasy. I am home in the here and now. The ingredients for happiness are present in this very moment, we can be happy now, no matter what is going on around us. In fact, we can only be happy now. When I was in college and high school I suffered so intensely because I believed the thought that I had to be someone. Now, I am both somebody and nobody.

But even flushed with a spiritual high, I felt the world crowding in. Anxiety, old thoughts of failure. *Where would I go? What would I do?* Broke, jobless. But I had something now that could never be taken away from me. A nameless, formless something.

EPILOGUE

"The kingdom of God is not coming with signs to be observed; nor will they say, 'Lo, here it is!' or 'There!' for behold, the kingdom of God is in the midst of you."

– Luke 17:21

Over the two years after leaving the property I would participate in another thirteen sesshin, eight of which took place during a five-month residential training period at the Great Vow Zen Monastery in Clatskanie, OR. Meditation practice broadly speaking and Zen practice in particular became the primary focus of my life. There were times in my residency when I reached states of such ecstatic bliss and non-separateness that I felt as if I had laid down my small self and picked up eternity. I was convinced, for a period of a few magical days, that I would never suffer again. Alas, these states did not last, and in a short time became only dead memories.

Nonetheless, something has irrevocably changed. The practice of Zazen has given me my life back. When I started Zen practice my sobriety was fragile, less than a year old, and the rage, depression and relapses I describe in the book were all-too-common. Zen helped me to discover that this life, just as it is, possesses everything I need. At the highest level, there are no problems, even as the relative, physical, and psychological world is filled with torrents of pain and lack. Of course, I do not live in a war zone. I have, in large measure, been spared from the worst life has to offer. I have never gone hungry from lack of money or famine. I have never been left out in the cold with no possibility of shelter. I have not gotten cancer, I have not even lost a member of my immediate family. So I do not think the solution to all life's problems is simply to "meditate more." And I, as well as anyone else who sincerely practices Zen, would never say that the problems of the world should simply be accepted with a kind of blase "nothing matters" spiritual indifference.

Zen says fundamentally that you have to begin, as Descartes did, with complete doubt about everything–with a complete "not knowing." Only then can you find the real answer. The faith of the Buddhists is fundamentally the faith of no separation. That in fact the separate self is utterly illusory, and it's not even a mystical idea, or a dogma, but one that you can touch through your own direct experience in the most tangible way imaginable. So that the truth is revealed to you in its sweeping whole and shatters you such that nothing is ever the same again. When the self diminishes, the world opens up unendingly.

It's important to note that, in the end, Zen does not change a person. It helps them discover who they really are. There is an old Zen saying describing the evolution of a practice life that goes like this: "At first, mountains are mountains and streams are streams. Then mountains are not mountains and streams and are not streams. In the end, mountains are once again mountains, and streams once more streams." At first, I found this inscrutable. But now I don't. When we start to see past our conceptual models of reality (I am "me" and everything else is "other"), the world looks radically different. But as practice develops you begin to realize that it was always this way, you just didn't see it before.

I am not here to say that Zen is THE path. It is rife with its own scandals, and I have heard from many people who have been burned or seriously traumatized by sexual assaults, physical abuse, and the like. The practice of Zen does make one "perfect," and its hierarchical DNA is sometimes painfully rigid and distasteful. I do not even say that Zen will always be my path. I only want to say that it has given me more than I even knew it was possible to have, and for that, I am eternally grateful.

"Gate Gate Para Gate Para Samgate Bodhi Svaha!" (Gone, gone to the other shore, completely gone, awakening, amen!)